Soil Biology & Ecology: The Basics

Authored by

Dan Răzvan Popoviciu

"Ovidius", University Constanța
România Faculty of Natural Sciences
and Agricultural Sciences
Romania

Soil Biology & Ecology: The Basics

Author: Dan Răzvan Popoviciu

ISBN (Online): 978-981-5313-29-1

ISBN (Print): 978-981-5313-30-7

ISBN (Paperback): 978-981-5313-31-4

© 2024, Bentham Books imprint.

Published by Bentham Science Publishers Pte. Ltd. Singapore. All Rights Reserved.

First published in 2024.

need for a court order if at any point you breach any terms of this License Agreement. In no event will any delay or failure by Bentham Science Publishers in enforcing your compliance with this License Agreement constitute a waiver of any of its rights.

3. You acknowledge that you have read this License Agreement, and agree to be bound by its terms and conditions. To the extent that any other terms and conditions presented on any website of Bentham Science Publishers conflict with, or are inconsistent with, the terms and conditions set out in this License Agreement, you acknowledge that the terms and conditions set out in this License Agreement shall prevail.

Bentham Science Publishers Pte. Ltd.
80 Robinson Road #02-00
Singapore 068898
Singapore
Email: subscriptions@benthamscience.net

BENTHAM SCIENCE

CONTENTS

PREFACE

Atlhough few people acknowledge it, soil is one of the environments hosting the highest biodiversity on this planet. A multitude of micro-and macroorganisms, bacteria, fungi, protists, plants and animals populate the various types of soil.

Yet, a really remarkable thing about soil is not just its enormous biodiversity, but also the variety and complexity of interactions among present organisms. At this level, we can find complex symbioses, competition, predation and parasitism. These interactions are essential to the continuous recycling of bioelements, in decomposing organic matter and making available again its various components.

Thus, soil has a crucial contribution to the very existence of Earth's biosphere. It provides nutritional support to all land-based ecological communities and, is also the basis of any agricultural production, thus, of our everyday food.

This is why knowledge of all these aspects of soil biology and ecology is important to naturalists. This book is conceived as a guide to students, specialists and all people interested in natural sciences.

Dan Răzvan Popoviciu
"Ovidius", University Constanța
România Faculty of Natural Sciences
and Agricultural Sciences
Romania

CHAPTER 1

Soil as a Living Habitat, General Considerations

Abstract: Soils cover most of the Earth's landmasses. Soil is a complex system, under continuous evolution and in perpetual relation to the atmosphere, hydrosphere, lithosphere, and biosphere. It is polyphasic, composed of a solid (mineral and organic) fraction, but also of liquid and gaseous fractions. A key aspect is its stratification into several horizons. This complex structure determines the living conditions being provided to the local biota, but also a major diversification of soil types on our planet.

Keywords: Classification, Life conditions, Soil, Stratification, Structure.

INTRODUCTION

Understanding soil biota requires, first of all, understanding soil as a living environment.

The key aspects of this are defining and delineating soil from other environments, knowing its characteristics, its structural features, and the life conditions it offers to inhabiting organisms.

Defining Soil

A key issue in studying this environment is how to clearly define and delimit it.

According to the Soil Science Society of America, soil can be briefly defined as *"The unconsolidated mineral or organic material on the immediate surface of the earth that serves as a natural medium for the growth of land plants"* [1].

The same society also gives a more precise definition, stating that soil is *"The unconsolidated mineral or organic matter on the surface of the earth that has been subjected to and shows effects of genetic and environmental factors of climate (including water and temperature effects), and macro- and microorganisms, conditioned by relief, acting on parent material over a period of time"* [1].

According to this definition, soil consists of both organic and inorganic components, which are subjected to continuous transformations, due to various environmental factors specific to our planet. Thus, the soil is clearly distinct from the *regolith* covering the surfaces of other planets in our Solar System – a layer of variable thickness, made up of mobile mineral fragments, but devoid of organic matter (or, at least not in substantial amounts), lifeforms and lacking exposure to a hydrosphere or even atmosphere [2].

Natural Resources Conservation Service (government entity subordinated to the United States Department of Agriculture), defines soil as "*Soil is a natural body comprised of solids (minerals and organic matter), liquid, and gases that occur on the land surface, occupies space, and is characterized by one or both of the following: horizons, or layers, that are distinguishable from the initial material as a result of additions, losses, transfers, and transformations of energy and matter or the ability to support rooted plants in a natural environment.*" [3].

Thus, the soil is formed of diverse components, has its specific layering, and is under continuous evolution, but it is also characterized from a functional point of view, by its ability to support plant life. The latter is connected to a key feature, typical to soil, that makes it clearly distinct from non-soils: fertility.

Even more important, NRCS states there are some physical boundaries between soils and other environments. The upper limit is the interface between the soil and air or a shallow water layer.

In aquatic environments, it is necessary to distinguish soil from *sediments* (sand, mud, *etc.*). The arbitrary limitation, according to NRCS is that the water layer should be less than 2.5 m thick so that the underlying material could be considered as soil. This would correspond to the maximum insertion limit of rooted water plants [3].

It is also important to define the lower limits of soil. Unlike underlying materials, the soil is characterized by a continuous interaction with the atmosphere and hydrosphere. Most lifeforms (including plant roots) dwell within a thin layer of Earth's lithosphere. This although there are living beings (mostly microorganisms) that can be found up to 5 km deep [4].

So, as a practical maximum lower limit, soil scientists take a depth of 2 m [3].

Soil Characteristics

There are several key features that define soil:

• Soil is a **system**. This means that it includes various types of components, integrated in a functional ensemble.

• It is a **natural** system because it is formed under the influence of natural, biotic, and abiotic factors.

• It is **complex** because the factors conditioning its genesis and structure are numerous.

• It is **polyphasic**, its genesis involves different successive temporal stages.

• It is h**eterogeneous**, being formed of components having different physical states (mainly solid, but also liquid and gaseous).

• It is **polydisperse**, meaning that its solid phase – dominant – is found under different degrees of dispersion: coarse dispersions (suspensions: sand and dust grains), colloidal dispersions (such as some heavily soluble hydroxides, humus, and clay), and molecular/ionic dispersions (soluble salts).

• It is an **open** system, being constantly involved in matter and energy exchange processes with Earth's lithosphere, hydrosphere, atmosphere, and biosphere.

• It is a **polyfunctional** system, performing multiple functions [5].

Morphological Characterization of Soil

As a complex system, soil is made up of different components. This complexity can be seen, for instance, in its vertical stratification (as soil consists of several **horizons**).

Horizon succession usually follows the scheme shown in Fig. (**1**) (obviously, this is a general model, while variations can occur from one soil type to another; some horizons may be missed, while others are present).

Thus, we may successively encounter:

• **O horizon**, superficial, rich in organic matter. It is mostly developed in forest areas, as well as in some grasslands (pastures, prairies). Its presence is due to plant tissue decomposition (especially leaves from woody plants). It can be subdivided into three categories, or sub-horizons, depending on the degree of organic matter decomposition: plant litter (Ol), fermentation horizon (Of), and humification horizon (Oh).

• **A horizon**, also called surface horizon or topsoil, contains a mix of organic and mineral matter.

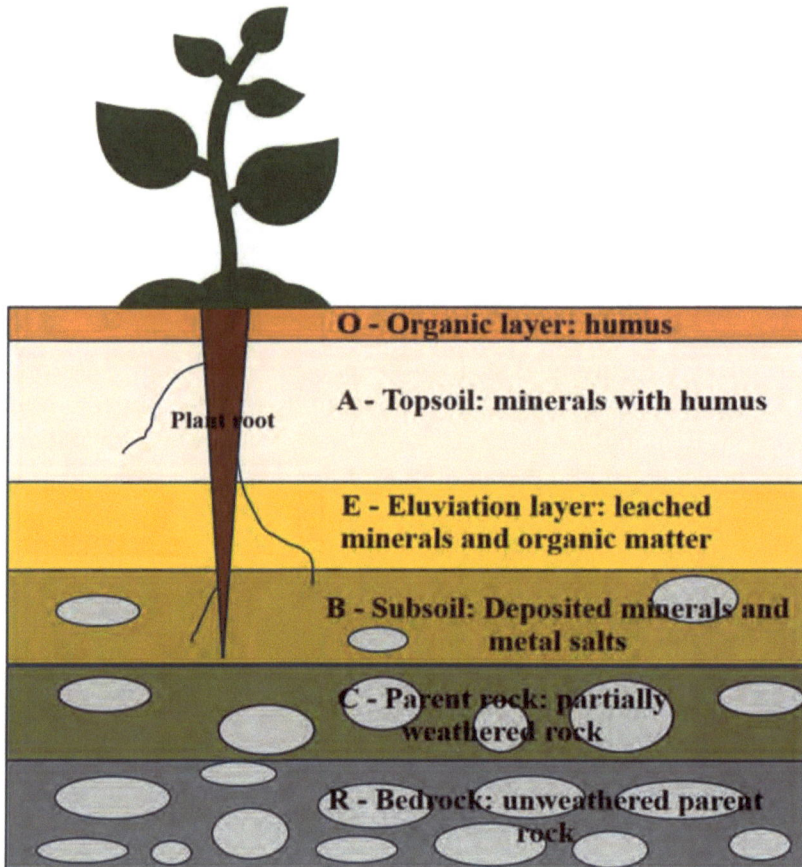

Fig. (1). The main horizons that compose a typical soil profile according to Science Facts [6].

• **E horizon** has a low content of clays, iron and/or aluminium compounds and stable minerals. It is formed through eluviation ("leaching") of the mineral content by water. On the other hand, it is enriched in silica.

• **B horizon** (subsoil) is the layer where clays, metal oxides, *etc.* coming either from the bedrock or from upper horizons (if present), or even formed *in situ* tend to accumulate. Usually, iron oxides give it a reddish color.

• **C horizon** is a mineral one, with low or zero organic matter content and a low influence on atmospheric, hydrospheric, or biospheric processes. This is where carbonates coming from upper horizons tend to crystallize.

• **R horizon** is the bedrock. Depending on geographical location, it can be found at a depth of a few centimeters or a few meters below the surface [7].

Each horizon can have subdivisions and there can also occur specific horizons (P horizon – peanut, specific to peatlands, G horizon – gleic, saturated with water, *etc.*) [5], that make the object of pedology.

In characterizing soils, an important aspect is their structure, which allows for distinguishing several types of soils. Structure is given by the assembly, or lack of assembly of component particles into aggregates. Thus, there are glomerular, granular, prismatic, polyhedric angular and subangular, columnar, lamellar soils, *etc.* A good soil structure is considered to be the one that allows air and water to permeate (Fig. **2**) [5].

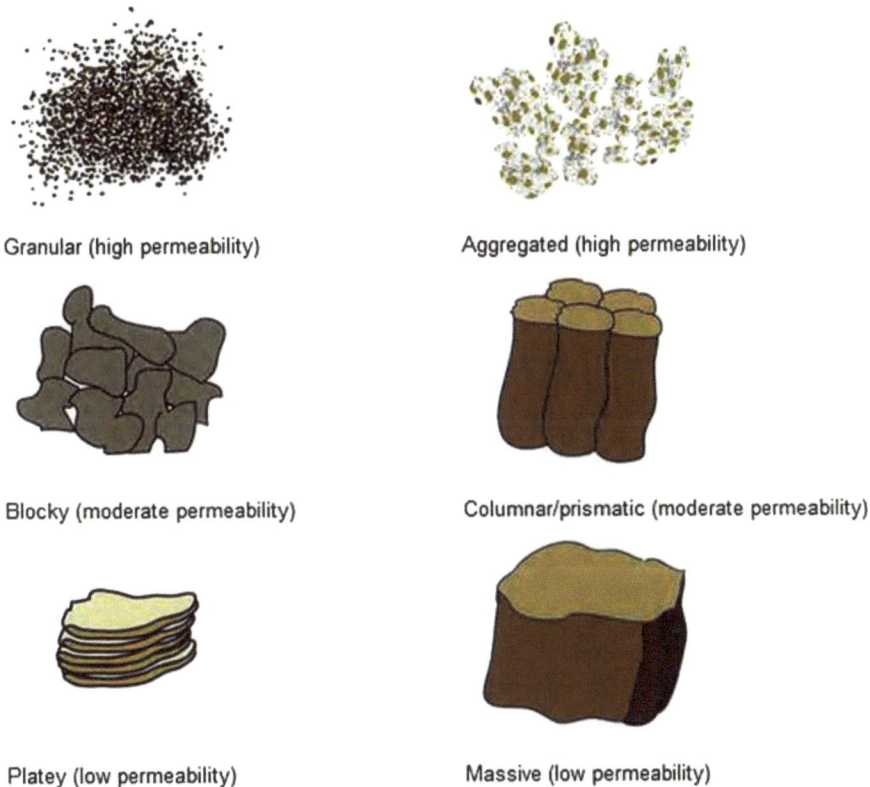

Granular (high permeability)

Aggregated (high permeability)

Blocky (moderate permeability)

Columnar/prismatic (moderate permeability)

Platey (low permeability)

Massive (low permeability)

Fig. (2). Soil types according to structure and permeability to water [8].

Considering the composition, a typical soil is made up, on average, of around 50% solid matter (45% being mineral and just 5-10% organic matter). The remaining 50% (40-60%) consists of interstitial spaces (pores), where the gaseous fraction (air) and the liquid one (water) are hosted, each forming 20-30% of the total mass [9].

Thus, any soil is formed of the following components:

• Solid inorganic matter (dominant), comprising both rock fragments and primary minerals (derived from rock disaggregation) and secondary minerals formed due to the weathering of primary ones.

• Solid organic matter, comprising dead organisms, under different stages of decomposition (but also, obviously, living microorganisms) and organic substances newly synthesized at soil level (humic compounds, or simply **humus**).

• Soil solution (water containing variate amounts of dissolved mineral salts). Soil water can be found in the following forms: **hygroscopic water** (with a strong physical bound, due to adhesion forces, to soil grains), **pellicular water** (weakly bound, covering soil grains), **capillary water** (contained in soil pores) and **gravitational water** (free, easily replenished due to rain, easily accessible to plants, but also easy to be lost through leaking and evaporation), of which a fraction sinks towards more profound soil layers [5, 7].

• The gaseous component is, basically, air coming from the atmosphere, but with a somewhat different composition, due to specific biological or chemical processes. Thus, soil air usually contains 78.5-80% nitrogen (compared to 78% in the atmosphere), 10-20% oxygen (compared to 21%), 0.2-3.5% carbon dioxide (in the atmosphere 0.04%), also hosting relatively large amounts of water vapor, hydrogen sulfide, methane, ammonia [5].

Another key aspect is texture. Soil texture is due to the distribution of various granulometric classes of soil particles, of which we can mention gravel (grains over 1 mm in diameter), sand (0.01-1 mm, with various subclasses), dust, mud, and colloids, commonly known as clays (a component made up of grains below 0.01 mm and chemically active).

According to texture, we can distinguish sandy, sandy-loamy, loamy-sandy, loamy, loamy-clayey, clayey-loamy, clayey, and heavy clayey soils [5].

Finally, another important consideration in soil characterization is water content. Soils can be unsaturated (liquid water does not fill interstitial spaces completely), saturated, or even flooded (water level is above the upper soil interface; (Fig. **3**). This is an extremely important aspect, that regulates oxygen permeability and the distribution of soil microbiota.

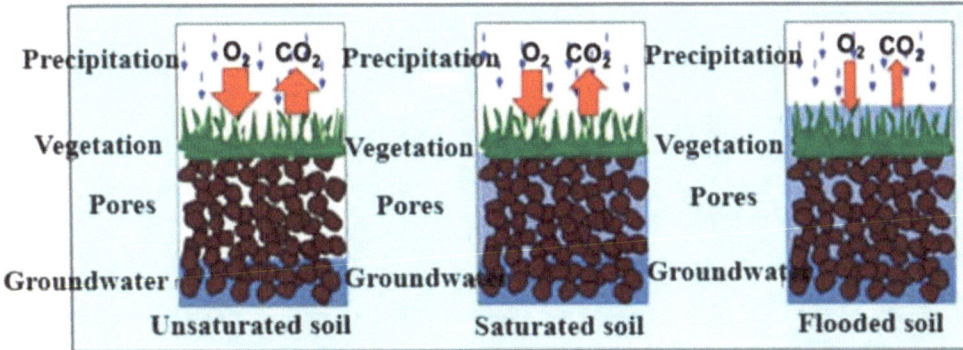

Fig. (3). Water saturation levels of soil [10].

Soil Classification

Soil classification is done according to several criteria.

One of the most important is the presence, absence, degree of development, and succession of the above-mentioned horizons. However, other factors and pedogenetic processes matter too (Fig. **4**).

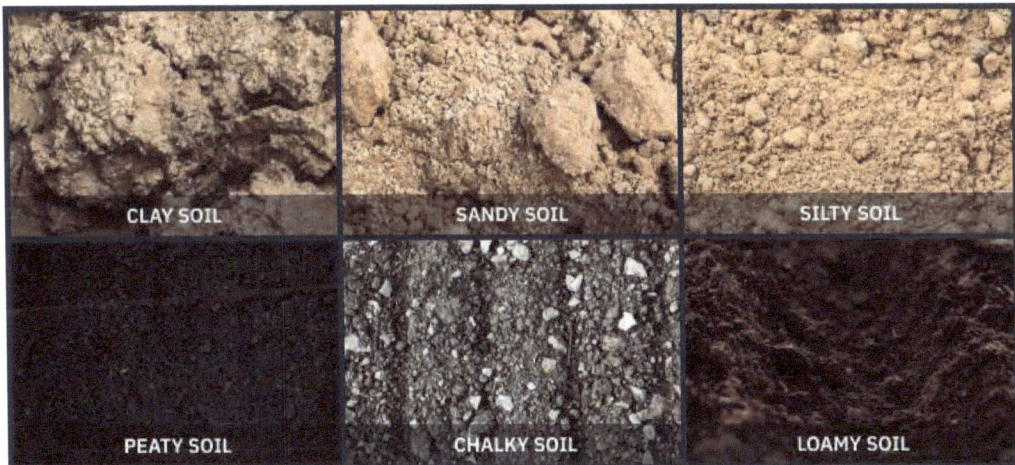

Fig. (4). A few types of soil [11].

Classifications may vary, according to the different pedological schools, but, basically, we may distinguish among major units such as the chernozems, phaeozems, kastanozems, luvisols, planosols, podzols, umbrisols, cryosols, cambisols, vertisols, calcisols, gypsisol, solonetzes, solonchaks, gleysols, *etc.*, each with its corresponding subclasses [5].

From a practical point of view, the most important classification criterion is fertility and agricultural potential, with chernozems (steppe soils) ranking among the highest (Fig. **5**).

Global Soil Regions

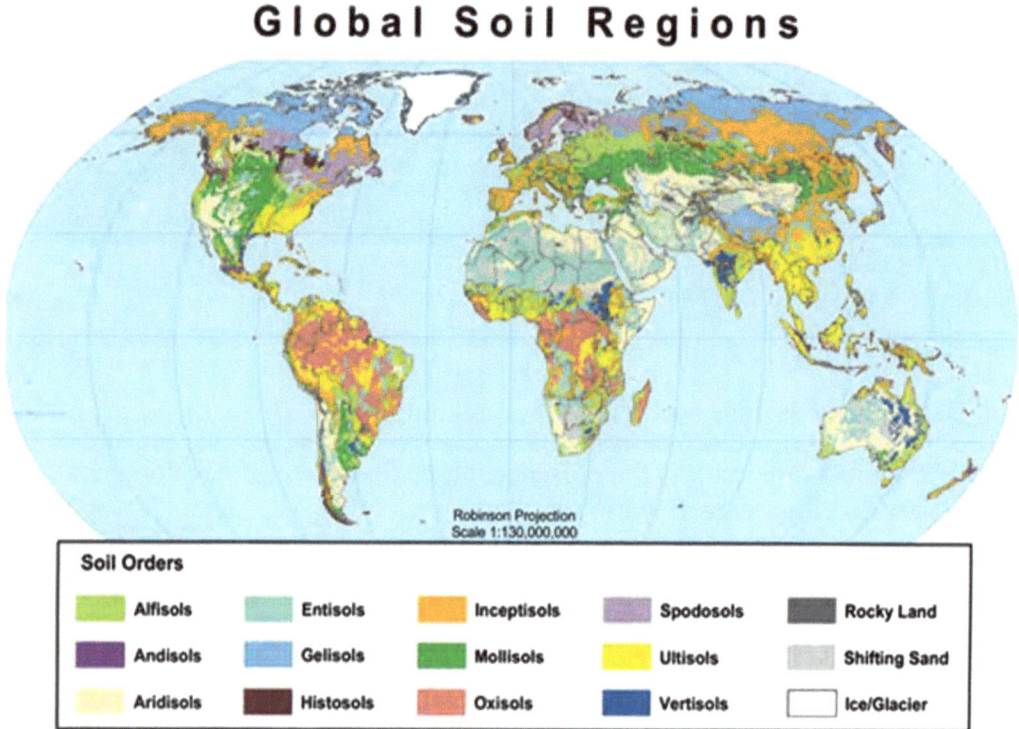

Fig. (5). The global distribution of the main soil types [12].

Environmental Factors Influencing Life in the Soil

Among the main factors are:

• **Temperature** is an extremely important factor, influencing liquid water availability, solubility and diffusion of various nutrients, enzyme functioning, *etc.* Each organism has its own thermal optimum and its own degree of tolerance to values outside this optimal range. Basically, except for some hot volcanic soils, most types of soil worldwide fit into the general biological optimum of 0-60°C [13].

• The **pH** of soil solution is also important for the availability of certain mineral nutrients, also affecting some biological processes. Just as for temperature, each species has its own pH optimum. Regular variation limits are between 3 and 8.5. Most organisms, especially multicellular ones (animals, plants), are sensitive to extreme values [13].

• **Salinity** refers to the concentration of salts dissolved in soil solution. It affects the ability of living organisms to absorb water and may cause osmotic stress and osmotic shock to sensitive species.

• **Moisture**, meaning the water content of the soil has both a direct influence on life (water is a key resource to all metabolic processes) and also an indirect one, determining soil oxygenation or the mobility of certain microorganisms.

• **The mineral composition** is important, minerals being valuable nutrients for organisms; however, some may become toxic when in excess.

• **Organic matter** provides a nutritive substrate to heterotrophic organisms.

• **Light** is particularly important to photosynthesizing organisms. The other living beings are indirectly affected, through the thermal effect of sunlight (infrared radiation) or the disruptive effects of ultraviolet radiation, which makes some organisms require chemical (specific pigments) of microtopographic (taking shelter in/beneath pebbles, *etc.*) screening.

• **Pollution** is a factor of growing importance nowadays. Among the most damaging pollutants are hydrocarbons, including their halogenated or hydroxylated derivatives (compounds derived from the breakdown of plastic, industrial solvents, *etc.*), heavy metals, various pesticides in excess, *etc.* Pollutants can be inorganic, such as heavy metal compounds, that are generally damaging to the cell structures of all organisms, when in excess. However, there are extremely numerous classes of organic pollutants, deriving from fuels, solvents, paints, cleaning and disinfecting products, pesticides, antibiotics and other pharmaceuticals . There are many ways in which such compounds can affect soil life. Some (like hydrocarbons) lower soil permeability to oxygen and water. Others are directly toxic to living organisms. Others have a selective effect on soil microbiota, inhibiting some organisms while stimulating others, thus influencing the way soil functions as a system. While pollution can affect the diversity and distribution of soil microbiota, its most visible effects are on the flora and fauna [13, 14].

All these factors vary at a global level. Some of these variations can be seen in a latitudinal or altitudinal gradient, determining a characteristic zonation of vegetation, but also of associated soil types (Fig. **6**). Other variations are present at a local level, causing significant differences in life conditions over distances of a few meters or even less.

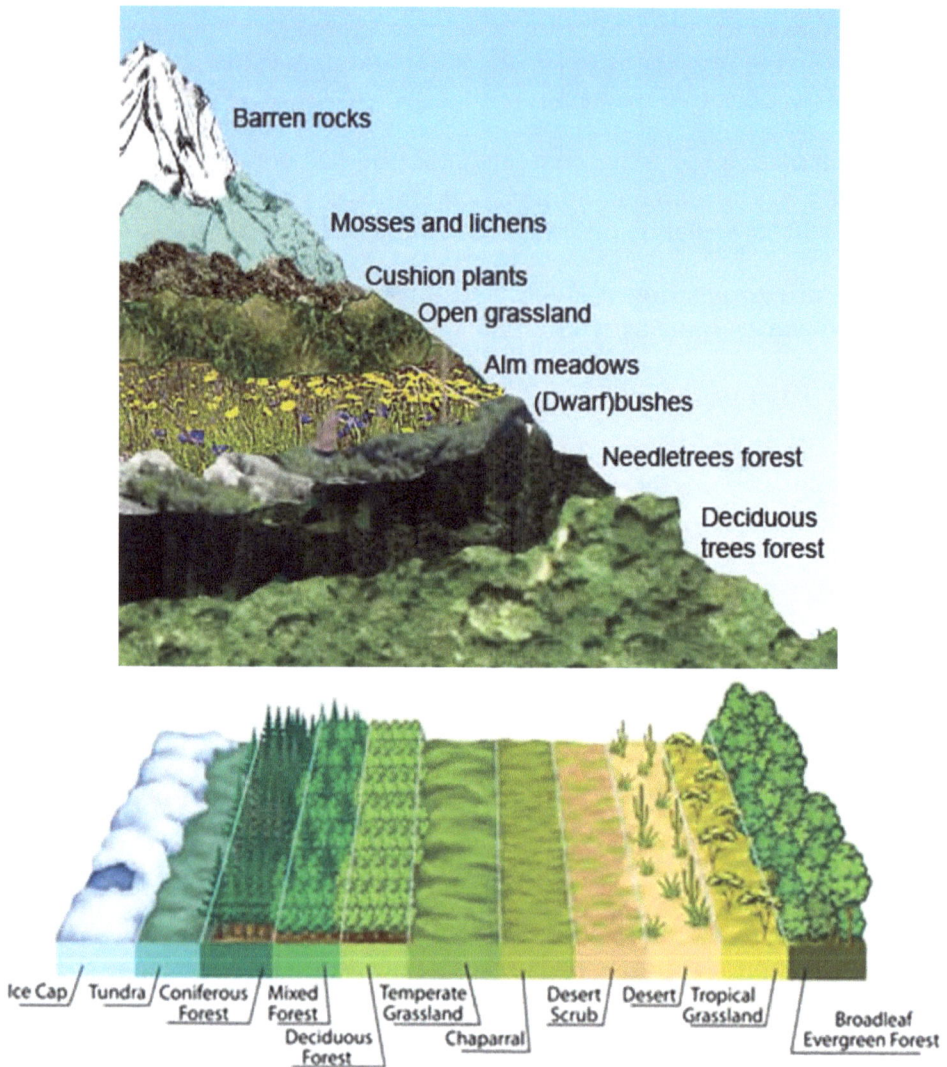

Fig. (6). Altitudinal [15] and latitudinal [16] ecological zones.

CONCLUSION

Soil is a complex type of environment, covering most of the Earth's landmasses. It is composed of both inorganic and organic fractions and its existence is due to micro- and macrobiota.

It is made up of specific layers, has a diverse structure and, besides the solid components, also contains a liquid fraction (soil solution) and a gaseous one.

Life in soils is affected by a wide variety of factors, from mineral composition and organic matter to light and temperature. There are major variations in these factors, on latitudinal, altitudinal, and zonal basis, leading to a major diversity of associated life.

REFERENCES

[1]   Soil Science Society of America, Soils Overview. SSSA, 2022. Available from: https://www.soils.org/files/about-soils/soils-overview.pdf

[2]   Meyer, C., Lunar regolith. NASA Lunar Petrographic Educational Thin Section Set, 2003. Available from: https://curator.jsc.nasa.gov/lunar/letss/regolith.pdf

[3]   Keys to soil taxonomy. 12th ed., Washington, DC: USDA-NRCS 2014.

[4]   Escudero C, Oggerin M, Amils R. The deep continental subsurface: the dark biosphere. Int Microbiol 2018; 21(1-2): 3-14.
[http://dx.doi.org/10.1007/s10123-018-0009-y] [PMID: 30810923]

[5]   Stadnic, S., Pedologie (Ştiinţa solului: geneza, proprietăţile, clasificarea, geografia). Curs de prelegeri. Universitatea de Stat "Alecu Russo" din Bălţi, 2010. 162.

[6]   Soil Horizons. Science Facts, 2023. Available from: https://www.sciencefacts.net/soil-horizons.html

[7]   Schoonover JE, Crim JF. An introduction to soil concepts and the role of soils in watershed management. J Contemp Water Res Educ 2015; 154(1): 21-47.
[http://dx.doi.org/10.1111/j.1936-704X.2015.03186.x]

[8]   Shanstrom, N., What is soil structure and why is it important? DeepRoot, 2021, Available from: https://www.deeproot.com/blog/blog-entries/what-is-soil-structure-and-why-is-it-important-2/

[9]   Soil Nutrient Management for Maui County, Soil composition. University of Hawai'i. College of Tropical Agriculture and Human Resources, 2022. Available from: https://www.ctahr.hawaii.edu/mauisoil/a_comp.aspx

[10]   T.H.V. Phan, Mechanism of Arsenic release in ecosystems of Southeast Asia delta: Mekong Delta Vietnam. Ph.D thesis, Université Grenoble Alpes, 2017. 179.

[11]   Cherlyinka, V., Types of soil in agriculture to grow crops efficiently. EOS Data Analytics, 2022. Available from: https://eos.com/blog/types-of-soil

[12]   United States Department of Agriculture – Natural Resources Conservation Service, Global UDA Soil Taxonomy, 2010. Available from: ftp://ftp-fc.sc.egov.usda.gov/NSSC/Soil_Taxonomy/maps.pdf

[13]   Furtak K, Gałązka A. Edaphic factors and their influence on the microbiological biodiversity of the soil environment. Adv Microbiol 2019; 58(4): 375-84.
[http://dx.doi.org/10.21307/PM-2019.58.4.375]

[14]   Joswig JS, Wirth C, Schuman MC, *et al.* Climatic and soil factors explain the two-dimensional spectrum of global plant trait variation. Nat Ecol Evol 2021; 6(1): 36-50.
[http://dx.doi.org/10.1038/s41559-021-01616-8] [PMID: 34949824]

[15]   Zonation. Virtual Classroom Biology. Radboud University Nijmegen, Available from: https://www.vcbio.science.ru.nl/en/virtuallessons/landscape/zonation

[16]   Distribution of life on Earth. GuyHowTo, 2021, Available from: https://www.guyhowto.com/distribution-of-life-on-earth

CHAPTER 2

Soil Biodiversity, Microbiota

Abstract: Microorganisms form the bulk of soil biota. Having densities of hundreds of millions per gram, bacteria are the dominant organisms. They are the starting point of most trophic chains, they ensure a major part of soil functionality as an ecosystem and they effectively create soil, especially by breaking down organic matter. Their taxonomic diversity is enormous, such as the ecological one: heterotrophs, photoautotrophs, chemoautotrophs, *etc.* Besides them, there are also archaea, viruses, different types of microalgae, and the eclectic group we usually call "protozoans".

Keywords: Archaea, Bacteria, Microalgae, Protozoa, Subcellular entities.

INTRODUCTION

Soils are environments that host an impressive biodiversity (Fig. **1**). Indeed, numerous micro- and microorganisms use soil as a home (permanently or temporarily), but also as a source of food. Among the different lifeforms that belong to soil biota, microorganisms are clearly dominant, in terms of number and biomass, but also functionality.

Just as in any other environment, biodiversity can be characterized using standard ecological indices. Abundance (A) is the number of individuals belonging to a given taxon. Dominance (D) is the percentual ratio between the number of individuals in a certain species and the total number of individuals in a soil sample. We can distinguish between subrecedent (<1.1%), recedent (1.2-2%), subdominant, dominant (2.1-5%), and eudominant (>10%) species. Constancy (C) is the percentual ratio between the number of samples featuring that species and the total sample number; there are accidental (1-25%), accessory (25.1-50%), constant (50.1-75%), and euconstant (>75.1%) species. The ecological significance index (W) is calculated as C×D/100; there are accidental (<0.1%), accessory (0.1-5%), and characteristic (>5.1%) species [2].

Bacteria

Bacteria are procaryotic unicellular organisms, extremely diverse in terms of biology and ecology. They are the dominant life domain on Earth, in all existing habitats, including soils.

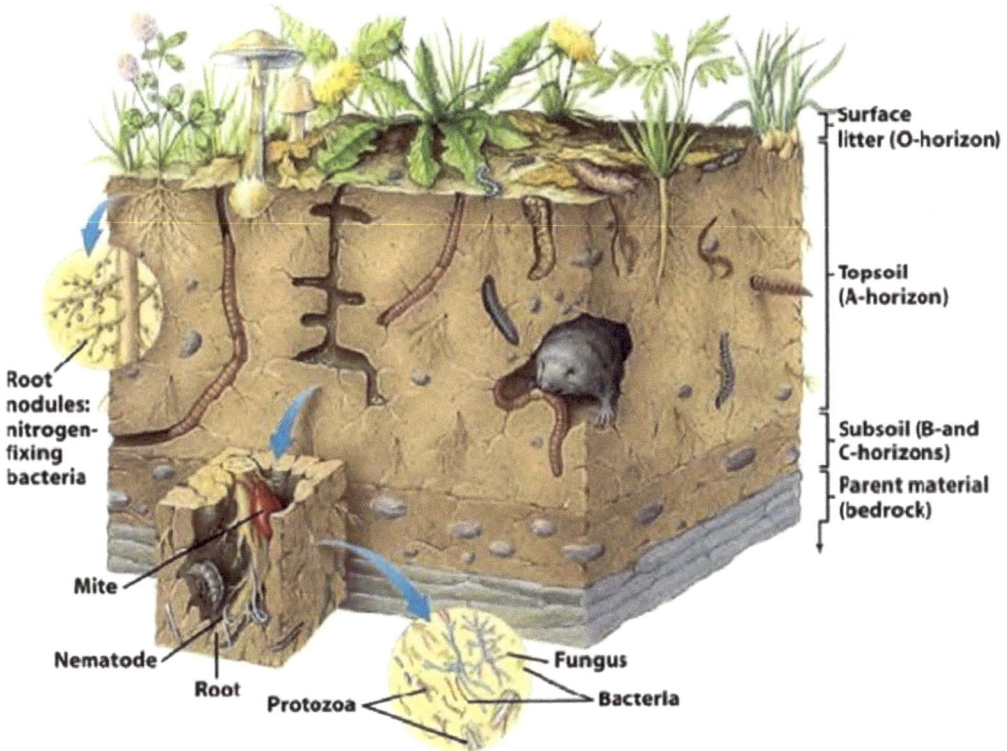

Fig. (1). Soil biodiversity [1].

Their density can be extremely variable, the limits being somewhere around 4×10^6, respectively 2×10^9 bacterial cells per gram of soil (dry mass), but can go up, under certain conditions, to about 10^{10} bacteria per gram. However, values around 10^8 cells per gram are the most common in most soil types [5, 6].

Regarding their general diversity, somewhere around 4×10^3-5×10^4 species can be found in a single gram of soil (although, of course, defining and delimiting bacterial species can be a complex topic) [5].

The density, diversity, and composition of soil microbiota depend on a wide array of factors. Among these are depth (which determines oxygen permeation), soil grain size (determines the available space, permeation of water and oxygen), mineral composition, the amount of organic matter (thus, available food), temperature, water content, and vegetation (involved in complex interactions with the local microbiota). An arid sandy soil will undoubtedly host much fewer bacteria than a muddy one. However, the differences can become significant even over small distances [5, 7].

The distribution of bacterial cells in the soil is far from uniform. The main determining factor here is the microtopography of soil grains (Fig. **3**). Pores, micro fissures, and other sheltered spaces tend to enlarge the surface available for bacterial adhesion, at the same time favoring the accumulation of organic matter.

While some bacteria are mobile, due to cilia or flagella, freely moving around in the pellicular and interstitial water, many adhere to the solid substrate, sometimes forming compact aggregates. Among adhesion mechanisms are electrostatic attraction between the components of cell walls and chemical compounds in the soil and exopolysaccharides, which cover the cell wall, either as a rigid capsule or as adhesive filaments (Fig. **3**) [8].

The ecological roles bacteria play are extremely variate.

According to their metabolism, more precisely, to the food and energy sources they employ, there are four main categories.

Photoautotrophic bacteria produce their food from atmospheric carbon dioxide, which gets fixed into organic structures by using sunlight energy. In this category, we can find cyanobacteria and a few other groups of bacteria, only present in superficial layers (where light can penetrate) of some particular soil types, especially moist ones.

Photoheterotrophs are photosynthesizing, but cannot use carbon dioxide as the sole carbon source, requiring various organic substrates. Although present in soils (*Rhodopseudomonas* sp., for instance), they are not particularly common.

Chemoautotrophs use reduced inorganic substrates to fix carbon dioxide. This category includes nitrifying and iron-oxidizing bacteria, present in many types of soil.

Chemoheterotrophs get both their necessary carbon and energy from organic substrates. Some are strictly specialized, being able to feed on just a few types of compounds, while others are rather multivalent. Within this category fits decomposing bacteria, dominant in soils, which are responsible for the very existence of soil [10].

Among ecological roles, we can mention the production of the organic components of soil, through decomposition. Also, soil microbiota mobilizes certain nutrients from their insoluble form, making them available to plants. On the contrary, other bacteria can mineralize certain chemicals, including toxins or pollutants.

Bacteria are essential to the continuous recycling process of the major bio elements: carbon, nitrogen, phosphorus, *etc.*

Their metabolites can regulate soil permeability or impermeability to water, while also contributing to natural filtering processes.

Some species are kept under control, through antibiosis, competition or hyperparasitism, and various phytopathogenic microorganisms (including some that affect crops).

Finally, some bacteria have biotechnological applications [10].

From a taxonomic and phylogenetic point of view, we can distinguish several major groupings (Fig. **2**).

Proteobacteria

These are Gram-negative bacteria (their cell wall features an outer membrane; (Fig. **4**). They usually form more than a quarter of the total soil microbiota, sometimes even over 40%.

This diverse group comprises several, quite different subdivisions, like α-Proteobacteria (among others, this group hosts the nitrogen fixer *Rhizobium* sp., but also nitrifiers like *Nitrospira* and *Nitrobacter*), β-Proteobacteria (with *Burkholderia, Alcaligenes, Thiobacillusetc.*), γ-Proteobacteria (*Pseudomonas* sp.), δ-Proteobacteria (with sulfate reducers in the genus *Desulfovibrio*, among others), ε-Proteobacteria (like *Helicobacter* sp.) [7, 10].

Acidobacteria

These are also gram-negative bacteria, usually acidophilic and often difficult to cultivate, thus long neglected by researchers. And yet, they are ubiquitous, often forming 20% or more of soil microbiota and seemingly playing key roles in decomposition processes. Among others, the group comprises genera like *Acidobacterium, Koribacter, Solibacter, etc* [10, 13].

Cyanobacteria

These are bacteria that, despite their phylogenetic position, have a Gram-negative cell wall structure. They are oxygenic photosynthesizing organisms, due to the presence of chlorophyll a. They are solitary or colonial (many species forming filamentous colonies), and some species can form symbioses with fungi or plants.

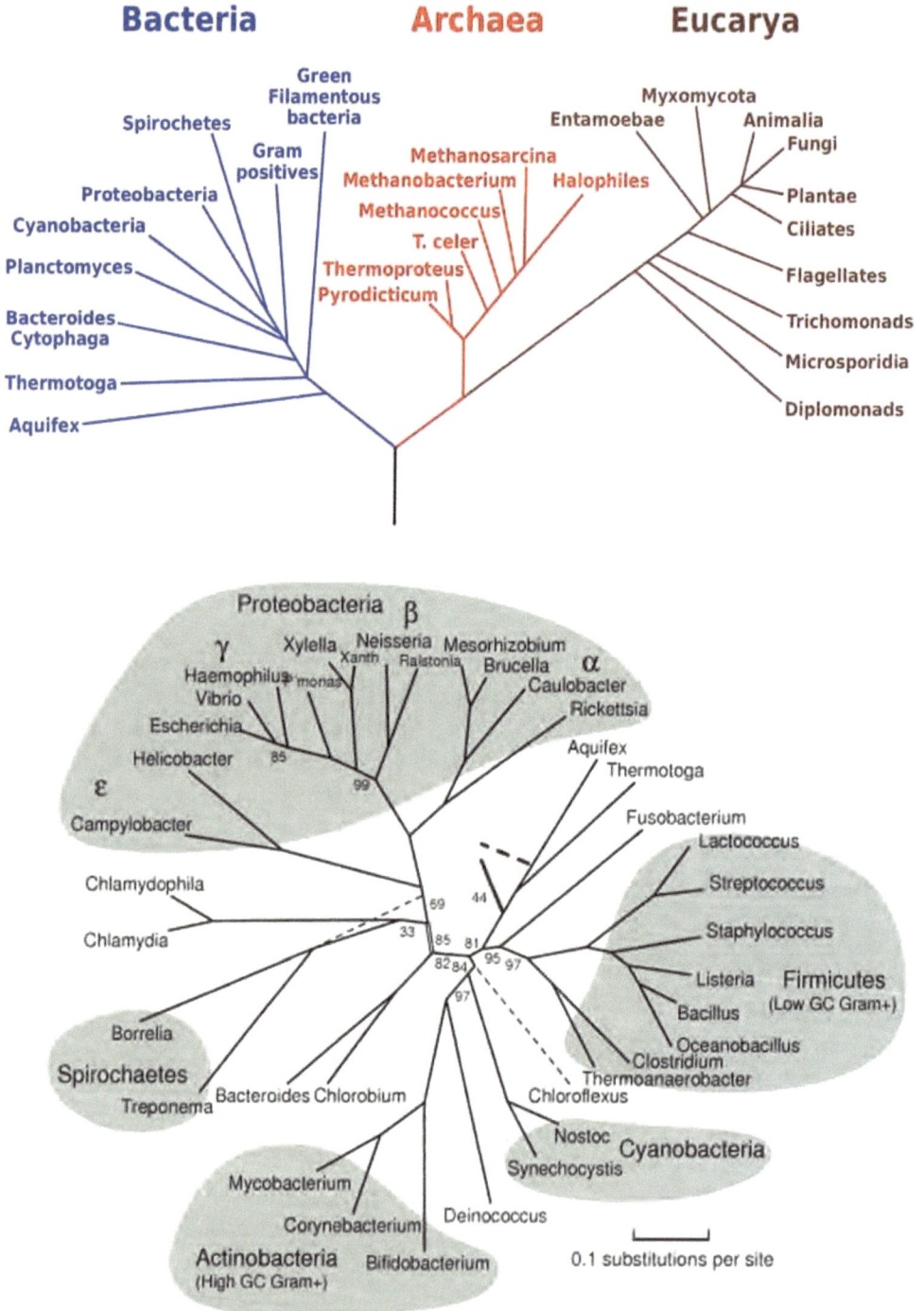

Fig. (2). Bacteria in the phylogenetic tree of life [3] and their own detailed phylogenetic tree [4].

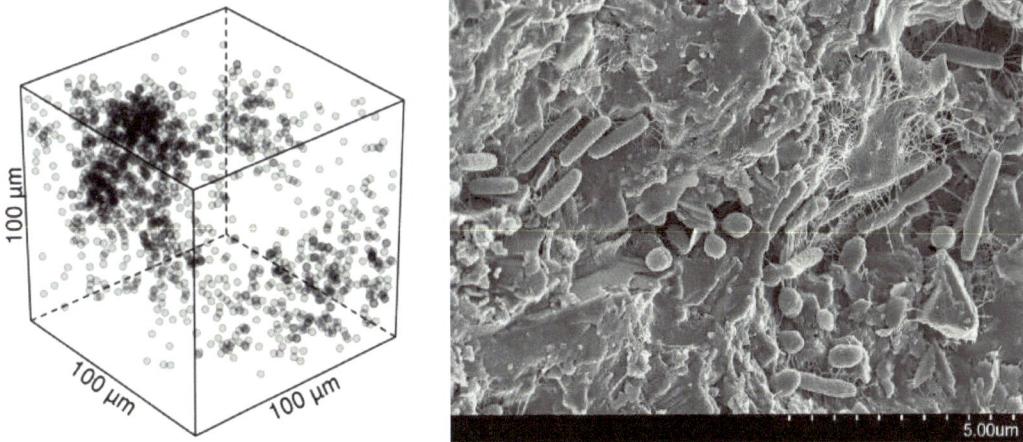

Fig. (3). The heterogenous spatial distribution of bacteria in the soil [5] and electron microscopy image of bacteria adhering to soil grains through polysaccharidic filaments [9].

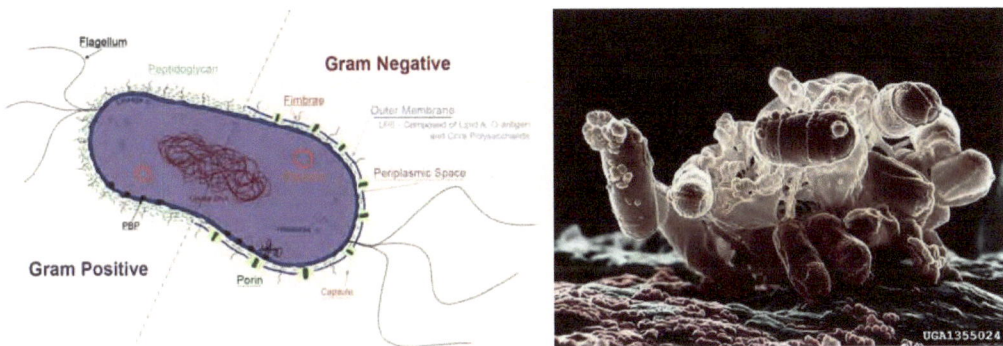

Fig. (4). Differences between Gram-negative and cele Gram-positive bacteria [11] and an electron microscopy image of some proteobacteria [12].

Their numbers are usually rather low in soils, although cyanobacteria can become more abundant in moist soil. From about 10^2, cyanobacterial density can reach up to 10^6-10^7 cells/cm^2 in wetland areas such as paddy fields [14]. Obviously, their photoautotrophic way of life forces them to populate only the upper soil layers, exposed to sunlight.

Among the most common genera are *Aphanocapsa, Leptolyngbya, Lyngbya, Microcoleus, Nostoc, Phormidium, Stigonema, Synechococcus, Synechocystis* (Fig. **5**) [15, 16].

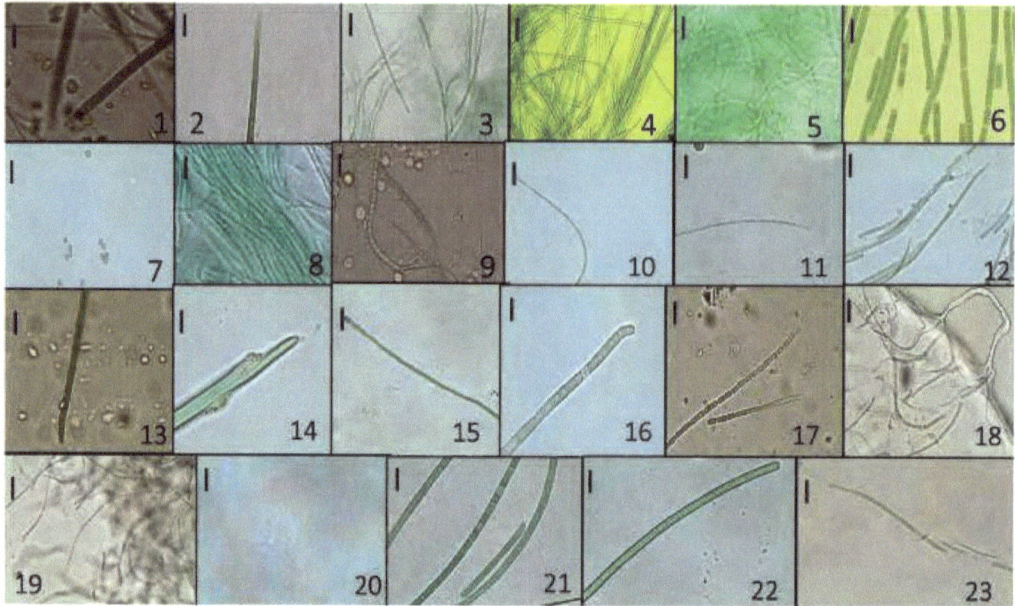

Fig. (5). Various cyanobacteria isolated from arid soils [16].

Regarding their ecological roles, cyanobacteria are, in the first place, primary producers, but many species are also able to fix atmospheric nitrogen into organic structures, being relatively important to the productivity of certain soil types [14]. In arid regions, they take part in the formation of biocrusts, one of the main forms of the desert "vegetation" [16].

Chlorobacteria (Chloroflexi)

These are a rather diverse group of bacteria, including some anoxygenic photoautotrophic species ("green non-sulfur bacteria"), but also some heterotrophic ones. They can form 1-2% of soil microbiota, although in some cases they may reach 16% [7, 10].

Firmicutes

They are Gram-positive bacteria, either rod-shaped (bacilli) or spherical (cocci), with a thick and rigid cell wall, often producing endospores (forms of resistance to adverse conditions). Most are heterotrophic, either aerobic or anaerobic.

They are another important component of soil microbiota, comprising anywhere between 1 and 40% [7, 17].

Actinobacteria

Actinobacteria are one of the main lifeforms in soil, with up to 25% of the local microbiota [7, 10, 17]. Gram-positive microbes, with a less-developed cell wall than Firmicutes, are capable of spore-formation and have a filamentous shape. While some species have slightly elongated cells, others can form widely branched, single-cell networks, with a huge absorption area, similar to fungal mycelia (for this reason, they are also called "actinomycetes").

They are aerobic heterotrophs, living freely or sometimes forming symbioses with plant roots, actively involved in organic matter decomposition, but also in processes like organic and inorganic phosphorus mobilization. Some species in the *Streptomyces* genus, produce antibiotic compounds [10, 18].

ARCHAEA

Formerly known as "archaebacteria", archaea are currently considered a distinct domain of life on Earth. Prokaryotic, unicellular organisms, with various shapes (Fig. **6**), sometimes colonia, are present in all types of soil, with variable densities, going up to 10% of the total microbiota.

Among the most common are methanogens (genera *Methanosarcina*, *Methanosaeta*, *Methanocella*), found in hypoxic, moist, swampy soils, or anoxic niches in other types of soil. Together with other types of microorganisms, they are involved in anaerobic decomposition processes. Methanogenic archaea are responsible for producing biogenic methane.

Other archaea (such as *Nitrososphaera* sp.) are involved in the aerobic oxidation of ammonia. There are also some species taking part in the sulfur and iron cycles. Finally, some extremophilic archaea inhabit salty, acid, or hot (volcanic) soils [10, 20].

SUBCELLULAR ENTITIES

At the border between living and non-living beings, there are a few known or just assumed entities.

Viruses

Having genetic material and, usually, a proteic shell (capsid), but lacking a metabolism and totally dependent on their host for reproduction, with sizes of tens or hundreds of nanometers, viruses challenge the very definition of life.

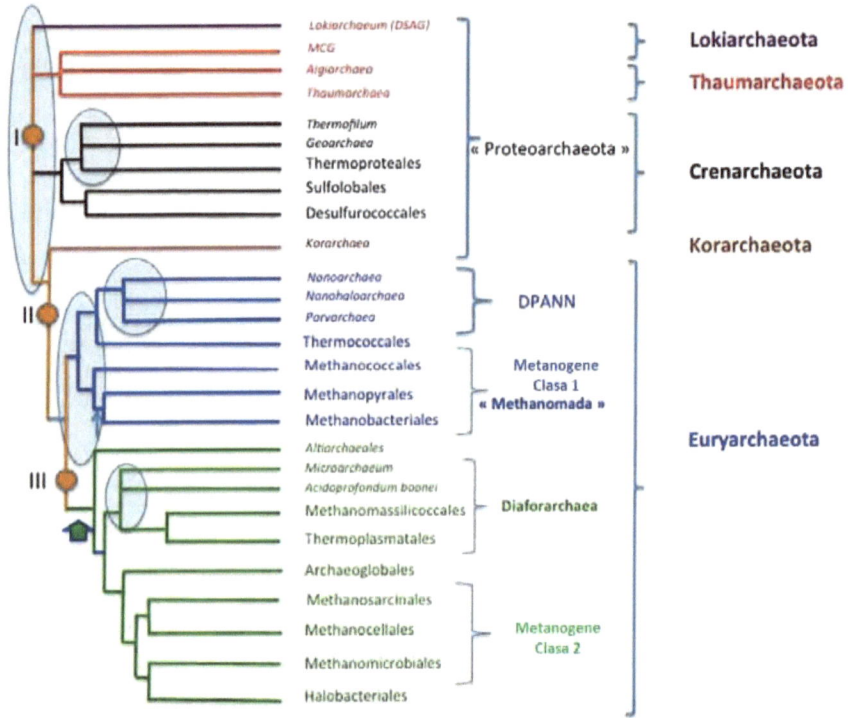

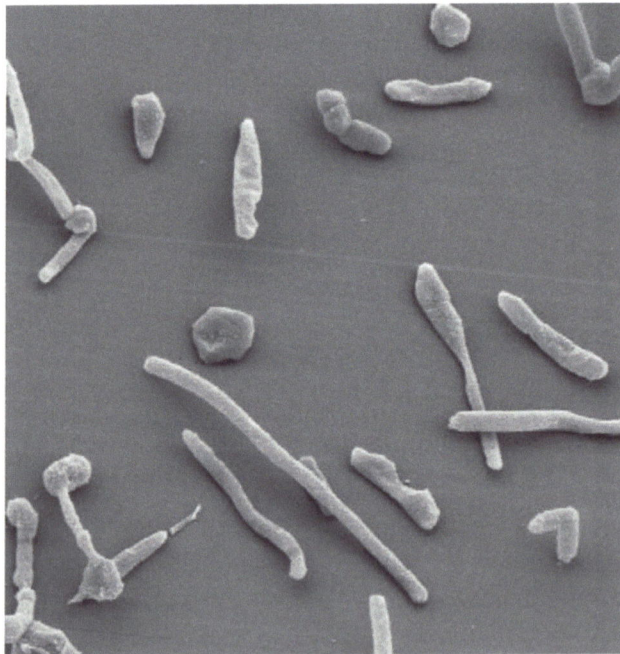

Fig. (6). Phylogenetic tree of archaea [19] and different shapes of archaea isolated from soil [20].

Although often ignored, viruses are extremely numerous in soils, reaching densities equal to those of bacteria (up to 10^{10} viral particles per gram of soil). By far, the most numerous are bacteriophages (Fig. **7**), having prokaryotic organisms as hosts. By analogy with aquatic environments, researchers consider that 1-4% of observable bacterial cells are infected, each one releasing, on average, 10 new viral particles.

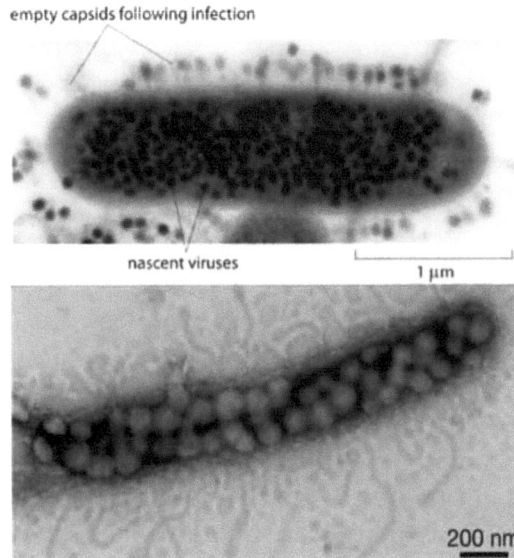

empty capsids following infection

nascent viruses

1 μm

200 nm

Fig. (7). Bacteriophages infecting soil bacteria [21].

Viruses can have lytic life cycles (the virus forces its host to rapidly reproduce it, which leads to cell destruction during the release of new viruses), lysogenic cycles (they temporarily integrate the host's genome), or pseudo lysogenic ones (while proceeding towards viral lysis, the host cell can still reproduce itself) [22].

The distribution and propagation of viruses depend on soil characteristics. Viruses can be considered colloidal particles, moved around by soil solution, but that can concentrate, through adsorption, in some areas. Clay minerals, due to their electrostatic charges and organic matter, due to hydrophobic interaction with viral capsids, can influence this distribution.

Among bacterial taxonomic groups most attacked by bacteriophages are Proteobacteria, Acidobacteria, and Verrucomicrobia.

Regarding their ecological roles, viruses are involved in organic matter recycling, but also in the horizontal transfer of genetic information between different strains and species of microorganisms. An estimated 5-25% of the carbon synthesized by primary producers will, at some point, be involved in cell destruction caused by viruses, at different levels of trophic chains [21 - 23].

Nanobacteria/Nanobes

Until recently, scientists considered that a minimum diameter of 0.2 μm would be a prerequisite of cell life, taking into account the normal sizes of cell components. This, however, goes against various reports of organisms smaller than that.

Currently, there are several bacterial taxa (especially within the so-called "CPR group" – *candidate phyla radiation*), but also "nanoarchaea" with sizes below 0.04 μm. We could also add starvation forms of some normal-sized bacteria, that under adverse conditions can reach similar sizes (0.05-0.06 μm). Although difficult to culture and identify, such organisms could form a significant, if not major part of the microbiota in most environments – soil included [24, 27 - 29].

Yet there are reports of even more mysterious and hard to understand lifeforms. Known as *nanobacteria* or, especially when having a filamentous shape, *nanobes*, they were identified by several authors in the most diverse environments: human body, residual water, soil, rock surface, or rock cores extracted from great depths and seem to be often involved in mineralization processes. Their size can go down to 20 nm, making it impossible for them to have a regular cell structure, as we know it (Fig. **8**). Not even ribosomes could fit inside such cells.

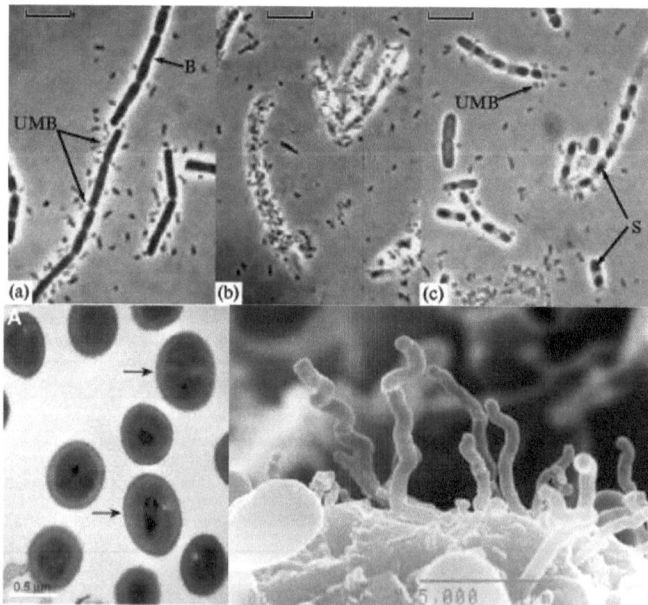

Fig. (8). Ultramicrobacteria (UMB) [24] *versus* nanobacteria [25] and nanobes [26].

All these reports were contested, some researchers suggest the use of despite their obviously organic look, crystals, (partially) self-replicating organo-mineral complexes, *etc.* Their discoverers claim to have found nucleic acids inside these "nanoorganisms" – thus explaining their self-replication. Contesters claim that external contaminations and merely apparent reproduction occur due to mineral crystallization [24, 27, 30].

The somewhat paradoxical conclusion is that such nanoorganisms might not exist, but if they do, due to their low size, they would not only be a part of new, unknown, domains of life, but they would very likely be the dominant lifeforms in most terrestrial ecosystems, including soils.

MICROALGAE

Algae is an eclectic, diverse, and polyphyletic group of eukaryote organisms. Their common features are the ability to photosynthesize and their preference towards aquatic, or at least moist environments (Fig. **9**).

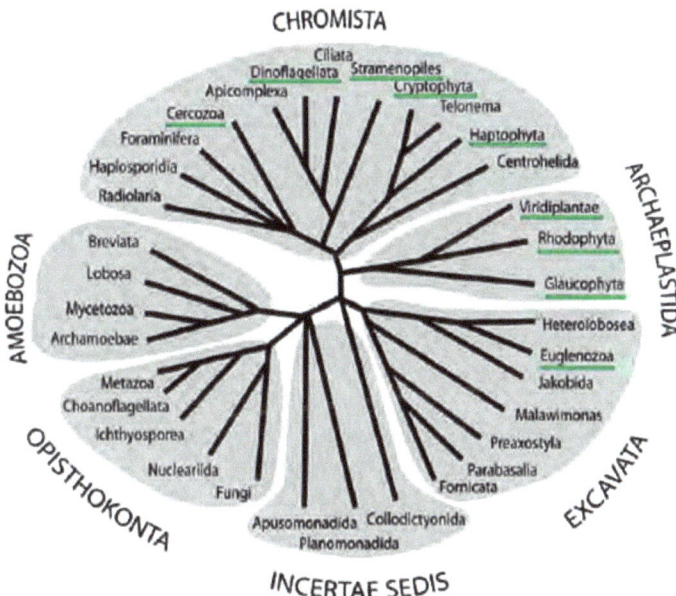

Fig. (9). The phylogenetic tree of eukaryotes. Groups that contain photosynthesizing organisms are underlined in green [31].

For obvious reasons, when such organisms are found in soil biota, they only inhabit the superficial layers (where there is acces to sunlight), in areas with enough water content. Also, soil algae are almost exclusiverly unicellular.

Their density varies, from close to 0 to 10^8 cells/g, although common values are 10^3-10^4 cells/g.

As an ecological role, they are primary producers and contribute to organic matter production in soil (although it is a limited contribution), but mostly to the ecological succession of vegetal communities, by colonizing pristine substrates (barren rock, for instance).

Other functions include nitrogen fixation and stabilization of the upper soil layers, thus lowering erosion [32].

Green Algae (Chlorophyta)

Green algae are one of the main groups of photosynthesizing microorganisms found in soil. Closely related to plants, possessing chloroplasts with chlorophyll a and b, these lifeforms are usually unicellular, solitary or colonial, bearing flagella or not.

Among the most common genera found in European soils are *Bracteacoccus*, *Chlorella*, *Coccomyxa*, *Chloropyrula*, *Chlamydomonas*, *Chloroidium*, *Chromochloris*, *Dictyococcus*, *Interfilum*, *Klebsormidium*, *Neocystis*, *Pseudomuriella* and *Scenedesmus* (Fig. **10**) [34].

In certain wetlands, paddy fields, or tropical soils, pluricellular filamentous forms may occur, such as members of the genera *Klebsormidium* and *Ulothrix* [33].

Diatoms

The other most important group of soil algae is represented by diatoms (class Bacillariophyceae, phylum Ocrophyta).

Exclusively unicellular organisms, possessing chlorophyll a and c and having their characteristic silica shell, made of valves, diatoms are widespread in many types of environments, including soils.

The density and specific composition of diatom populations vary significantly according to soil type and local environmental conditions, including the impact of anthropic activities (agricultural practices, pollution, *etc.*), some of them being considered valuable bioindicators of soil quality.

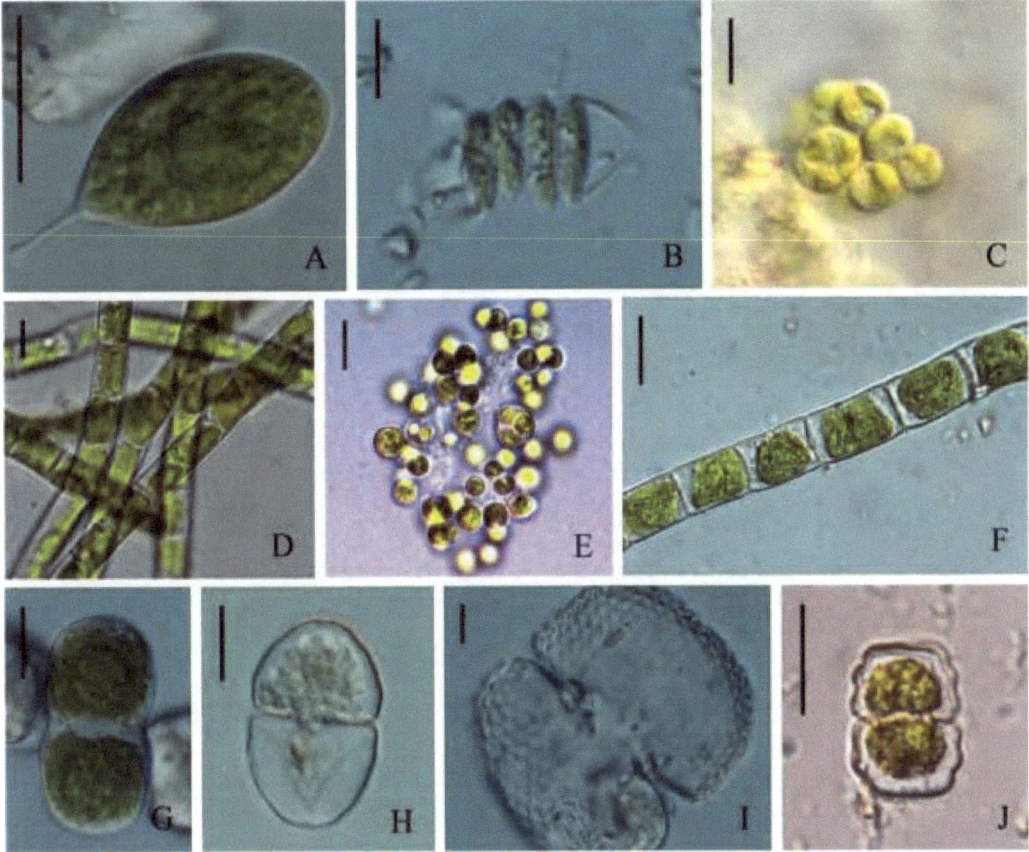

Fig. (10). A few green algae that may be found in upper soil layers: A. *Characium* sp., B. *Scenedesmus* sp., C. *Chlamydomonas* sp., D. *Klebsormidium* sp., E. *Chlorella* sp., F. *Ulothrix* sp., G. *Actinotaenium* sp., H-J. *Cosmarium* sp [33].

While at the surface of some wetland, alluvial soils, we may find species that are rather specific to aquatic environments, in dry soils only the most adapted diatoms can thrive; fro example, species having valves that properly protect them against ultraviolet rays and retain water. Among the most common land diatoms are species belonging to the genera *Navicula, Nitzschia,* and *Pinnularia*; Fig. (**11**) [33, 35].

Yellow-green Algae (Xanthophyceae)

These are members of the same phylum, Ocrophyta, as the diatoms, also possessing chlorophyll a and c. Although widespread globally, they generally prefer very moist soils. The group contains both unicallular (*Botrydiopsis* sp.), and multicellular filamentous algae (*Botrydium* sp., *Tribonema* sp., *Vaucheria* sp.; Fig. (**12**) [32, 36].

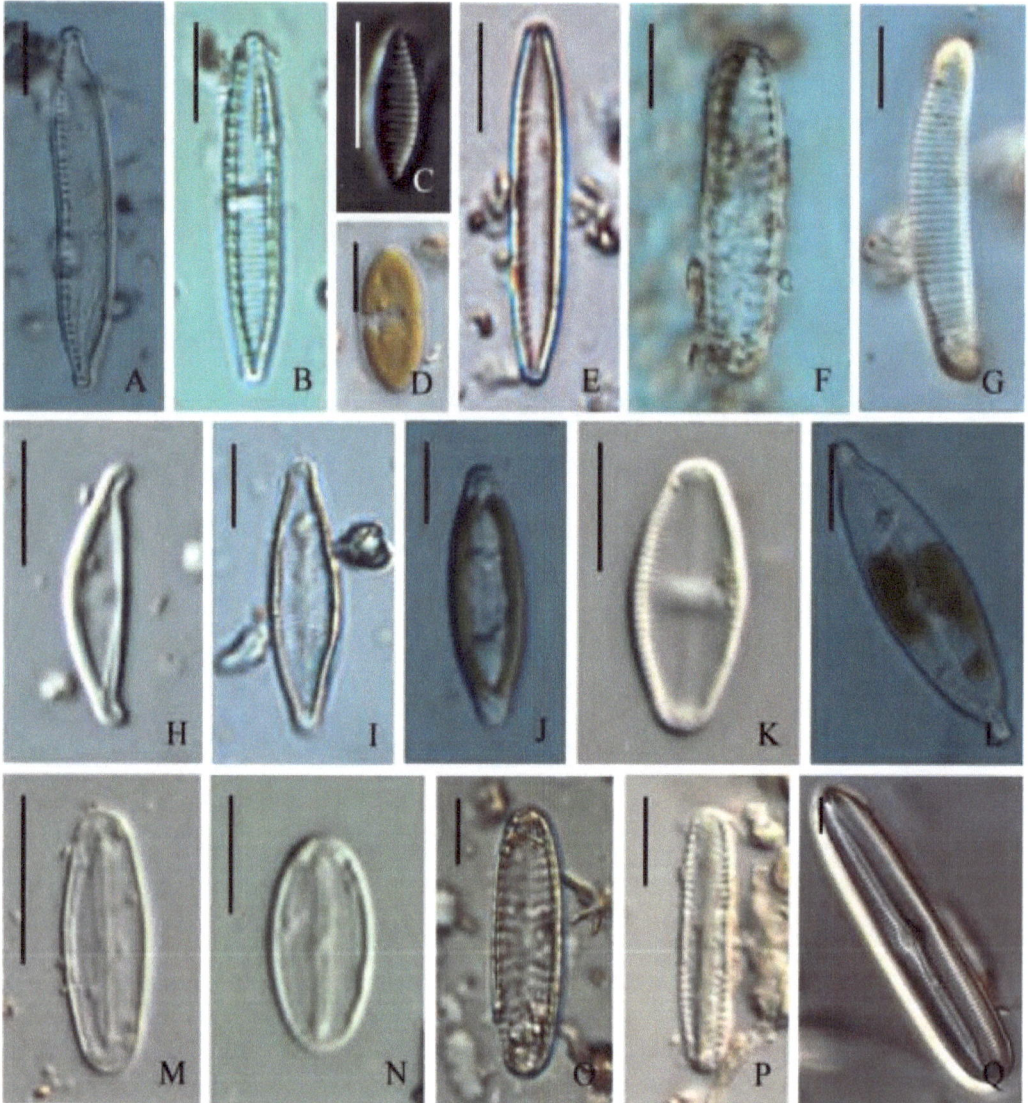

Fig. (11). Some diatoms found in upper soil layers: A. *Hantzschia* sp., B-E. *Nitzschia* sp., F. *Encyonema* sp., G. *Eunotia* sp., H. *Amphora* sp., I-N. *Navicula* sp., O-Q. *Pinnularia* sp [33].

Other Algae

Other groups, much less represented include Eustigmatophyceae (unicellular, related to yellow-green algae and diatoms, within phylum Ochrophyta), Dinophyceae (dinoflagellates, unicellular, mobile organisms), Cryptophyceae (biflagellate unicellular organisms), or some red algae (Rhodophyta), especially unicellular forms belonging to the genus *Cyanidium* [32, 36].

Fig. (12). Two genera of yellow-green algae occurring in some types of soil [37].

PROTOZOA

Just like algae, protozoa are actually an extremely eclectic and polyphyletic group of organisms. We could define them as the ensemble of eukaryotic unicellular lifeforms that lack a photosynthetic apparatus. So, they have a saprophytic, predatory or parasitic way of life.

There are somewhere between 1,600 and 4,000 protozoan species present in this environment, while their density is around 10^4-10^6 cells/gram of soil. Size varies between 5 and 500 μm.

Their roles in soil ecology are numerous. First of all, protozoa are the main bacteria grazers (especially ciliates and amoebae), eating more than half of the overall bacterial mass, while also being prey to other, larger, organisms (nematodes). Thus, they not only form a key component of trophic chains but also keep certain groups of bacterial populations under control. Furthermore, much of the organic nitrogen they consume is released with their dejections, as ammonium ions (NH_4^+), easily accessible to plants [38 - 40].

Usually, protozoans are divided into several large morphological groups, even if they do not have much taxonomic relevance.

Testate Amoebae

These are a polyphyletic group, comprising very diverse subdivisions of the phyla Amoebozoa, Cercozoa, and not only.

Their common feature is the mineral test, made of silica or calcium carbonate, protecting their cells. Tests are either formed of endogenous material by agglutinating mineral particles from the environment on a sticky extra membranary sheath (Fig. **13**).

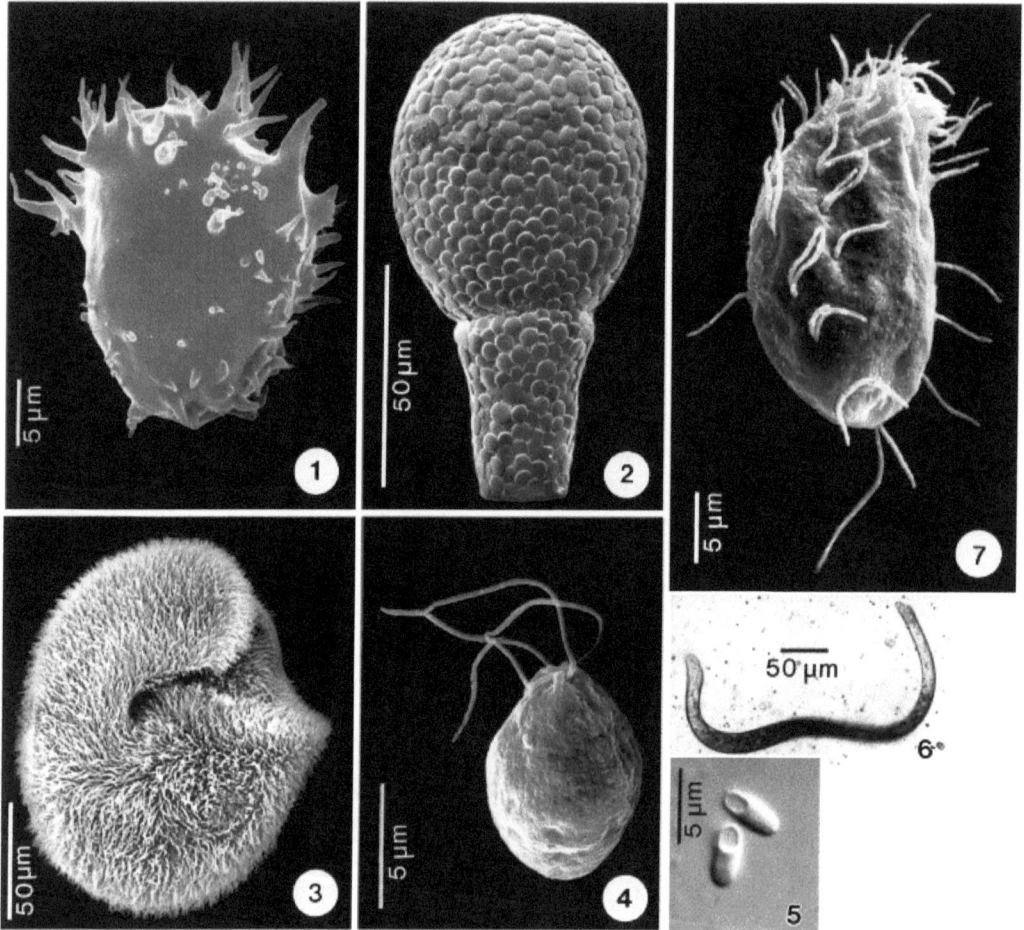

Fig. (13). Few examples of soil protozoa: 1. a naked amoeba (*Mayorella* sp.), 2. a testate amoeba (*Nebela* sp.), 3. ciliate (*Bresslauides* sp.), 4. flagellate (*Polytomella* sp.), 5. sporozoan parasitising ciliates (*Ciliatosporidium* sp.), 6. filamentous ciliate (*Circinella* sp.), 7. fungivore ciliate (*Pseudoplaytophrya* sp.) [38].

They are one of the most common groups of protozoa in soil, with densities ranging from a few hundred and up to 10^4-10^5 cells/g in soils rich in organic matter.

Due to their large cells, they definitely possess the highest overall biomass of all types of soil protozoa [38].

Naked Amoebae

In this category, we can find an even wider variety of taxonomic groups of eukaryotes. They all share the classic amoeboid shape, continuously changing due to their cells forming pseudopods (used in both moving and feeding; (Fig. **13**).

Not surprisingly, this highly variate group seems to be the most abundant, with densities of 10^3-10^6 cells per gram of soil. They are usually bacterivores, although some may feed on other protozoa and even fungi. They can feed by phagocytosis or perforation and can use even the tiniest available spaces inside or between soil grains [38, 40].

Flagellates

Another extremely polyphyletic group is because many eukaryote phyla host members that are mobile through 1-2 or even more flagella (Fig. **13**). There are at least 260 species (strictly speaking of heterotrophic flagellates) isolated and determined in soils up to now, with extremely variable densities, from close to 0 and up to one million cells/g.

However, they are also very small (5-20 μm), so their contribution to overall biomass is quite limited [38, 40].

Ciliates

Unlike previous groupings, this one is monophyletic, from a taxonomic point of view (phylum Ciliophora). Around 2,000 species are known to inhabit soils (many yet to be described), all having massive, binucleated cells, moving by using their numerous cilia (Fig. **13**). They prefer superficial layers of soil and humid areas (larger cells require more water to move), where they can become the main group of bacterivore organisms, surpassing naked amoebas. They are not necessarily very abundant (up to 10^4/g), but they compensate by their high cellular biomass.

While almost 40% feed on bacteria, there are also predatory ciliates (about one-third; they feed on other protists, and fungi – some species being even strictly specialized on fungi) or omnivores (20%). There are a few anaerobic species, thriving in hypoxic soils [38, 40].

Sporozoa

More precisely, phylum Apicomplexa, comprises extremely diverse parasitic unicellular organisms. In soil, they are mostly present as parasites of ciliates, nematodes, annelids, *etc.*, [38].

CONCLUSION

Soil life is clearly dominated by microorganisms. While soil hosts its own microbiota, it is the very microbiota that creates and shapes soil.

Bacteria are, as far as we know, the dominant lifeforms, and among them, Proteobacteria, Acidobacteria, Firmicutes, and Actinobacteria are the main taxonomic groups found in soils. Besides them, subcellular entities such as viruses and the hypothetical nano organisms may equal or even outnumber bacteria.

Archaea and the taxonomically diverse "protozoans" are other key components of soil life, while microalgae can form significant populations, but only in upper soil layers.

REFERENCES

[1]   Van der Berg, M., All about soil – Part 2: Soil food web. Equine Permaculture, 2018, Available from: https://equinepermaculture.com/blog/2018/11/18/all-about-soils-part-2-soil-food-web/

[2]   Trotuş E, Mincea C, Pintilie PL, Amarghioalei RG, Zaharia R. New data on knowledge of pest entomofauna and ecological parameters for rapeseed, sunflower and corn crops. Rom J Plant Prot 2022; 15: 66-77.
[http://dx.doi.org/10.54574/RJPP.15.08]

[3]   Eisen, J., Fact sheet: rRNA in evolutionary studies and environmental sampling. Microbenet: The Microbiology of The Built Environment Network, 2022, Available from: https://microbe.net/simple-guides/fact-sheet-rrna-in-evolutionary-studies-and-environmental-sampling/

[4]   Bern M, Goldberg D. Automatic selection of representative proteins for bacterial phylogeny. BMC Evol Biol 2005; 5(1): 34.
[http://dx.doi.org/10.1186/1471-2148-5-34] [PMID: 15927057]

[5]   Raynaud X, Nunan N. Spatial ecology of bacteria at the microscale in soil. PLoS One 2014; 9(1): e87217.
[http://dx.doi.org/10.1371/journal.pone.0087217] [PMID: 24489873]

[6]   Vieira FCS, Nahas E. Comparison of microbial numbers in soils by using various culture media and temperatures. Microbiol Res 2005; 160(2): 197-202.
[http://dx.doi.org/10.1016/j.micres.2005.01.004] [PMID: 15881837]

[7]   Feng H, Guo J, Wang W, Song X, Yu S. Soil depth determines the composition and diversity of bacterial and archaeal communities in a poplar plantation. Forests 2019; 10(7): 550.
[http://dx.doi.org/10.3390/f10070550]

[8]   Nkoh NJ, Liu ZD, Yan J, Cai SJ, Hong ZN, Xu RK. The role of extracellular polymeric substances in bacterial adhesion onto variable charge soils. Arch Agron Soil Sci 2020; 66(13): 1780-93.
[http://dx.doi.org/10.1080/03650340.2019.1696016]

[9]   Turco, R., Are soil bacteria harmful? Soils Matter, Get the Scoop!, 2014, Available from: https://soilsmatter.wordpress.com/2014/09/02/the-living-soil/

[10]   Aislabie J, Deslippe JR. Soil microbes and their contribution to soil services. In: Dymond JR, Ed. Ecosystem Services in New Zealand – Conditions and Trends. Lincoln: Manaaki Whenua Press 2013; pp. 143-61.

[11]   Robinson, C., Bacterial structures. MedBullets, 2022, Available from: https://step1.medbullets.com/microbiology/104001/bacterial-structures

[12]   Garge, S., Proteobacteria. Alchetron, 2020, Available from: https://alchetron.com/Proteobacteria

[13]   Kalam S, Basu A, Ahmad I, *et al.* Recent understanding of soil acidobacteria and their ecological significance: A critical review. Front Microbiol 2020; 11: 580024.
[http://dx.doi.org/10.3389/fmicb.2020.580024] [PMID: 33193209]

[14]   Roger, P.A., Rice field cyanobacteria: Ecology, contribution to soil fertility and practical utilisation. În Morot-Gaudry J.F. (ed.), Nitrogen Assimilation by Plants : Physiological, Biochemical and Molecular Aspects, Science Publishers, Enfield, 2001, pp. 199-226.

[15]   Redkina VV, Shalygina RR, Korneykova MV. Microfungi, algae and cyanobacteria in soils polluted with fluorine (Kola Peninsula, Russia). Czech Polar Rep 2020; 10(1): 94-109.
[http://dx.doi.org/10.5817/CPR2020-1-9]

[16]   Hakkoum Z, Minaoui F, Douma M, Mouhri K, Loudiki M. Impact of human disturbances on soil cyanobacteria diversity and distribution in suburban arid area of Marrakesh, Morocco. Ecol Process 2021; 10(1): 42.
[http://dx.doi.org/10.1186/s13717-021-00303-7]

[17]   Zhang G, Chu X, Zhu H, Zou D, Li L, Du L. The response of soil nutrients and microbial community structures in long-term tea plantations and diverse agroforestry intercropping systems. Sustainability (Basel) 2021; 13(14): 7799.
[http://dx.doi.org/10.3390/su13147799]

[18]   Ghorbani-Nasrabadi R, Greiner R, Alikhani HA, Hamedi J, Yakhchali B. Distribution of actinomycetes in different soil ecosystems and effect of media composition on extracellular phosphatase activity. J Soil Sci Plant Nutr 2013; 13(ahead): 0.
[http://dx.doi.org/10.4067/S0718-95162013005000020]

[19]   Forterre P. The universal tree of life: an update. Front Microbiol 2015; 6: 717.
[http://dx.doi.org/10.3389/fmicb.2015.00717] [PMID: 26257711]

[20]   Global Soil Biodiversity Initiative, Archaea. In Global Soil Biodiversity Atlas, 2019. Available from: https://static1.squarespace.com/static/5b9033f1f8370a3700df6f4b/t/5be32923758d46e25fd81465/1541 613863280/GSBAtlas_ch2_Archaea.pdf

[21]   Kuzyakov Y, Mason-Jones K. Viruses in soil: Nano-scale undead drivers of microbial life, biogeochemical turnover and ecosystem functions. Soil Biol Biochem 2018; 127: 305-17.
[http://dx.doi.org/10.1016/j.soilbio.2018.09.032]

[22]   Kimura M, Jia ZJ, Nakayama N, Asakawa S. Ecology of viruses in soils: Past, present and future perspectives. Soil Sci Plant Nutr 2008; 54(1): 1-32.
[http://dx.doi.org/10.1111/j.1747-0765.2007.00197.x]

[23]   Trubl G, Jang HB, Roux S, *et al.* Soil viruses are underexplored players in ecosystem carbon processing. mSystems 2018; 3(5): 10.1128/msystems.00076-18.
[http://dx.doi.org/10.1128/msystems.00076-18] [PMID: 30320215]

[24]   Duda VI, Suzina NE, Polivtseva VN, Boronin AM. Ultramicrobacteria: Formation of the concept and contribution of ultramicrobacteria to biology. Mikrobiologiia 2012; 81(4): 415-27.
[PMID: 23156684]

[25]   Zhang MJ, Liu SN, Xu G, Guo YN, Fu JN, Zhang DC. Cytotoxicity and apoptosis induced by nanobacteria in human breast cancer cells. Int J Nanomedicine 2014; 9: 265-71.
[PMID: 24403832]

[26]   Bruckner, M., Nanobacteria and Nanobes- Are They Alive? Microbial Life – Educational Resources, 2022. Available from: https://serc.carleton.edu/microbelife/topics/nanobes/index.html

[27]   Velimirov B. Nanobacteria, ultramicrobacteria and starvation forms: A search for the smallest metabolizing bacterium. Microbes Environ 2001; 16(2): 67-77.
[http://dx.doi.org/10.1264/jsme2.2001.67]

[28]   Luef B, Frischkorn KR, Wrighton KC, *et al.* Diverse uncultivated ultra-small bacterial cells in groundwater. Nat Commun 2015; 6(1): 6372.
[http://dx.doi.org/10.1038/ncomms7372] [PMID: 25721682]

[29]   Nicolas, A.M., Jaffe, A.L., Nuccio, E.E., Taga, M.E., Firestone, M.K., 3,4, Banfield, J.F., Unexpected diversity of CPR bacteria and nanoarchaea in the rare biosphere of rhizosphere-associated grassland soil. bioRxiv, 2020.
[http://dx.doi.org/10.1101/2020.07.13.194282]

[30]   Urbano P, Urbano F. Nanobacteria: Facts or Fancies? PLoS Pathog 2007; 3(5): e55.
[http://dx.doi.org/10.1371/journal.ppat.0030055] [PMID: 17530922]

[31]   Sutak R, Botebol H, Blaiseau PL, *et al.* A comparative study of iron uptake mechanisms in marine microalgae: iron binding at the cell surface is a critical step. Plant Physiol 2012; 160(4): 2271-84.
[http://dx.doi.org/10.1104/pp.112.204156] [PMID: 23033141]

[32]   Metting B. The systematics and ecology of soil algae. Bot Rev 1981; 47(2): 195-312.
[http://dx.doi.org/10.1007/BF02868854]

[33]   Lin CS, Chou TL, Wu JT. Biodiversity of soil algae in the farmlands of mid-Taiwan. Bot Stud (Taipei, Taiwan) 2013; 54(1): 41.
[http://dx.doi.org/10.1186/1999-3110-54-41] [PMID: 28510880]

[34]   Hodač, L., Green algae in soil: assessing their biodiversity and biogeography with molecular-phylogenetic methods based on cultures. Teză de Doctorat, Georg-August-Universität Göttingen, 188, 2015.

[35]   Foets J, Wetzel CE, Teuling AJ, Pfister L. Temporal and spatial variability of terrestrial diatoms at the catchment scale: controls on communities. Peer J 2020; 8: e8296.
[http://dx.doi.org/10.7717/peerj.8296] [PMID: 31915584]

[36]   Venter A, Levanets A, Siebert S, Rajakaruna N. A preliminary survey of the diversity of soil algae and cyanoprokaryotes on mafic and ultramafic substrates in South Africa. Aust J Bot 2015; 63(4): 341-52.
[http://dx.doi.org/10.1071/BT14207]

[37]   Example of yellow green algae. ExamplesOf.net, Available from: https://www.examplesof.net/2014/04/example-of-yellow-green-algae.html

[38]   Foissner W. Soil protozoa as bioindicators: pros and cons, methods, diversity, representative examples. Agric Ecosyst Environ 1999; 74(1-3): 95-112.
[http://dx.doi.org/10.1016/S0167-8809(99)00032-8]

[39]   Bonkowski M. Soil protozoa as bioindicators: pros and cons, methods, diversity, representative examples. New Phytol 2004; 162: 617-31.
[http://dx.doi.org/10.1111/j.1469-8137.2004.01066.x] [PMID: 33873756]

[40]   Hoorman, J.J., The role of soil protozoa and nematodes. Fact Sheet, Agriculture and Natural Resources, Ohio State University, 2011. Available from: https://citeseerx.ist.psu.edu/viewdoc/download?doi=10.1.1.231.647&rep=rep1&type=pdf

CHAPTER 3

Soil Biodiversity, Macrobiota

Abstract: The most abundant multicellular organisms in the soil are fungi (although the group also contains unicellular members – yeasts). Fungi are an extremely diverse group of heterotrophic organisms. Most are saprophytic, playing key roles in decomposition and pedogenesis processes. We can add parasitic species, as well as lichens, and photoautotrophic symbiotic associations. Similar to an organization and way of life are mycetozoa and pseudofungi (oomycetes and their relatives). Plants are present in the soil only through their underground organs (roots, rhizomes, bulbs, *etc.*), but have an essential contribution to the genesis and functioning of soil, once their various underground and aboveground components decompose. Finally, animals are some of the main consumers of soil. Here we may find nematodes, annelids, insects, and other arthropods and some species of vertebrates that use soil as a temporary or permanent living environment.

Keywords: Animals, Fungi, Mycetozoa, Pseudo fungi, Plants.

INTRODUCTION

While microbial life may be dominant on Earth, in terms of numbers, other lifeforms are also key components of the biosphere.

Plants, animals, and fungi contribute with their large individual biomasses but also fill in important ecological positions: primary producers, predators, but also important decomposers.

Soils are no exception to this.

Fungi

Fungi are eukaryotic organisms, quite related phylogenetically to animals. Usually, their body is pluricellular and mycelian, formed of an extremely branched array of hyphae, which gives fungi a huge absorption surface. In some groups, parts of the hyphae come together forming pseudo-tissues called plectenchyma and even complex structures such as macroscopic fruiting bodies.

At the other end, some fungi (especially yeats) are single-celled and colonial, with an intermediate version of species bearing pseudo-hyphae. Very often, fungi have complex life cycles.

Up to now, at least 80,000 species and over 8,000 genera are known, of which most dwell in soils, at least partially. They form a consistent part of soil biota. Researchers estimate that fungi form 10-30% of the overall mass of rhizospheres (the soil region neighboring plant root systems).

Fungi can be either saprophytic or parasitic. They can live freely in complex symbiotic associations, such as lichens (associations with microalgae) and mycorrhizae (associations with plant roots, which will be described in another chapter) [1].

While the densest populations are found in rhizospheres, fungi are widespread in soils. Yet, they mostly inhabit the upper layers, respectively the plant litter and O horizon, due to their saprophytic regime and the need to get organic matter.

Fungi have a remarkable ecological plasticity, colonizing a wide variety of soils, from tropical rainforests to the driest deserts.

Their ecological roles are numerous. First of all, mycelial networks can perform a mechanical function, stabilizing mobile soils, which is extremely obvious in some arid regions of the world [2].

However, most of all, as decomposers, fungi are essential to the breakdown of dead organic matter and its reinsertion in trophic chains, thus, to the biogeochemical cycles of carbon and nitrogen. Fungi are able to decompose even some of the hardiest organic substances, such as lignin. They are also among the first organisms involved in breaking down plant material fallen onto the soil surface: dead leaves, fruits, *etc.*

By decomposing woody material, they create microecosystems that allow other organisms to settle in. In addition, as symbionts of plant roots, they enhance water and mineral absorption, and plant productivity, but also resistance to disease and adverse pedological conditions. Last but not least, parasitic fungi are also important for trophic chains at the soil level [2].

Fungal taxonomy is extremely complicated (Fig. **1**), but, traditionally, this phylum is divided into three main groups: Zygomycota, Ascomycota, and Basidiomycota, to which we may add the Deuteromycota, a mysterious and probably polyphyletic grouping of all fungi that seemingly lack any kind of sexual reproduction.

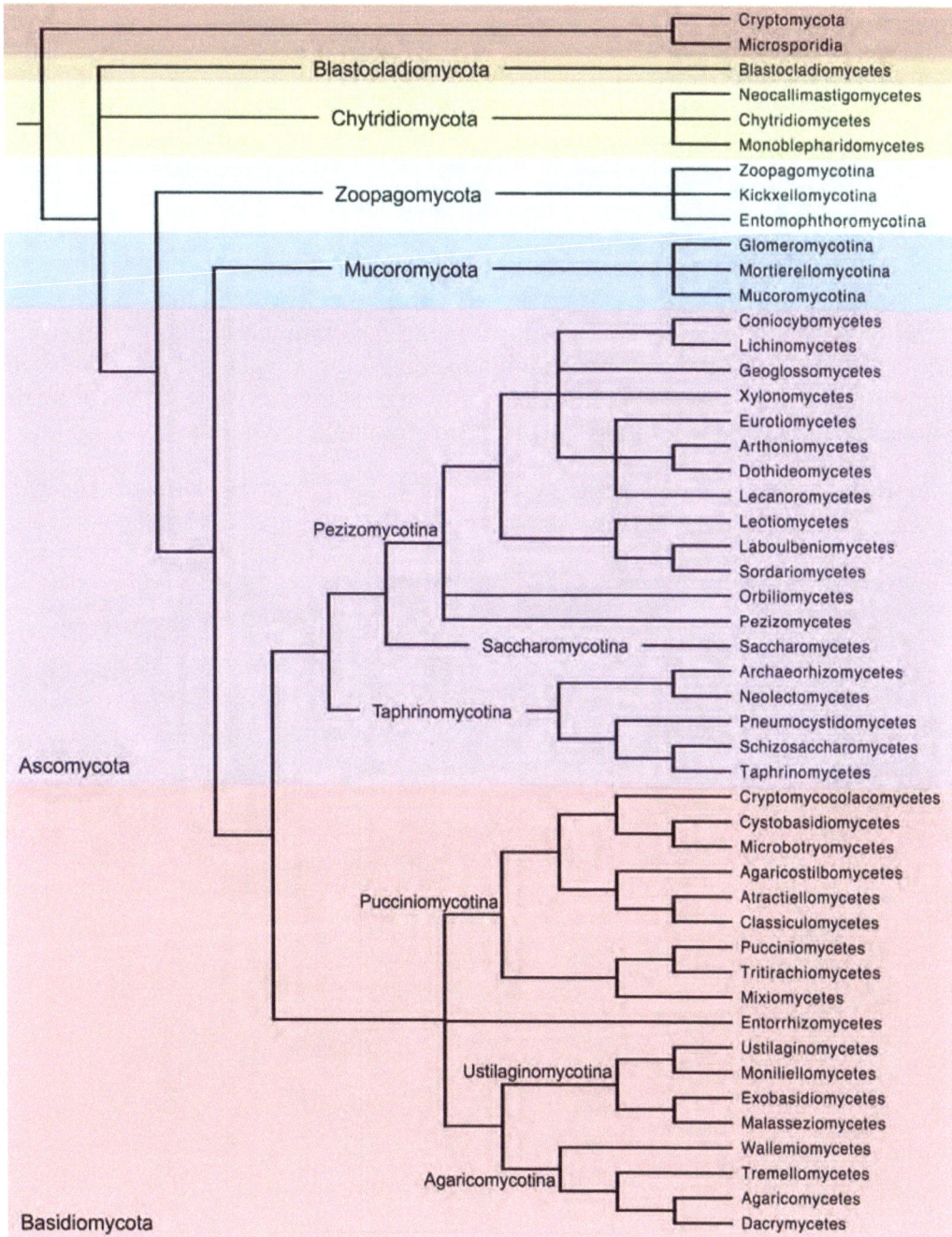

Fig. (1). The phylogenetic tree of fungi [3].

Zygomycetes

Currently considered an extremely diverse and paraphyletic ensemble, zygomycetes are a group of mycelial fungi, with often non-septate mycelia, with no fruiting bodies or other macroscopic organs, with cell walls mostly made of chitosan and having zygophores as sexual organs – terminations of some hyphae which can produce spores (zygospores) after uniting two by two.

Most of them are saprophytic organisms, especially spread in environments rich in organic matter and with a certain amount of oxygen. In soils, their proportion can vary, from a few percent (2%), to becoming the dominant fungal group (over 50%). This depends on the soil type, climate conditions, vegetation, and tillage (in agroecosystems). It was found that plowing increases the proportion of zygomycetes, while other types of tillage are rather unfavourable [4 - 6].

Among the most common genera of zygomycetes found in soil are *Absidia*, *Fennellomyces*, *Mortierella* (Fig. **2**), *Mucor, Umbelopsis,* and *Zygorhynchus* [5].

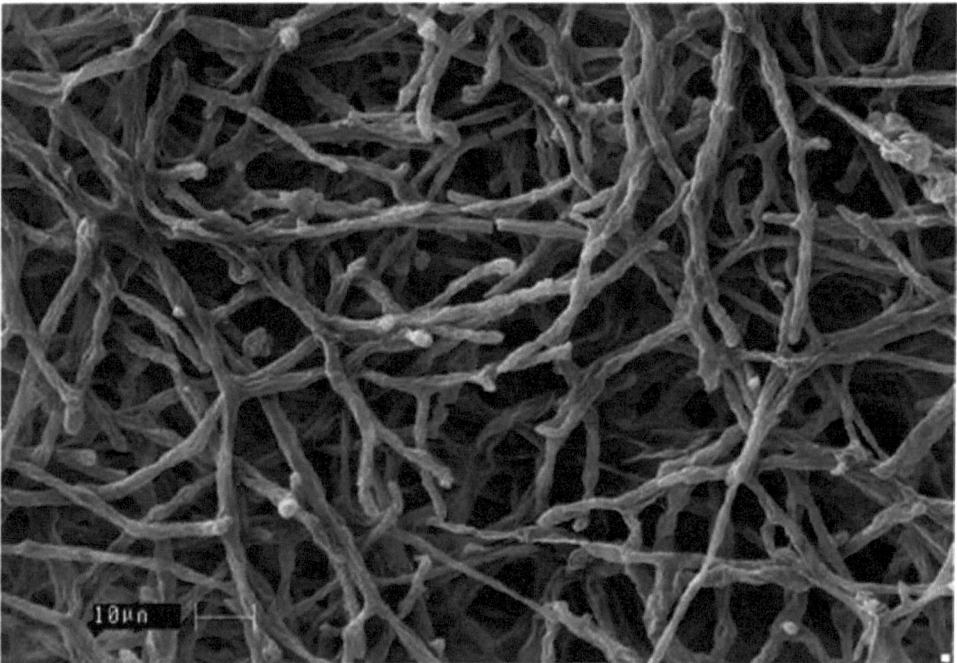

Fig. (2). *Mortierella alpina*, one of the most common zygomycetes in soil, seen in electron microscopy [7].

Ascomycetes

These are an extremely diverse group of fungi, most of them have septate mycelia and reproduction by ascospores. Yet, some of them are unicellular – yeasts. Others are involved in symbioses, in lichens of mycorrhizae. Others (*Morchella* sp., *Peziza* sp., *etc.*) have visible fruiting bodies that can sometimes be edible. They can be saprophytic, parasitic, or endophytic (they grow, totally, partially, or just in some stages of their life cycle, inside plant tissues, without causing damage).

Their proportion may reach, in some types of soil, 80-90% of the total fungal taxa [6, 8].

Despite the extraordinary diversity of this group (Fig. **3**), researchers show that a rather limited number of genera form the bulk of ascomycete communities in most soils around the world: *Alternaria, Aureobasidium, Cadophora Chaetomium, Cladosporium, Curvularia, Exophiala, Fusarium, Knufia, Leohumicola, Penicillium, Podospora, Talaromyces,* and *Trichoderma* [9].

Fig. (3). Diversity of ascomycetes: A. *Orbilia* sp., B. *Aleuria* sp., C. *Ophioparma* sp., D. *Lichinella* sp., E. *Thaxterriella* sp., F. *Arthonia* sp., G. *Prolixandromyces* sp., H. *Neurospora* sp., I. *Cudonia* sp., J. *Eupenicillium* sp., [3].

Yeasts are a very peculiar group of ascomycetes, often of great biotechnological interest. These unicellular fungi are widespread in all kinds of soils, including those featuring extreme conditions: acidic, alkaline, salty, volcanic, cold, *etc.* Nevertheless, their density is never too high, but usually around 10^3-10^4/g.

Their metabolism is often specialized in decomposing sugars. They can be either saprophytic or parasitic. Among the most common genera are *Saccharomyces, Candida, Hanseniaspora, Metschnikowia,* or *Ogataea* [10].

Basidiomycetes

These are another extremely diverse group. At one end, there are unicellular basidiomycetes, which easily confound with yeasts. This is especially the case with some members of the order Tremellales (*Cryptococcus, Rhodotorula, Trichosporon, Apiotrichum,etc.*). Saprophytes or parasites have a more versatile metabolism than yeasts and are quite widespread [10].

However, most basidiomycetes are mycelial fungi, this group includes most of the species with a visible fruiting body.

Considering their specific abundance, they are usually a minority fraction (often below 10%) of soil microbiome, and among them, unicellular forms are dominant [6, 9]. Yet, they compensate through their higher biomass.

The enormous diversity (Fig. **4**) of basidiomycetes is not of concern for the current book, however, their importance needs to be mentioned. Many species are symbionts of plant root systems, enhancing plant growth (see the subchapter dedicated to mycorrhizae); others are efficient decomposers of organic matter, including some hardy compounds, such as lignin; their complex enzymatic apparatus makes them suitable for various biotechnological applications; last but not least, many species (*Agaricus* sp., *Boletus* sp., *Craterellus* sp., *etc.*) are edible.

Chytridiomycetes

Unicellular, once considered protozoa, producing flagellate spores, saprophytic or sometimes parasitic, species of phylum Chytridiomycota form another important component of the soil microbiome.

Their remarkable tolerance to hostile conditions helps them to become dominant in some cases, such as in high-altitude soils. Some of the most common genera are *Allomyces, Catenaria, Chytridiomyces, Spizellomyces, Rhizophlyctis* (Fig. **5**), and *Rhizophydium*. Some, such as *Synchytrium endobioticum* (the agent of potato black swab disease) are parasitic, infecting the underground organs of plants [11, 12].

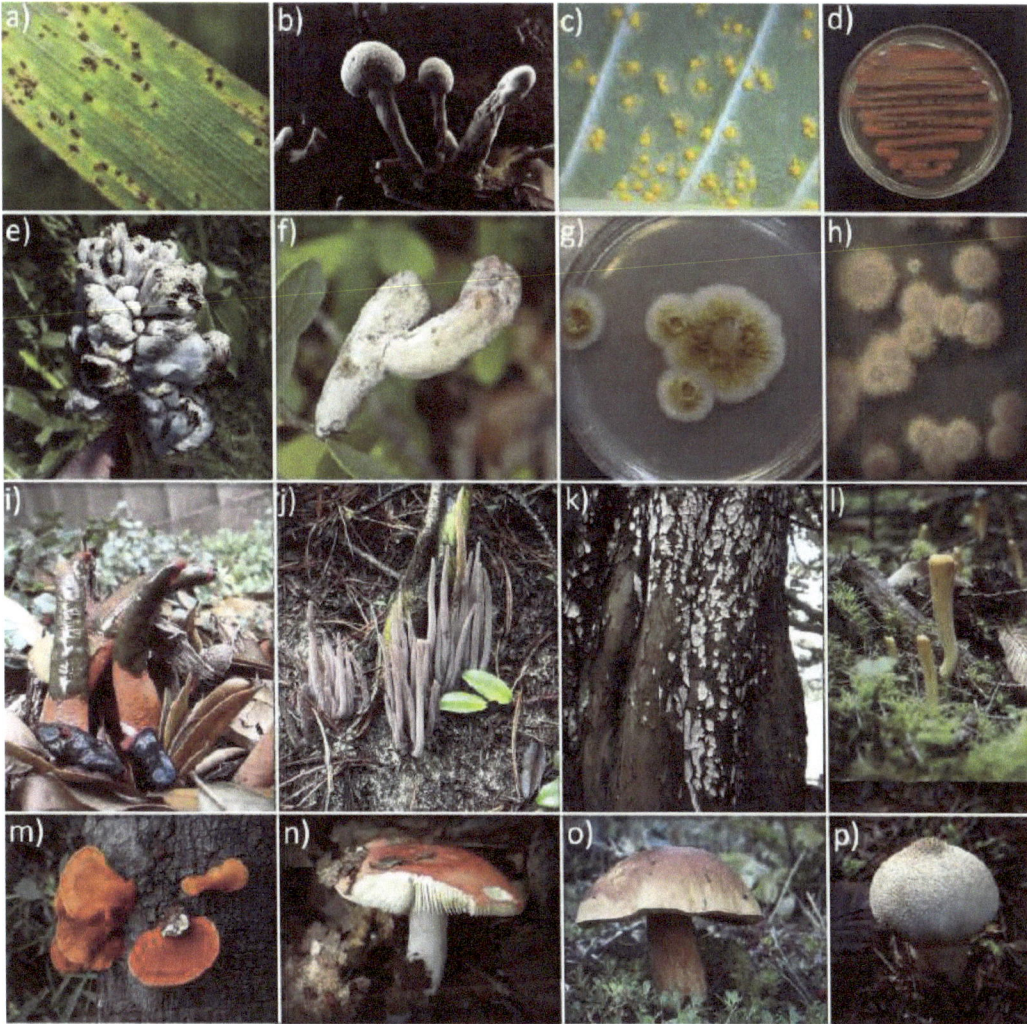

Fig. (4). Diversity of basidiomycetes: A. *Puccinia* sp., B. *Phelogena* sp., C. *Coleosporium* sp., D. *Symmetrospora* sp., E. *Ustilago* sp., F. *Exobasidium* sp., G. *Moniliella* sp., H. *Wallemia* sp., I. *Phallus* sp., J. *Clavaria* sp., K. *Amylostereum* sp., L. *Clavariadelphis* sp., M. *Pycnophorus* sp., N. *Russula* sp., O. *Boletus* sp., P. *Lycoperdon* sp., [3].

Lichens

Lichens are photoautotrophic symbiotic associations between mycelial fungi and green microalgae or, much less often, cyanobacteria. The fungus involved is usually an ascomycete, rarely a basidiomycete.

Having different shapes and different ecological requirements, lichens are extremely variate and inhabit a wide array of ecosystems.

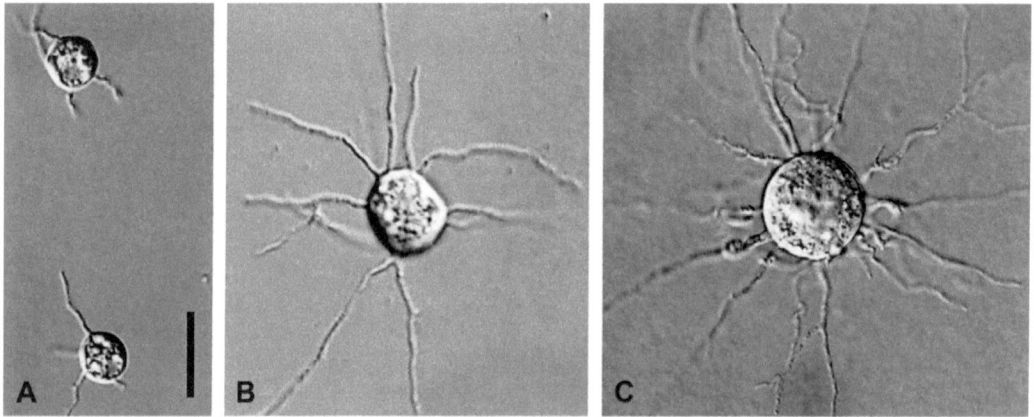

Fig. (5). *Rhizophlyctis rosea*, one of the most common chytridiomycetes in soil [13].

One of the key roles they play is that of pioneer species within primary ecological successions: lichens are among the first organisms that can colonize a new environment (for example a barren rock or an abandoned building wall) and initiate the pedogenetic process. This means that, through physical (using rhizines) and chemical (by secreting organic acids) disaggregation, favouring particulate mineral and organic matter, and finally, through their decomposition after death, lichens produce the first thin layer of soil, that in turn, allows other, more associations of organisms to settle [14].

Lichens (Fig. **6**) contribute to the stabilization of upper soil layers, while also stimulating rainwater infiltration [16].

Finally, in some arid regions of our planet (both typical deserts and semideserts, but also circumpolar or alpine areas), lichens, together with fungi, microalgae, cyanobacteria, and bryophytes form the dominant type of vegetation (with a soil coverage up to 70%): biological crusts, also called cryptobiotic crusts, due to the difficulty to spot them on field, but also due to their ability to maintain very low metabolic rates during unfavorable seasons [17].

False fungi

There are some groups of organisms bearing a mycelial or syncytial body, which reproduce through spores and sometimes produce fruiting bodies resembling those of fungi, and yet, they are not fungi. Saprophytes or parasites, organisms have their place in soil biota.

Fig. (6). Some common lichens [15].

Mycetozoa

Organisms belonging to the subphylum Mycetozoa are part of the much more diverse phylum Amoebozoa and, thus, related to most amoebae. This group comprises micro- or macroscopic organisms, usually known as slime molds.

Their life cycle is complex and comprises both unicellular and multicellular (dictyostelids and the microscopic protostelids) or plasmodial stages (myxogastrids).

Their bodies can reach, especially in myxogastrids (Fig. **7**), sizes of tens of centimeters, with a mycelial aspect and spongy-gelatinous texture. This brings them common names such as "dog vomit mold" (*Fuligo septica*).

Saprophytic forms are important due to their participation in decomposition processes. For instance, it is now known that dictyostelids are among the main organisms responsible for breaking down plant litter in tropical and temperate forests. Others specialize in the biodegradation of woody material [18 - 20].

Fig. (7). Slime molds (Mycetozoa) [21].

Pseudofungi

This group, belonging to phylum Heterokonta, thus related to brown, golden, and yellow-green algae and diatoms, contains the class **Oomycetes** and the smaller Hyphochytridiomycetes, both having species found in soil biota.

Oomycetes (Fig. **8**) are organisms usually having a mycelial body, rarely septate, with an extended array of hyphae, with sporangia, but with cellulosic cell walls. The group contains parasites of plants or fungi (*Phytophthora* sp., *Pythium* sp.), saprophytes, as well as species with an intermediate way of life (such as hemibiotrophic, organisms that feed on both dead and living plant tissue). They can be a major component of the biota in plant rhizospheres.

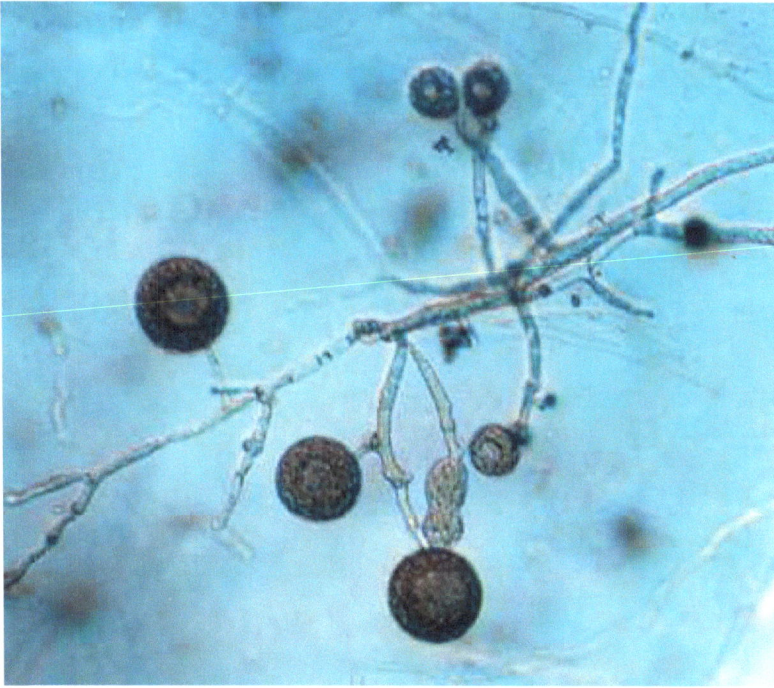

Fig. (8). *Phytophthora* sp., mycelium with resting spores (chlamydospores) [24].

Among the most common genera are *Aphanomyces*, *Globosporangium*, *Hyaloperonospora*, *Peronospora*, *Phytophthora*, and *Pythium*. Their practical importance is given by the parasitism of some (affecting crop plants like potato, beet, onion, some Cucurbitaceae, *etc.*, and also plants of silvicultural interest) and the hyperparasitism of others (helping us control some pathogens) [22, 23].

Plants

Plants are some of the main contributors to soil biota, providing living space to various microorganisms, in the region neighbouring their root systems (a region called ***rhizosphere***), while also being the source of most available organic matter, through the decomposition of dead plant organs and through secreting root exudates.

This group comprises bryophytes (mosses), pteridophytes (ferns), gymnosperms, and angiosperms, whose diversity is not the object of the current book.

Still, plants are present in soils just by part of their body. Roots are branched organs, whose main function is absorbing water and nutrients. Each species has a particular shape, and horizontal and vertical extension of its root systems, adapted to its specific nutritional requirements (Fig. **9**).

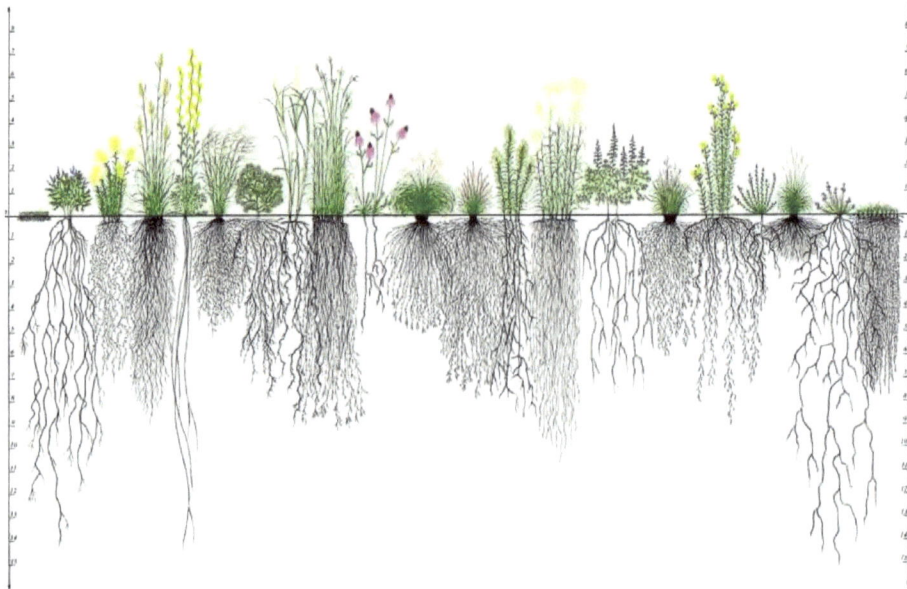

Fig. (9). Various shapes of root systems [25].

Besides roots, there is a wide variety of underground stems, useful in food storage, resistance to unfavorable weather conditions, and vegetative reproduction: rhizomes, bulbs, bulbo-tubers, tubers, or underground stolons (Fig. **10**).

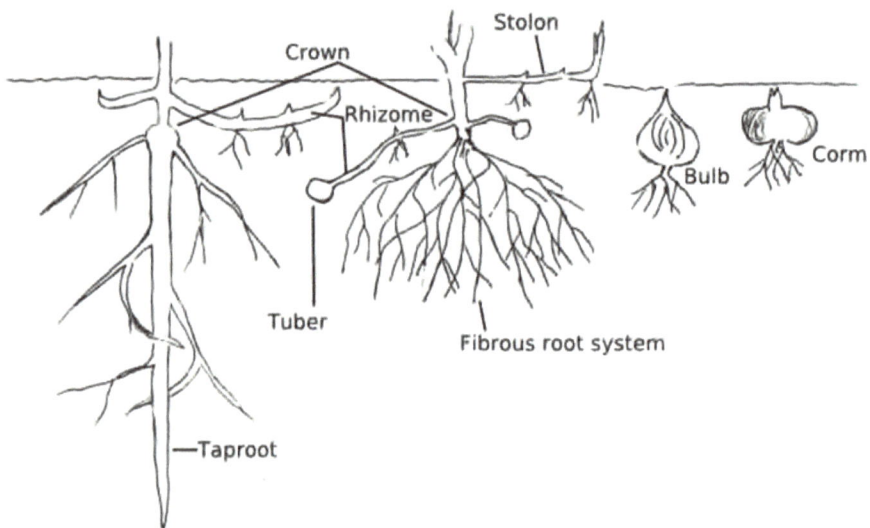

Fig. (10). Types of underground plant organs [26].

Animals

Many animal species use soil as their home. For some this is true for all their life, for others, just in some of their ontogenetic stages and, finally, there are animals using soil only as a temporary shelter.

The animal kingdom hosts the upper links of trophic chains: consumers of various degrees.

Nematodes

The most abundant and diverse animals in the soil are, by far, nematodes. Over 2,200 genera and 15,000 species are known, and widespread in all terrestrial ecosystems.

Worm-shaped organisms are extremely small-sized (most have between 0.05-1 mm in length) and, for this reason, reach major densities, of tens of such animals in each gram of soil (Fig. **11**). Due to their metabolism requiring oxygen, 90% of them inhabit the upper 15 centimeters of soil layers. However, where oxygen is able to permeate deeper, nematodes were identified up to a few kilometers below ground level.

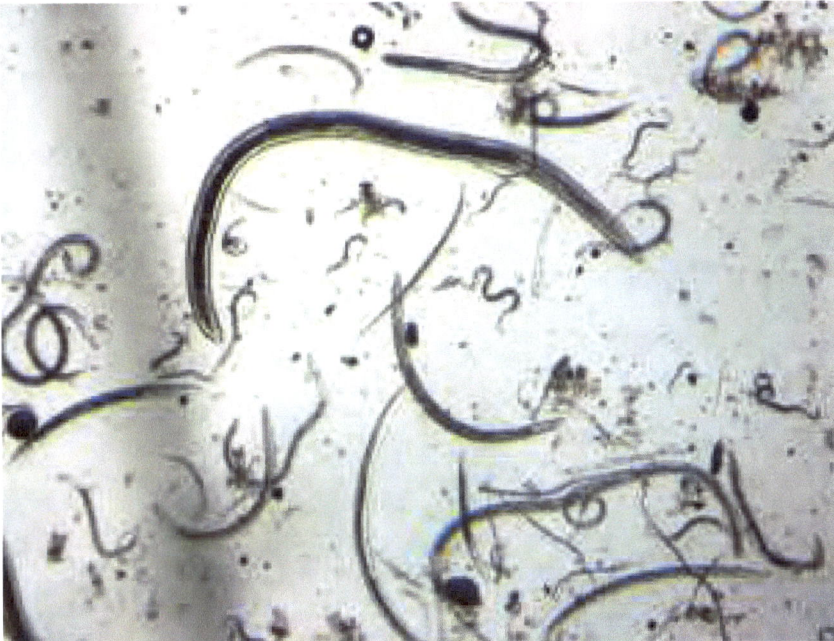

Fig. (11). Nematodes isolated from soil [33].

Considering their nutritional regime, there are several major groups of nematodes. Bacterivores are extremely small-sized and a tube-shaped buccal apparatus, that allows them to eat bacteria dwelling on soil grains. About one-third of soil nematode populations belong to this category, mostly species of the order Rhabditida.

Herbivores constitute around half of the total population, mostly belonging to orders Aphelenchida, Dorylaimida, and Tylenchida. Part of them live at the interface between soil and plant roots, feeding on their tissues. Others are endoparasitic, invading plant organs and causing various diseases [27, 28].

Fungivores (especially from order Aphelenchida) make up to 15% or even more; they use their sharp mouthpieces to pierce fungal cells and eat their content.

Predatory nematodes (Mononchida, Dorylaimida) form a minority; they feed on small animals, similar in size to them – usually other nematodes – or protozoans, *etc.* There are also omnivorous species [28].

The role nematodes play in soil ecology is an extremely important one. Not only they are key intermediate links in most trophic chains (serving as food for larger animals), but they directly contribute to the decomposition and mineralization of organic matter. For instance, excess nitrogen taken from their food (such as the protein-rich bacteria) is excreted as ammonium ions, easy to be absorbed and metabolized by plants. Nematodes also ensure the propagation of some microorganisms over much longer distances than they would be able to move on their own.

Some nematodes are parasites of plants, attacking roots and other underground organs and causing damage to agricultural crops. Furthermore, some are also vectors to some phytopathogenic viruses, thus increasing their damage. Potato, tobacco, tomato, beet, soybean, peas, or corn are among the most common victims of such infections [29, 30].

However, even parasitic nematodes may have a positive influence on soil, by causing the release of some carbon and nitrogen amounts from plant tissues in neighbouring soil, these in turn serving as food to many other organisms [31].

Nematode populations in the soil are sensitive to mechanical and chemical treatments, as well as to pollution; this way many species can be used as bioindicators [29, 32].

Annelids

Segmented, worm-shaped organisms, extremely common in most types of soil, annelids are a key component of soil biota.

The most common are oligochaete annelids, of which, in temperate soil two families are dominant: Lumbricidae (proper earthworms) and Enchytraeidae (potworms; smaller than earthworms). The most common genus is *Lumbricus* (especially *L. terrestris*), but *Aporrectodea*, *Dendrobaena*, and *Octolasion* are also frequently found. In temperate Europe, some of the largest individuals found (1-2 meter long) belong to the genus *Octodrilus*, but in tropical families such as Megascolecidae and Microchaetidae, there are real giants: *Megascolides australis* (up to 3-3.5 m) or *Microchaetus rappi* (an individual found in South Africa had no less than 6.7 m length; Fig. **12**) [34, 35].

Large or small, these animals are extremely important to soil health. Some species thrive at the interface between proper soil and plant litter. Others dig shallow horizontal galleries, while proper earthworms dig deeper burrows, feeding on organic compounds and microorganisms in the soil.

All these animals play an important role in organic matter decomposition and making large amounts of carbon and nitrogen bioavailable again. By digging, they alter the normal stratification of soil, allowing organic material from plant litter to be drawn and broken down into deeper layers. Burrows also allow oxygen to permeate up to greater depths, stimulating microbial activity (a phenomenon called **bioturbation**). This loosening of soil also enhances the drainage of excess rainwater. Practically, annelid activity creates a particular micro ecosystem called **drilosphere**, consisting of the actual burrows and adjacent soil areas [34, 36].

However, annelid populations are sensitive to factors like soil acidification, pollution, or mechanical compaction [34].

Arthropods

Insects dominate animal life on Earth and soil is just one of the many environments they have adapted to. It is estimated that 90% of known species have at least one stage of their life cycle linked to soil. This can mean living at the soil-litter interface or in burrows dug in the soil.

Their diversity is enormous: blatoids, coleopterans, dermapterans, hemipterans, hymenopterans, isopterans, and orthopterans. Many of them, such as numerous species of Coleoptera, have a larval stage living underground and often damaging plant root systems.

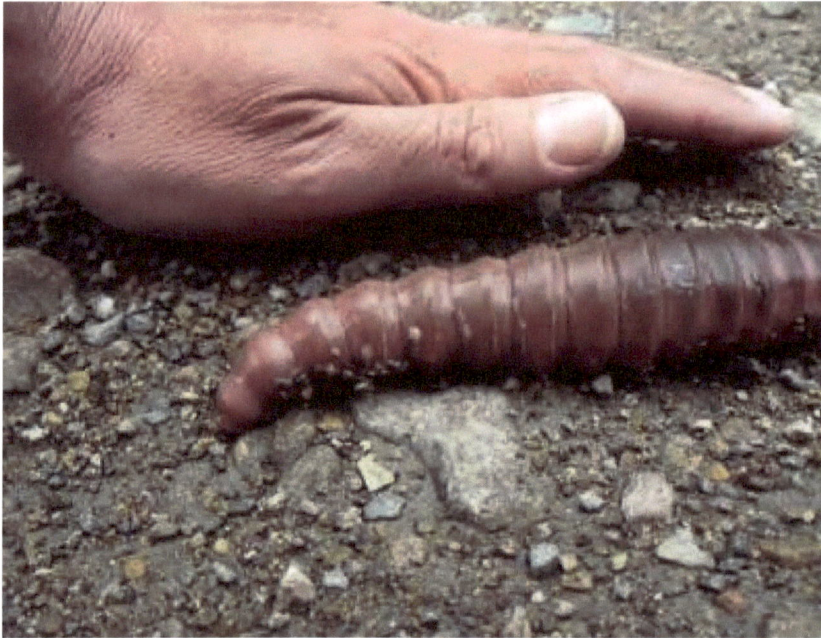

Fig. (12). *Microchaetus rappi*, the Goliath of annelids [35].

Besides this, insects are important links in trophic chains, contributing to dead plant organs decomposition, while their burrows allow oxygen to reach deeper soil layers [37, 38].

An extremely profound impact is that of colonies of social insects: ants and termites. These insects build structures that are often complex and remarkably large, featuring ventilation shafts, myriads of tunnels, and specialized chambers. A typical ant mound may vary between a few tens of centimeters and two meters in depth, with a considerable horizontal extension. Termite mounds can be even larger, with a depth of up to 5-6 meters and a radius that can go over 30 meters (Fig. **13**).

The result is a profound bioturbation effect, with a decrease in soil density, oxygenation of deep soil layers, and a change in pH (towards a more neutral one). The diversity of the microbial population dramatically increases and so does the amount of organic matter. This is due to both dejections and accumulation of dead insects (in dedicated areas of the colony), as well as their ability to grow fungi (using plant material as a substrate), as a food source.

The overall effect of such colonies on soil fertility and plant development in surrounding areas tends to be a positive one [39 - 42].

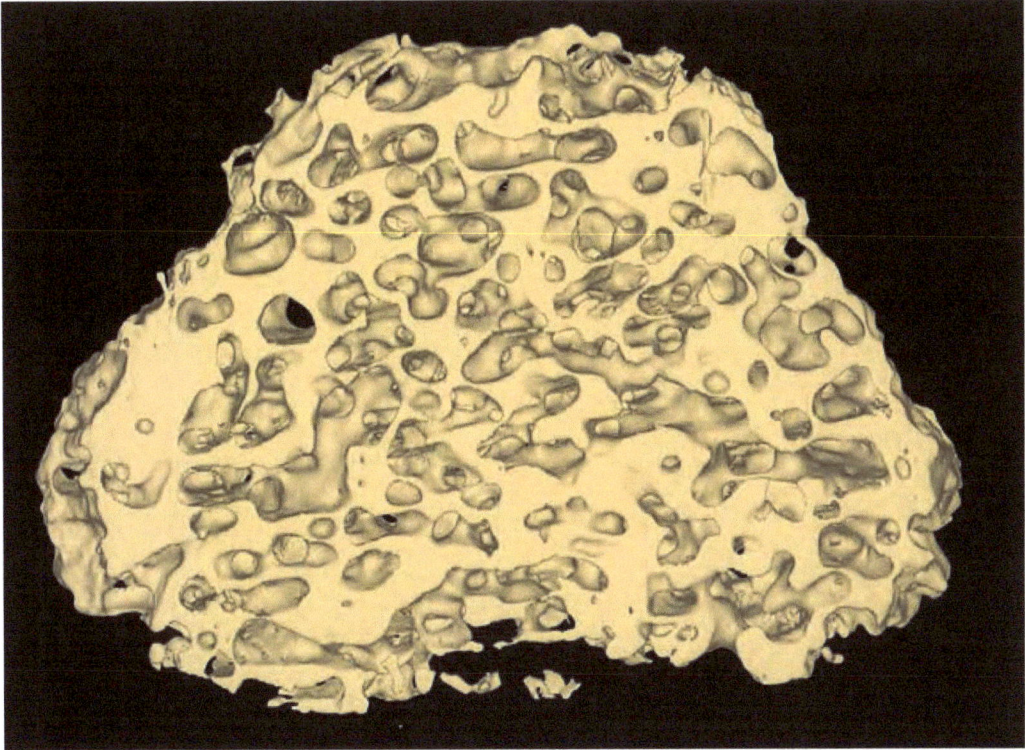

Fig. (13). Structure of an ant colony [43].

Besides insects, soils host populations of centipedes and millipedes, arachnids (acari, spiders, solifuges, scorpions), and crustaceans (some isopods) [37].

Vertebrates

There are numerous species of land vertebrates that spend different periods of their lives in soil. Local effects are, obviously, major ones, regarding bioturbation, oxygen and water permeation, organic matter input (secretions, dejections, food caches, *etc.*), and their impact on the microbiota.

Many species of **amphibians**, for instance, practice aestivation – a period of latency during the warmest season of the year – during which they bury themselves in soil, for a few weeks or months [44].

The same is true for some **reptiles**. Snakes, in particular, may have the ability to dig burrows. Some use them to spend a consistent part of their life, while others, such as the whole family Typhlopidae, are fully adapted to a subterranean way of life [45].

Mammals are also a common presence. A fox, for instance, digs dens where it takes shelter under unfavorable conditions, stores food, and raises its cubs. On the other hand, a hamster, a prairie dog, or a meerkat spend much larger shares of their lives in underground burrows (Fig. **14**).

Fig. (14). Some mammals with an (at least partial) underground way of life: mole (*Talpa europaea*), plains pocket gopher (*Geomys bursarius*), prairie dog (*Cynomys* sp.), wombat (Australian marsupial, *Vombatus ursinus*) [48], naked mole-rat (*Heterocephalus glaber*) [49].

At the extreme limit, moles, marsupial moles, mole-rats, and other species (belonging to rather diverse taxonomic groups) live quasi-exclusively in such galleries. Their atrophied eyes, body shape, and limbs adapted to digging, do not allow them to have any other way of life [46].

Maybe the most interesting adaptations are found in the naked mole-rat (*Heterocephalus glaber*) and its relative, the Damaraland mole-rat (*Fukomys damarensis*), blind rodents that live in complex underground colonies, hosting tens or even hundreds of individuals, with caste segregation reminding that of social insects (reproductive individuals, workers but also individuals that specialize in searching for neighboring colonies, for exogamous reproduction) [47].

CONCLUSION

Among multicellular soil biota, fungi (along with similar, mycelial organisms, such as Mycetozoa and Oomycetes) are clearly dominant. They are mostly decomposers, having a key role in the recycling of organic matter and pedogenesis. Some are also parasitic or even photosynthetic (when in symbiosis with microalgae, such as lichens).

Plants are only present in the soil through their underground organs, such as roots and tubers, but their contribution to soil creation is crucial, through their continuous organic matter input.

Animals are consumers, that fill in the upper levels of trophic chains. Nematodes, annelids, and insects are the main representatives of this kingdom. Through feeding, motion, and bioturbation, they play important roles in shaping soils.

REFERENCES

[1]   Bridge P, Spooner B. Soil fungi: diversity and detection. Plant Soil 2001; 232(1/2): 147-54.
        [http://dx.doi.org/10.1023/A:1010346305799]

[2]   Went FW, Stark N. The biological and mechanical role of soil fungi. Proc Natl Acad Sci USA 1968; 60(2): 497-504.
        [http://dx.doi.org/10.1073/pnas.60.2.497] [PMID: 16591652]

[3]   Spatafora JW, Aime MC, Grigoriev IV, Martin F, Stajich JE, Blackwell M. The fungal tree of life: from molecular systematics to genome-scale phylogenies. Microbiol Spectr 2017; 5(5): 5.5.03.
        [http://dx.doi.org/10.1128/microbiolspec.FUNK-0053-2016] [PMID: 28917057]

[4]   He J, Xu Z, Hughes J. Analyses of soil fungal communities in adjacent natural forest and hoop pine plantation ecosystems of subtropical Australia using molecular approaches based on 18S rRNA genes. FEMS Microbiol Lett 2005; 247(1): 91-100.
        [http://dx.doi.org/10.1016/j.femsle.2005.04.033] [PMID: 15927752]

[5]   Richardson M. The ecology of the Zygomycetes and its impact on environmental exposure. Clin Microbiol Infect 2009; 15(5) (Suppl. 5): 2-9.
        [http://dx.doi.org/10.1111/j.1469-0691.2009.02972.x] [PMID: 19754749]

[6]   Naumova N, Barsukov P, Baturina O, Rusalimova O, Kabilov M. Soil mycobiome diversity under different tillage practices in the South of West Siberia. Life (Basel) 2022; 12(8): 1169.
[http://dx.doi.org/10.3390/life12081169] [PMID: 36013348]

[7]   Vadivelan G, Venkateswaran G. Production and enhancement of omega-3 fatty acid from *Mortierella alpina* CFR-GV15: its food and therapeutic application. BioMed Res Int 2014; 2014: 1-9.
[http://dx.doi.org/10.1155/2014/657414] [PMID: 24982900]

[8]   Al-Sadi AM, Al-Khatri B, Nasehi A, Al-Shihi M, Al-Mahmooli I, Maharachchikumbura SSN. High fungal diversity and dominance by ascomycota in dam reservoir soils of arid climates. Int J Agric Biol 2017; 19(4): 682-8.
[http://dx.doi.org/10.17957/IJAB/15.0328]

[9]   Egidi E, Delgado-Baquerizo M, Plett JM, *et al.* A few Ascomycota taxa dominate soil fungal communities worldwide. Nat Commun 2019; 10(1): 2369.
[http://dx.doi.org/10.1038/s41467-019-10373-z] [PMID: 31147554]

[10]   Yurkov AM. Yeasts of the soil – obscure but precious. Yeast 2018; 35(5): 369-78.
[http://dx.doi.org/10.1002/yea.3310] [PMID: 29365211]

[11]   Gleason FH, Midgley DJ, Letcher PM, McGEE PA. Can soil Chytridiomycota survive and grow in different osmotic potentials? Mycol Res 2006; 110(7): 869-75.
[http://dx.doi.org/10.1016/j.mycres.2006.04.002] [PMID: 16876703]

[12]   Freeman KR, Martin AP, Karki D, *et al.* Evidence that chytrids dominate fungal communities in high-elevation soils. Proc Natl Acad Sci USA 2009; 106(43): 18315-20.
[http://dx.doi.org/10.1073/pnas.0907303106] [PMID: 19826082]

[13]   Letcher PM, Powell MJ, Barr DJS, Churchill PF, Wakefield WS, Picard KT. *Rhizophlyctidales*—a new order in *Chytridiomycota*. Mycol Res 2008; 112(9): 1031-48.
[http://dx.doi.org/10.1016/j.mycres.2008.03.007] [PMID: 18701267]

[14]   Kallison ER. A review of the contributions by lichen to building soil. IdeaFest 2021; 5: 6-10.

[15]   Redfern, L. Lichen: Exploring microecosystems in your backyard. Following Deer Creek, Available from: http://followingdeercreek.com/lichen-exploring-microecosystems-in-your-backyard/

[16]   Tunç E, Çetindemir B. The effect of lichens on aggregate soil stability. Int J Energy Eng Sources 2022; 7(1): 40-51.

[17]   Rosentreter, R., Bowker, M., Belnap J., 2007. A Field Guide to Biological Soil Crusts of Western U.S. Drylands. U.S. Government Printing Office, Denver, 104.

[18]   Cavender JC, Cavender-Bares J, Rohl HR. Ecological distribution of cellular slime molds in forest soils of Germany. Bot Helv 1995; 105: 199-219.

[19]   Seephueak P, Petcharat V. The biodiversity of Dictyostelid cellular slime molds in rubber tree leaf litter in Southern Thailand. Mycosphere 2014; 5(6): 805-13.
[http://dx.doi.org/10.5943/mycosphere/5/6/10]

[20]   Glime, J. M. 2019. Slime Molds: Ecology and Habitats – Bark and Logs. In Glime, J. M. (ed.) Bryophyte Ecology, Michigan Technological University, Houghton, 2, 3.3.1-3.3.42.

[21]   Mason, D., The unexpected beauty of 'dog vomit' and other slime molds. The New York Times Magazine, 16.06.2020, Available from: https://www.nytimes.com/2020/06/16/magazine/the-unexpected-beauty-of-dog-vomit-and-other-slime.html

[22]   Fiore-Donno AM, Bonkowski M. Different community compositions between obligate and facultative oomycete plant parasites in a landscape-scale metabarcoding survey. Biol Fertil Soils 2021; 57(2): 245-56.
[http://dx.doi.org/10.1007/s00374-020-01519-z]

[23]   Blakney, A.J.C., Bainard, L.D., St-Arnaud, M., Hijri, M., Soil chemistry and soil history significantly

structure oomycete communities in Brassicaceae crop rotations. biorXiv, 2022.
[http://dx.doi.org/10.1101/2022.07.12.499733]

[24]   Fry WE, Grünwald NJ. Introduction to Oomycetes. The Plant Health Instructor 2010.
[http://dx.doi.org/10.1094/PHI-I-2010-1207-01]

[25]   Tsao DT. Overview of phytotechnologies. In: Tsao DT, Ed. Phytoremediation. Berlin: Springer 2003;
pp. 1-50.
[http://dx.doi.org/10.1007/3-540-45991-X_1]

[26]   Schonbeck, M., Weed identification tool and techniques. eOrganic, 18.01.2011, Available from:
https://eorganic.org/node/2732

[27]   Li Z, Chen X, Li J, *et al.* Relationships between soil nematode communities and soil quality as
affected by land-use type. Forests 2022; 13(10): 1658.
[http://dx.doi.org/10.3390/f13101658]

[28]   McSorley, R., Soil-inhabiting nematodes, Phylum Nematoda. University of Florida, IFAS Extension,
2022. Available from: https://edis.ifas.ufl.edu/pdf/IN/IN138/IN138-Dvcxsf1pjz.pdf

[29]   Neher DA. Role of nematodes in soil health and their use as indicators. J Nematol 2001; 33(4): 161-8.
[PMID: 19265875]

[30]   Evans, A., Soil dwelling free-living nematodes as pests of crops. Technical note. SAS, Edinburgh, 4,
2007.

[31]   Tu C, Koenning SR, Hu S. Root-parasitic nematodes enhance soil microbial activities and nitrogen
mineralization. Microb Ecol 2003; 46(1): 134-44.
[http://dx.doi.org/10.1007/s00248-002-1068-2] [PMID: 12739076]

[32]   Putri AH, Indarti S, Harjaka T. Diversity and abundance of nematodes in soil treated with solarization
treatments. Biodiversitas (Surak) 2021; 22(7): 2612-8.
[http://dx.doi.org/10.13057/biodiv/d220708]

[33]   Greenresilient, How to monitor soil health with DNA-metabarcoding of Nematode communities.
Greenresilient, 2021. Available from: https://www.greenresilient.net/service/videos/how-to-monit-
r-soil-health-with-dna-metabarcoding-of-nematode-communities.html

[34]   Pižl V, Schlaghamerský J. The impact of pedestrian activity on soil annelids in urban greens. Eur J
Soil Biol 2007; 43: S68-71.
[http://dx.doi.org/10.1016/j.ejsobi.2007.08.004]

[35]   Hiskey, D., South African worms can grow as large as 22 feet long. Today I Found Out, 2011,
Available   from: https://www.todayifoundout.com/index.php/2011/03/south-african-earthworms--
an-grow-as-large-as-22-feet-long

[36]   Andriuzzi, W.S., Ecological functions of earthworms in soil. Ph.D. thesis, Wageningen University,
160, 2015.

[37]   Hale FA, Vail KM. Lawn Insects: How to Control Them. Knoxville: University of Tennessee, Institute
of Agriculture 2020.

[38]   Juniarti F, Rusniarsyah L. Diversity of soil surface insects in three land use types in Sintang district,
West Kalimantan. IOP Conf Ser Earth Environ Sci 2022; 959(1): 012026.
[http://dx.doi.org/10.1088/1755-1315/959/1/012026]

[39]   Frouz J, Jilková V. The effect of ants on soil properties and processes (Hymenoptera: Formicidae).
Myrmecol News 2008; 11: 191-9.

[40]   Farji-Brener AG, Werenkraut V. The effects of ant nests on soil fertility and plant performance: a
meta□analysis. J Anim Ecol 2017; 86(4): 866-77.
[http://dx.doi.org/10.1111/1365-2656.12672] [PMID: 28369906]

[41]   Khan, A., Ahmad, W., Paul, B., Ecological Impacts of Termites. In Khan, M., Ahmad, W. (ed.)

Termites and Sustainable Management, vol. 1: Biology, Social Behaviour and Economic Importance. Springer, Cham, 2018; pp. 201-216.
[http://dx.doi.org/10.1007/978-3-319-72110-1_10]

[42]   Delgado-Baquerizo M, Eldridge DJ, Hamonts K, Singh BK. Ant colonies promote the diversity of soil microbial communities. ISME J 2019; 13(4): 1114-8.
[http://dx.doi.org/10.1038/s41396-018-0335-2] [PMID: 30607027]

[43]   Singer, E., The remarkable self-organization of ants. Quanta Magazine, 2014, Available from: https://www.quantamagazine.org/ants-build-complex-structures-with-a-few-simple-rules-20140409

[44]   West J. Importance of amphibians: A synthesis of their environmental functions, benefits to humans, and need for conservationmade field. 2018.

[45]   Shea GM. Waite's blind snakes (Squamata: Scolecophidia: Typhlopidae): identification of sources and correction or errors. Rec Aust Mus 1999; 51(1): 43-56.
[http://dx.doi.org/10.3853/j.0067-1975.51.1999.1294]

[46]   Partha R, Chauhan BK, Ferreira Z, *et al.* Subterranean mammals show convergent regression in ocular genes and enhancers, along with adaptation to tunneling. eLife 2017; 6: e25884.
[http://dx.doi.org/10.7554/eLife.25884] [PMID: 29035697]

[47]   Burda H, Honeycutt RL, Begall S, Locker-Grütjen O, Scharff A. Are naked and common mole-rats eusocial and if so, why? Behav Ecol Sociobiol 2000; 47(5): 293-303.
[http://dx.doi.org/10.1007/s002650050669]

[48]   Greene, P., 20 Animals that live underground (with pictures). Wildlife Informer, 2022. https://wildlifeinformer.com/animals-that-live-underground

[49]   Jemison, M., Building a naked mole-rat dream home at the Smithsonian's National Zoo. Smithsonian Insider, 2018, Available from:https://insider.si.edu/2018/08/building-a-naked-mole-rat-drea--home-at-the-smithsonians-national-zoo

CHAPTER 4

Cycles of Matter in Soil, Carbon Cycle

Abstract: The entire organic chemistry is based on carbon, an essential element in all substances that form living matter. The carbon cycle in soil comprises a wide variety of processes, involving diverse groups of micro- and macroorganisms. Photoautotrophy and chemoautotrophy are weakly represented, although they are not a negligible source of organic matter. The dominant process, however, is decomposition. Sugars, lipids, proteins, and other categories of compounds are being constantly degraded, through the enzymatic activity of various heterotrophic microorganisms, forming humus (a relatively stable organic complex) and, then, simpler and simpler products. In weakly oxygenated soils, specific phenomena such as methanogenesis and its reverse, methanotrophy, occur.

Keywords: Chemosynthesis, Carbon, Decomposition, Humus, Methanogenesis, Methanotrophy, Photosynthesis.

INTRODUCTION

As shown above, soil is a complex and open system, in which matter undergoes continuous transformations and which has a constant exchange of chemicals, organisms, and energy with other environments. And yet, like any other ecological system on Earth, it maintains its characteristics and equilibrium in the long term.

All these are due to the continuous recycling of the various biogenic chemical elements. Living beings are a key component of these cycles, through processes such as photo- and chemosynthesis, trophic relationships (prey-predator), and decomposition.

Organic matter is an essential component of soil and carbon is the essential component of organic matter. It includes hydrocarbons and derivatives, lipids, sugars (mono-, oligo-, polysaccharides), alcohols, ketones, acids, amino acids, peptides (mono-, oligo-, polypeptides), proteins, nucleotides, and nucleic acids.

Basically, soil contains organic matter under active decomposition, stabilized organic matter (meaning humus, with a low rate of breakdown processes) – each of these two fractions composing between 33 and 50% of the total mass, as well as fresh organic residues beginning their decomposition cycle (up to 10%) and, of course, the biomass of indigenous micro- and macroorganisms (below 5%) [1].

Besides organic matter, carbon is an important component of the atmosphere (as carbon dioxide, with a concentration of 0.04%) and also of hydrocarbon deposits in the deep lithosphere. Between these forms of carbon, organic and inorganic, there is a continuous biogeochemical circuit that involves among others the biosphere (including humankind), of which soil biota is a consistent part (Figs. **1** and **2**).

The carbon cycle includes a series of biological processes, including some that occur at the soil level: autotrophy (photosynthesis and chemosynthesis), decomposition, trophic relationships, and respiration. In the following subchapters, we will analyze some of them.

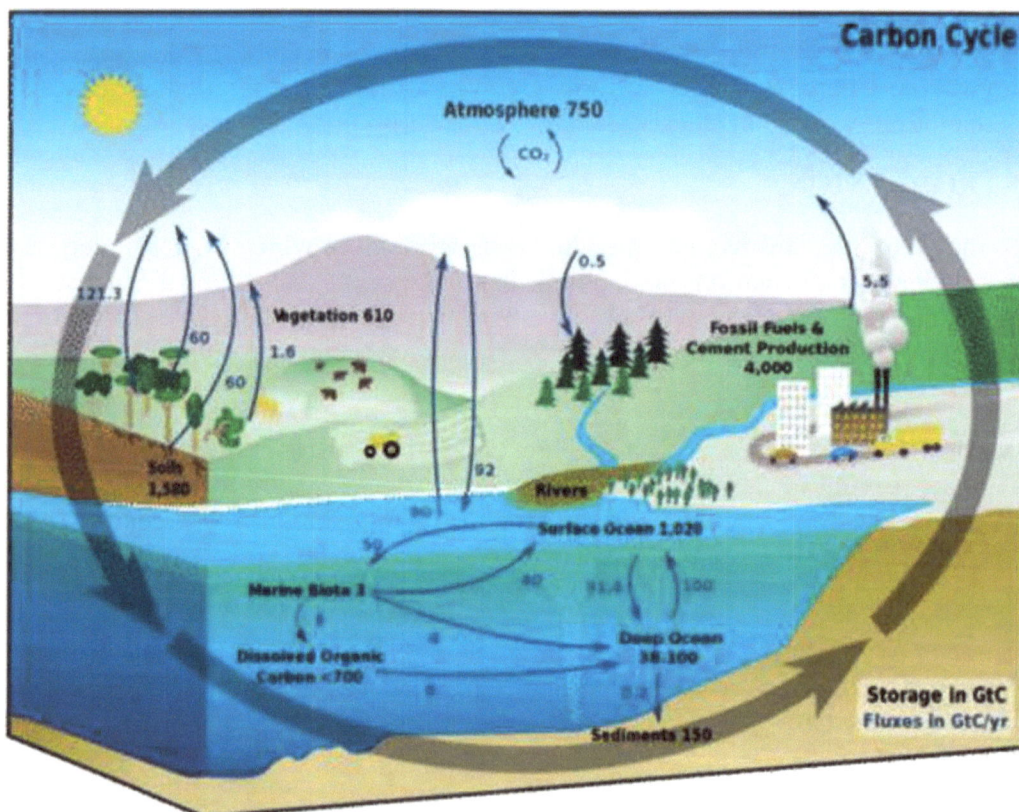

Fig. (1). The global carbon cycle [2].

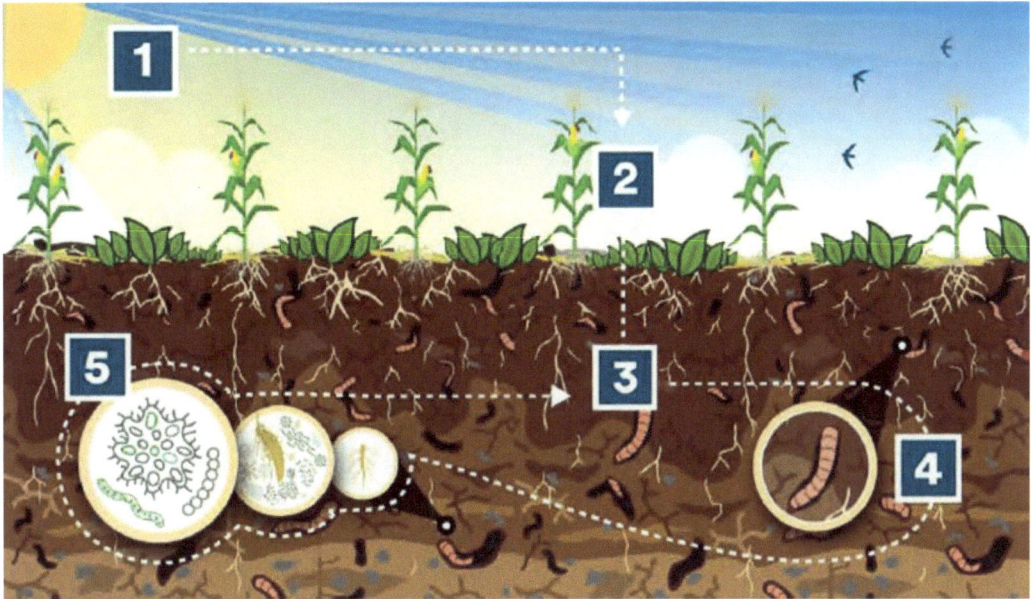

Fig. (2).   Soil carbon cycle: 1. atmospheric CO_2, 2. photosynthesis, 3. root exudate secretion, 4. descomposition and aggregation of organic matter by macroorganisms (nematodes, andelids), 5. microbial decomposition of organic matter [3].

Photosynthesis

Photosynthesis is the autotrophic feeding process, through synthesizing organic compounds from CO_2, by using sunlight energy, which in turn is aquired through specific assimilatory pigments (chlorophylls, bacteriochlorophylls, carotenoids, *etc.*)

It can be oxygenic (the most common form, found in cyanobacteria, algae, and plants, where water is the hydrogen donor; Fig. (**3**) or anoxygenic (in some groups of bacteria, having H_2S or other compounds as hydrogen donors).

Responsible for producing organic matter through this process, in soils, are bacteria (especially cyanobacteria), microalgae, and lichens, as shown in chapters 2-3. In some arid areas, these are the main sources of soil organic matter [6].

However, usually, just a small fraction of this process occurs in the upper layers of soil. In most terrestrial environments, plants are the main primary producers and the compounds they synthesize reach soil only by means of their root secretions or decomposition of dead organs.

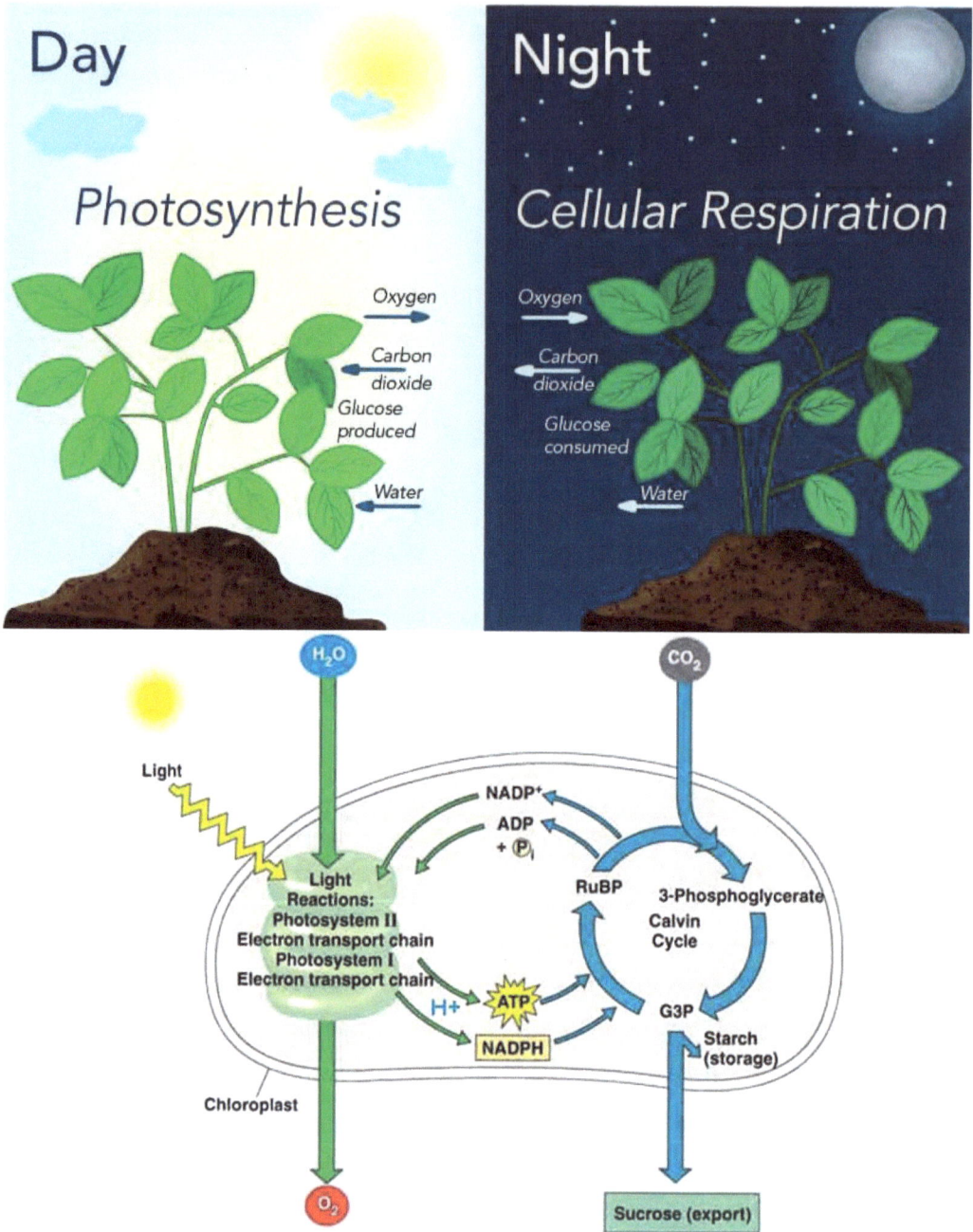

Fig. (3). Photosynthesis versus respiration in plants [4] and the diagram of photosynthetic processes in a chloroplast [5].

Chemosynthesis

Chemosynthesis is a form of autotrophic nutrition, in which carbon derived from an inorganic source (usually CO_2) is fixed in organic structures by using the energy generated through oxidizing certain chemical compounds.

Although the overall role of chemosynthesis in soil carbon economy is quite limited, chemosynthesizing microorganisms are rather widespread in all kinds of soils. Belonging to diverse groups of bacteria and archaea, they can use the energy obtained by oxidizing ammonium ions (NH_4^+), nitrite ions (NO_2^-), sulfides (S_2^-), or ferrous iron (Fe_2^+).

The proportion of chemoautotrophic microbiota tends to increase in desert, alpine, and circumpolar regions [6, 7].

Decomposition

The decomposition of organic matter derived from plants (and not only) is the main biological process undergoing at the soil level, a process that actually leads to the formation of the soil itself.

Decomposition can be defined as the removal of a particular carbon compound, a process that sums mineralization, assimilation, and alteration.

Mineralization means the release of carbon as CO_2, through respiration. Assimilation means retaining carbon in the organic structures of the decomposer. Alteration means transforming an organic substance into another [8].

Decomposition involves a wide variety of organic compounds and an equally wide variety of biochemical pathways.

The rate at which such processes occur is also extremely variable. Basically, fresh organic residues (plant litter, various dead plant organs, *etc.*), can be considered as fully incorporated into soil organic matter after about one year or less.

After that, other decay processes will lead to the formation of humus, a complex of more stable compounds. Decomposition still continues, but at a much lower rate (Figs. **4** and **5**).

Among the factors influencing this rate are the type of chemicals, their input rate, soil granulometry and moisture, temperature.

Organisms involved are also numerous: animals, fungi, but most of all, bacteria [8 - 11].

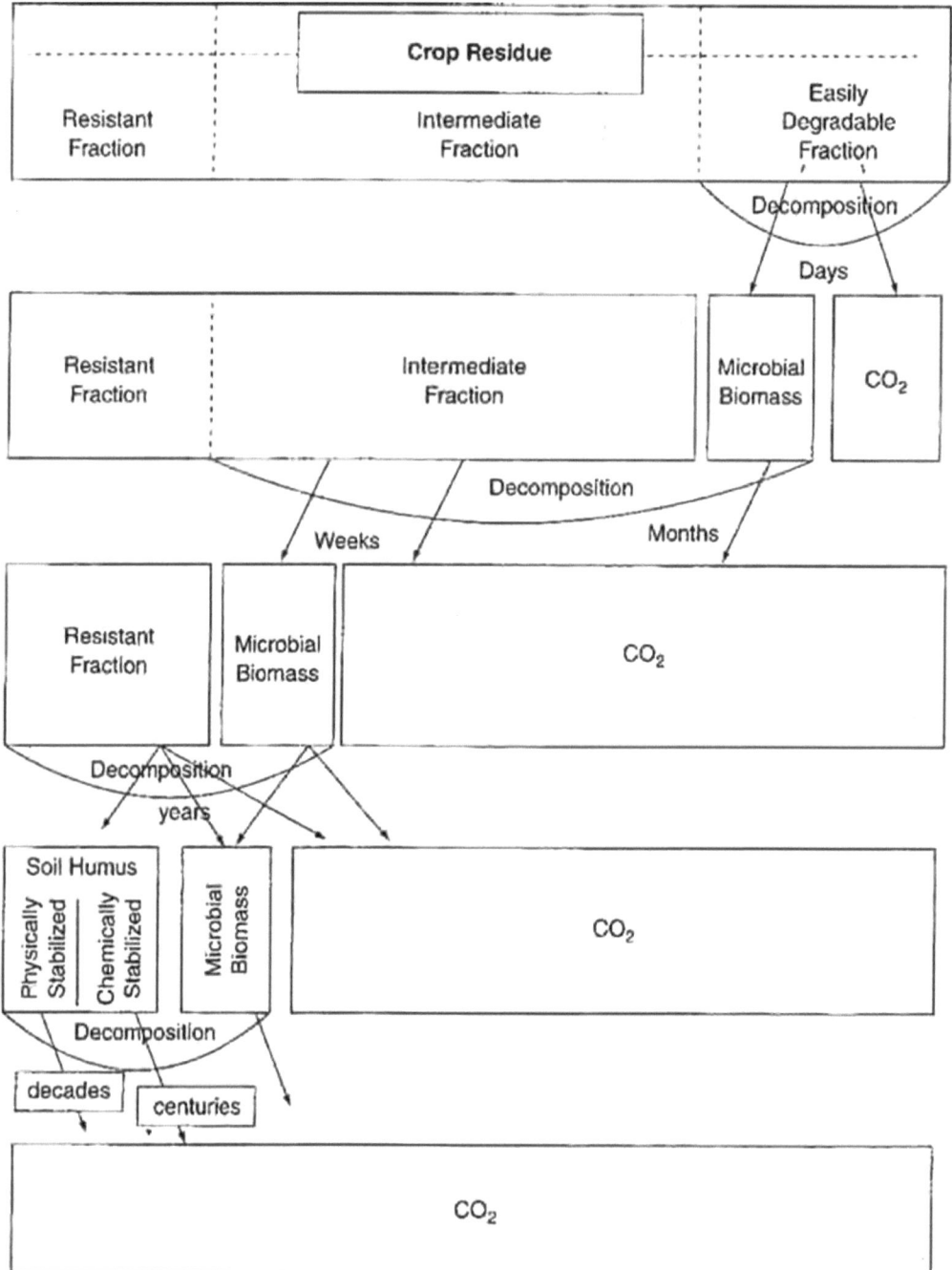

Fig. (4). Decay rate of organic matter in soil [12].

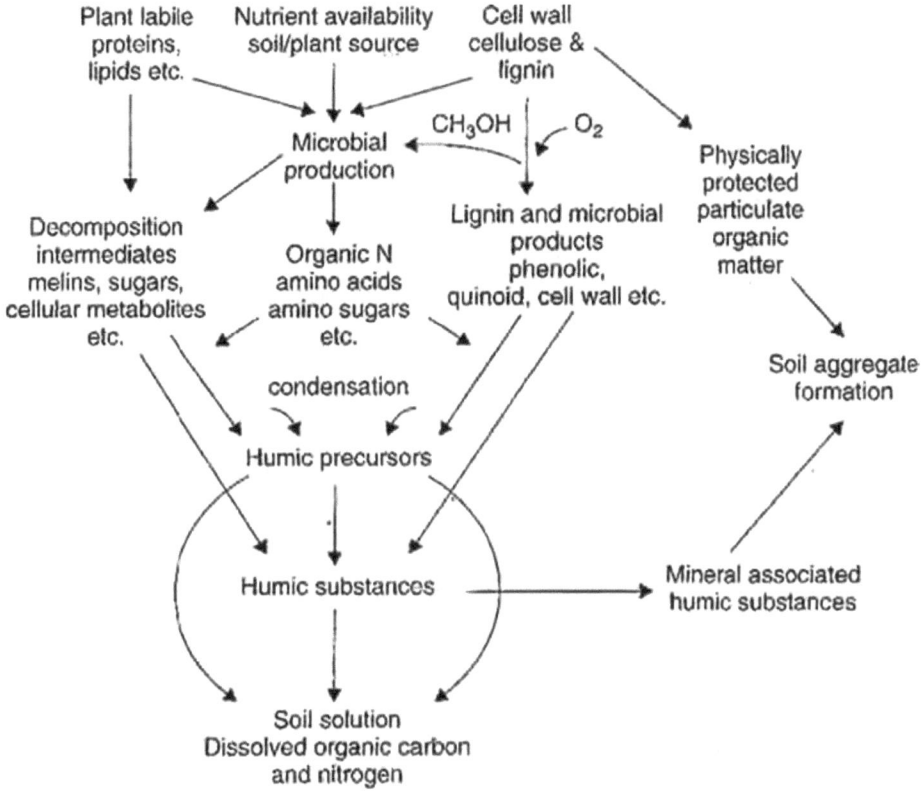

Fig. (5). Decomposition pathways of various organic compounds [12].

Decomposition of Polysaccharides

Cellulose is an essential component of vegetal matter, more precisely of plant cell walls. From a chemical point of view, it is a complex and extremely intricate polymer of glucose (Fig. **6**).

It is a relatively resistant compound, degradable only by some specific enzymes (cellulases). Among the orgnaisms producing such enzymes are bacteria (species of, *Clostridium, Cellulomonas, Thermomonospora, Ruminococcus, Bacteroides, Erwinia, Acetivibrio*), fungi (*Aspergillus, Rhizopus, Trichoderma*), but also some protists, annelids or insects (termites) that host cellulolytic symbionts, *etc.*

These microorganisms play an extremely important role in the soil carbon cycle, by releasing simple saccharides, which become available to the rest of soil microbiota. Also, from a biotechnological point of view, cellulolytic microorganisms contribute to the production of some biofuels (bioethanol, biogas) [9, 13].

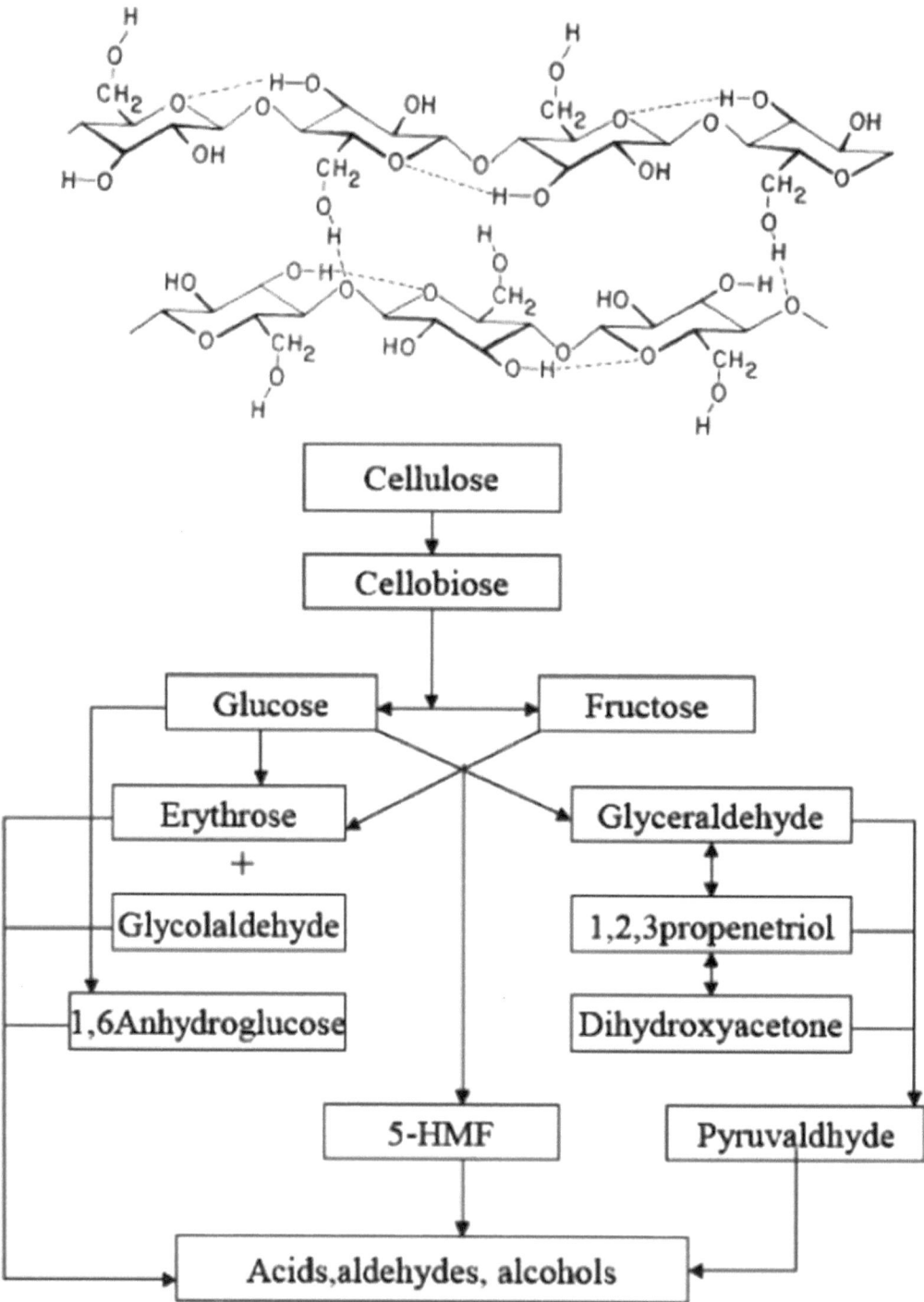

Fig. (6). Chemical structure of cellulose [14] and decomposition pathways [15].

Hemicelluloses are saccharidic polymers, whose structure mostly consists of xylose and arabinose units, together with some amounts of glucose, manose, galactose, and fructose. They form a consistent part of plant cell walls, binding together cellulose fibers. Also in plant cell walls, **pectins** are found, mostly made up of galacturonic acid. Finally, fungal cell walls, as well as cuticles of some invertebrates contain **chitin**, a nitorgenated polysaccharide based on N-acetylglucosamine (Fig. **7**). All these compounds are subject to decomposition by soil microbiota, at variable rates, depending on their chemical structure stability [9, 13, 16].

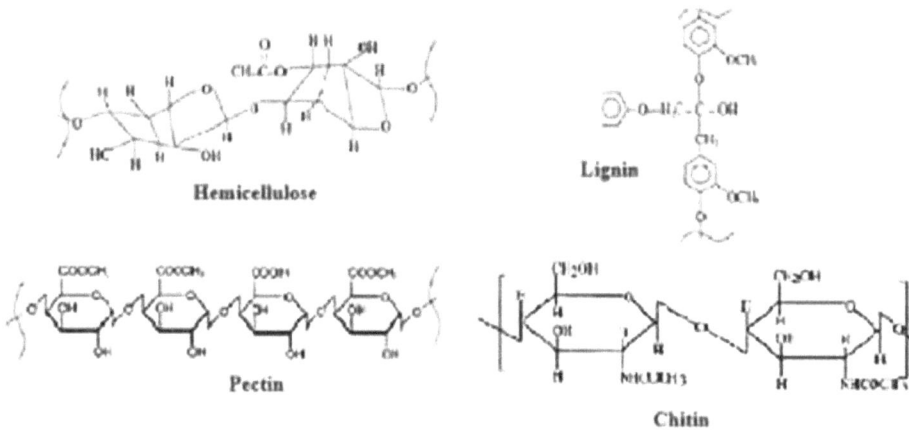

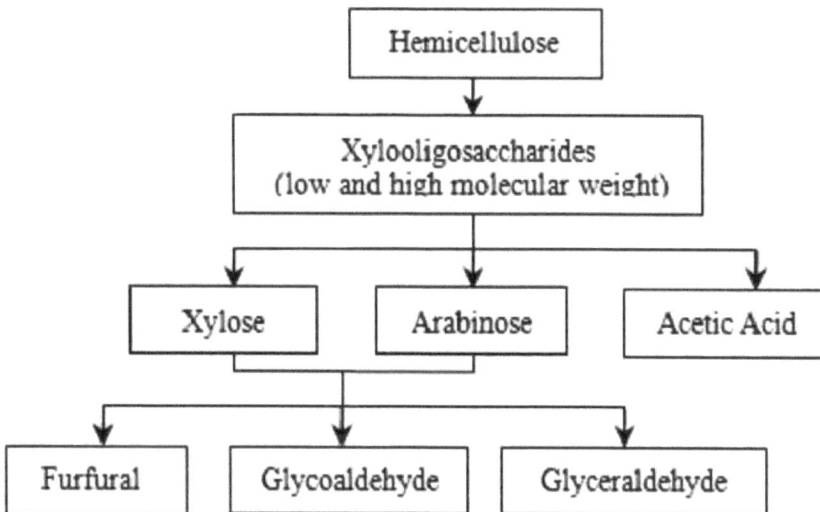

Fig. (7). Glucidic polymers commonly found in soil organic matter [16] and hemicellulose decomposition pathways [17].

Hemicelluloses are biodegraded more efficiently at an alkaline pH and higher temperatures. Besides thermophilic species, there are, of course, numerous mesophilic microorganisms able to break down these molecules at normal temperatures. They include some bacterial species (mostly actinomycetes, such as members of the genus *Streptomyces*), as well as some fungi, from genera like *Aspergillus*, *Phanerochaete*, *Talaromyces*, and *Trichoderma* [9, 18].

Oligosaccharides, such as glucose, fructose, arabinose, maltose, raffinose, rhamnose, sucrose or sau xylose are also found in the soil. Soluble and easily accessible to lifeforms, they are quickly consumed. The main sources are root exudates (of which they may make up 15-50%) and soil microbiota, as byproducts of other decomposition processes [9].

Decomposition of Lignin

Lignin is an extremely complex ensemble of organic heteropolymers, based on lignols (a class of phenolic acids) and carbohydrates. Lignin is an important component of plant cell walls, being associated with cellulose, especially in mechanic and vascular tissues. It is found in large amounts in woody organs but is not limited to these.

Basically, within the lignocellulosic complex which forms plant cell walls, lignin makes up 10-25% (40-60% being cellulose and 20-40% hemicellulose).

When plant organs die, lignin becomes an important biochemical component of soil, subject to decomposition processes. Obviously, it is mostly found in the litter, with a progressive decrease towards lower soil horizons (although there are some exceptions). Its proportion depends on neighboring vegetation, soil type, and climate factors. Because it is harder to break down (due to its heterogeneity), its percentage tends to increase during the first phases of decomposition [9, 19, 20].

There are various species of organisms able to degrade lignin or some of its fractions, by using specific or non-specific pathways (for instance, those normally dedicated to polyphenolic compounds or aromatic hydrocarbons; Fig. (**8**).

Among bacteria, we can mention some proteobacteria (α and γ) și actinomycetes (especially the genus *Streptomyces*), but also species of *Flavobacterium*, *Kocuria,* and *Staphylococcus*. Among fungi, numerous basidiomycetes possess the enzymatic apparatus needed to break down lignin (including some endophytic or parasitic ones). In soils, we may find species such as *Agaricus bisporus, Agrocybe praecox, Marasmius quercophilus, Phallus impudicus, Phanerochaete chrysosporium*, β-aryl ether and *Stropharia* sp. (Fig. **9**) [20, 21].

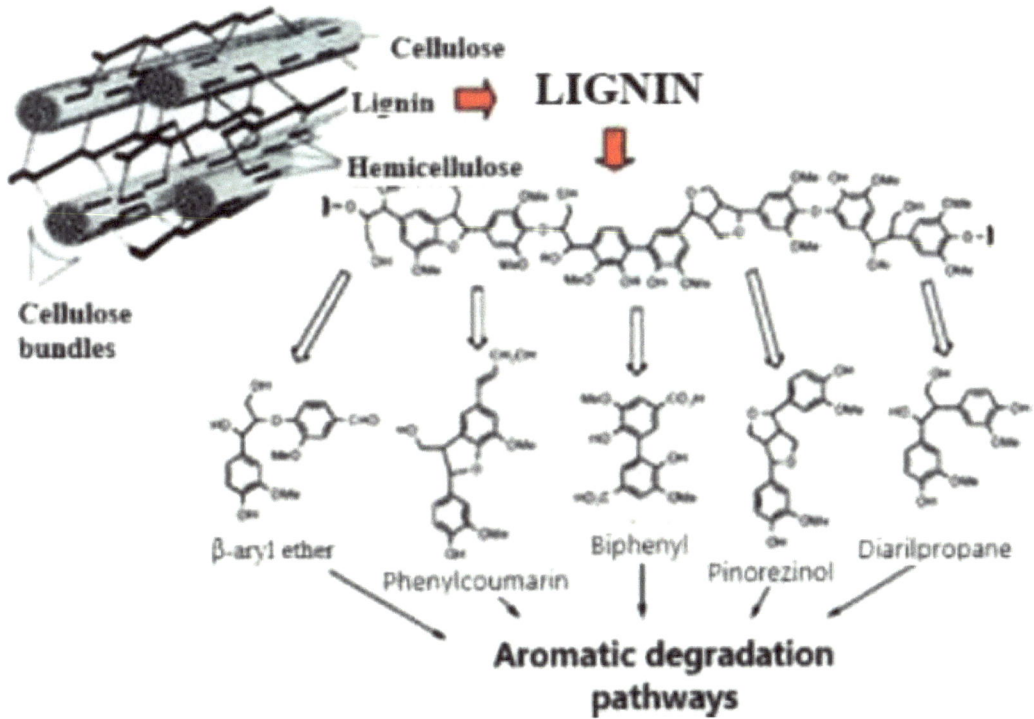

Fig. (8). Lignin decomposition pathways [22].

Fig. (9). Fungal species involved in lignocellulosic material decomposition: *Aspergillus* sp., [23], *Phanerochaete chrysosporium* [24], *Marasmius quercophilus* [25].

Decomposition of Proteins

Protein biodegradation is one of the key components of organic matter decomposition in soil. Proteins are complex organic compounds, made up of chains of amino acids. They are extremely important constituents of all organisms. Because these substances contain carbon as well as nitrogen, their breakdown is an important stage in the biogeochemical cycles of both elements.

The process requires synthesizing some specific enymes called proteases. They dismantle" proteic macromolecules into oligopeptides or amino acids, which in turn get involved in various metabolic pathways of those organisms (Fig. **10**).

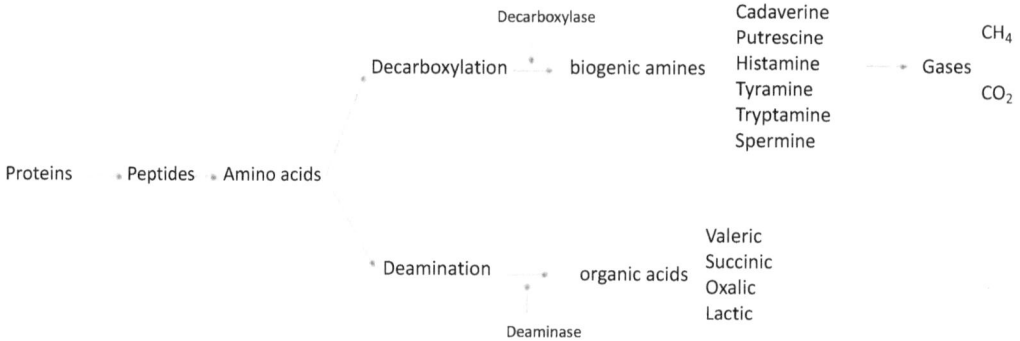

Decarboxylase

Decarboxylation · biogenic amines

Cadaverine
Putrescine CH_4
Histamine   ─ · Gases
Tyramine CO_2
Tryptamine
Spermine

Proteins   · Peptides · Amino acids

Deamination · organic acids

Valeric
Succinic
Oxalic
Lactic

Deaminase

Fig. (10). Protein decomposition pathways [29].

There are numerous proteolytic organisms. Among the most remarkable are, obviously, bacteria, such as members of the genera *Arthrobacter*, *Bacillus*, *Halomonas*, *Pseudomonas*, *Staphylococcus*, but, most of all, actinobacteria [26, 27]. Fungi (in particular species of *Aspergillus* and *Trichoderma*, but also some fungi involved in symbiotic relationships with plant roots) also play an important role in proteolytic processes [28].

Diverse functional types of proteases exist. Some act on terminal amino acids (exopeptidases, like amino acid-peptidases and carboxylases), others break the protein in the middle of its chain (endopeptidases, such as elastin, papain, pepsin, trypsina, and chymotrypsin).

Their action is significantly influenced by environmental factors such as temperature and pH.

Besides their essential role in organic matter recycling, proteolytic microorganisms, and their enzymes are of great biotechnological interest, with applications in the medical and pharmaceutical fields (wound cicatrization, for instance), decomposition of organic residues, production of biodetergents for cleaning and unclogging pipes, in textile, tanning, or food industry [26 - 28].

Research has shown that microorganisms are not solely responsible for protein decomposition. Plant roots, independent of the microbial symbionts might eventually host, and can secrete their array of proteolytic enzymes. Some are disseminated in the surrounding environment (rhizosphere), while others stick to the root-soil interface. They are of particular importance, allowing plants to use a consistent source of nitrogen, while also protecting them against some pathogens.

Among plant species known to produce significant amounts of proteases are *Allium cepa*, *Allium porrum*, *Cucumis sativus*, *Cucurbita pepo*, *Geranium pusillum*, *Hippopohae rhamnoides*, *Lactuca sativa*, *Raphanus sativus*, *Ruta graveolens*, and *Zea mays* [30].

Decomposition of Lipids

Lipids are one of the main classes of organic compounds that reach the soil. Of bacterial origin or derived from the decomposition of plant (or animal) organs, soil lipids include the typical triglycerides (made up of glycerol and fatty acids), phospholipids (the main constituents of cell membranes), cutin and suberin (compounds that are present in the cell walls of some plant tissues), plant waxes, individual fatty acids (mainly alkanoic acids, but also diacids and hydroxy acids), sterols, and n-alcohols. Similar in structure and decomposition pathways are hydrocarbons, terpenes, terpenoids, and resins (polymers of terpenes).

Their concentration is variable, but very often ranges between 1-6% of soil organic fraction (when considering "lipids" in the widest sense of the concept). Some of them, harder to biodegrade, become part of the humic component of soil, of which they can make up to 20%. One of the key sources of soil lipids is plant root decomposition since roots tend to be rich in such compounds. Lipids and similar compounds may have significant effects on water flow (some waxes may decrease permeability, especially in sandy soils) or seed germination and seedling growth (some lipids can have inhibitory or even toxic effects) [31 - 33].

Obviously, the main actors of lipid decomposition in soils are microorganisms. Because the extended lipid class is structurally variate, their breakdown occurs at different rates, by using different enzymes and metabolic pathways, by different lifeforms. If we strictly refer to typical lipids, such as triglycerides, their metabolization is quite easy, through hydrolysis, respectively, fatty acid beta-oxidation; a process that is fast and common to all organisms (Fig. **11**) [34].

Biodegradation of Hydrocarbons

Hydrocarbons are the simplest organic substances because they are exclusively composed of carbon and hydrogen. This does not mean that they cannot have complex, extended, and branched structures.

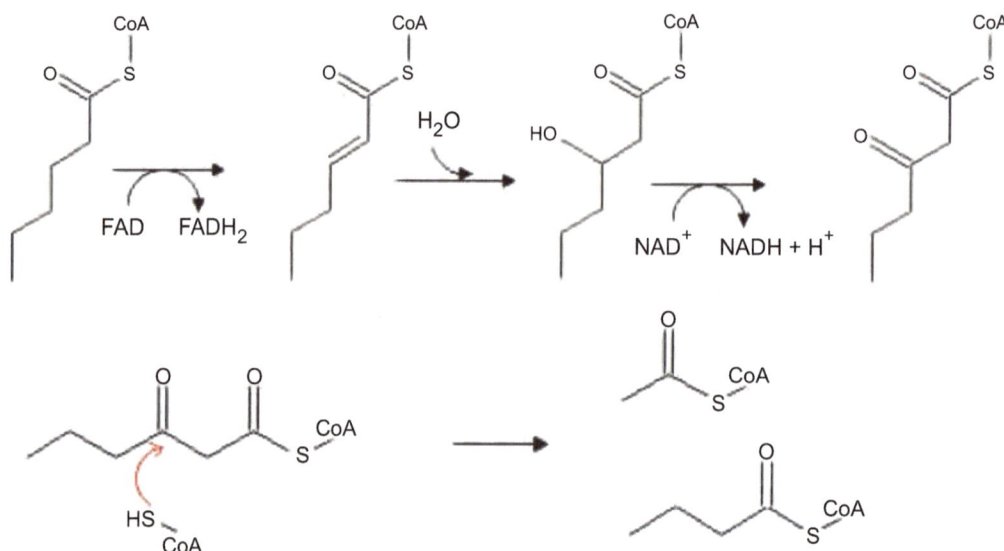

Fig. (11). Decomposition of fatty acids [35].

We can distinguish between several types, such as alkanes, cycloalkanes, alkenes, aromatic and polyaromatic hydrocarbons, asphaltenes or sulfonated hydrocarbons, *etc.*

Hydrocarbons may occur as byproducts of plant or microbial metabolism (some carotenoids, for instance, fit into this category), but their natural concentration in the soil is extremely low.

However, oil industry, with the various spills that can occur during drilling, transport, storage or processing, greatly increases the risk of soil contamination with such compounds. Plastic and its degradation byproducts are other extremely common pollutants. Last but not least, some halogenated hydrocarbons are used as pesticides.

Hydrocarbons, especially when in large amounts, are toxic to most organisms, interfering with the structure of cell membrane phospholipid layers. Furthermore, they can affect soil properties and most of all, their permeability to water and oxygen, major pollution events usually cause shallow anoxic layers to appear [36].

Yet, the very structural similarity between hydrocarbons and lipids allows certain microorganisms to metabolize these compounds. Specific enzymes can oxidize different types of hydrocarbons while resulting byproducts are then subjected to beta-oxidation or other biodegradation pathways.

Although not really a common feature, the ability to decompose hydrocarbons is found in some bacterial species (especially in genera *Achromobacter, Acinetobacter, Alcanivorax, Arthrobacter, Bacillus, Brevibacterium, Corynebacterium, Flavobacterium, Micrococcus, Nocardia, Pseudomonas, Vibrio*) and fungi (*Candida, Rhodotorula, Sporobolomyces*).

Some of them are strictly specialized in a limited number of hydrocarbons, while others (mostly species of *Pseudomonas*) can be rather polyvalent. The efficiency of the process is also variable.

This ability is especially important to perform ***bioremediation***. Bioremediation can be defined as the ecological reconstruction process through which natural microbiota is used to lower the concentration or toxicity of certain pollutants. It can be significantly influenced by environmental factors such as the physical state of the pollutant, its solubility, concentration, ambient temperature, nutrients – especially nitrogen and phosphorus, oxygen, *etc.* [36, 37].

Humus

The first stages of decomposition of some complex organic substances (lignin, polyphenolic compounds, cellulose) lead to the formation of humus, an essential component of the organic fraction of soil.

Humus is made up of both direct byproducts of decomposition and newly formed compounds. Humus, in turn, is also broken down, but at a much slower rate. It is characterized by a high affinity for cations (metal ions), an extremely important aspect of plant nutrition.

There are three main categories of humic compounds.

Humic acids have a high molecular mass, and a low number of oxygen atoms, are insoluble in water, and usually give the soil a black color.

Humic acids are lighter in color and soluble in water only at alkaline pH.

Fulvic acids, with a yellow-brown color, are soluble in water at any pH and contain more oxygen. The ratio between humic and fulvic acids concentration is a key index of soil fertility, with a clear advantage for soils richer in humic acids [9].

In time, the traditional vision defining humus as an "amorphous or colloidal" biochemical ensemble has evolved. Nowadays, researchers consider humus to be a complex mixture of the above-mentioned chemicals with cell fragments, dejections, and colonies of microorganisms [38].

Methanogenesis

Microbial methanogenesis is a process of anaerobic respiration, involving the oxidation of some chemical byproducts of decomposition processes: carbon dioxide, acetic and formic acids, methyl alcohol, methylamines, *etc.* The result of all these oxidations is methane (CH_4), a gaseous hydrocarbon.

This process requires anoxic or hypoxic conditions, thus moist soils in swamps, peat bogs, wetlands, and rice fields are the optimal locations for methanogens. This does not mean that there is no methanogenesis in other types of soils, due to the existence of hypoxic microniches or methanogenic microorganisms with a certain tolerance to oxygen (such as species of *Methanothrix*). The difference is that in most types of soil (for instance, in grasslands, and agroecosystems tundra), the effective amount of methane produced is low and usually surpassed by the amount consumed by other microorganisms. The process is more intense in the upper layers of soil [39 - 41].

Pollution may stimulate this process, for instance during hydrocarbon spills, by lowering soil oxygenation [42]. Some agricultural practices, such as applying certain fertilizers, tend to increase methane production, while others (pesticides, sulfur-rich fertilizers like bird manure, *etc.*) inhibit methanogenesis [40].

Methanogenesis is a feature uniquely found in some species of archaea, such as those in the genera *Methanobacterium*, *Methanobrevibacter*, *Methanococcus*, *Methanomicrobium*, *Methanosarcina*, and *Metanothrix* (Fig. **12**).

This process is of particular ecological importance. The methane produced diffuses through upper layers of soil (due to the concentration gradient), or passes through porous tissues inside plant roots and stems, reaching the atmosphere.

Methane is a greenhouse gas at least 25 times stronger than carbon dioxide, thus playing a role in global climate regulation. Of the 600 Tg released each year, 40% are due to natural sources. 145 Tg are produced in Earth's wetlands.

Methane is also the main component of "swamp gas" (together with H_2S and CO_2), which sometimes self-ignites. A similar phenomenon may occur in landfills, and wastewater of coal mines [39 - 41].

Methanotrophy

The opposite phenomenon to methanogenesis is methanotrophy: the biological oxidation of methane by certain microorganisms.

Fig. (12). Biochemical pathways of methanogenesis [43], *Methanothrix* sp., [44], and *Methanosarcina* sp., [45].

This oxidation leads to the production of methyl alcohol and, then, of formaldehyde. From here, various organic syntheses may start, but also the release of carbon dioxide. Most methanotrophs are aerobic, although some anaerobic species exist, that use nitrate, nitrite, sulfate, or iron ions as electron acceptors.

Metanotrophy is specific to some bacteria (*Methylobacter*, *Methylococcus*, *Methylomicrobium*, *Methylomonas*, among γ-proteobacteria, respectively *Methylocystis*, *Methylosinus*, among α-proteobacteria), but also to some archaes (Methanosarcinales, Methanomicrobiales) or even fungi (*Candida* sp.).

It is an extremely important process, keeping under control the natural methane emissions in swamps, peat bogs, paddy fields, tundras, *etc.* In many ecosystems (forests, grasslands, agroecosystems), metanotrophy dominates methanogenesis, so that the soils there work as a net sink for atmospheric methane [39, 40].

Of course, there are some determinant environmental factors: soil aeration, first of all, but also vegetation cover, pH (alkaline environments favor methanotrophy), temperature, and salinity (a major inhibiting factor).

Agroecosystems have lower methane consumption efficiency when compared to natural ecosystems. Also, pesticides are strong inhibitors, while fertilizers can have variate effects on methanotrophic microbiota (ammonium salts are inhibitors, while nitrates have a rather neutral effect).

Metanotrophs are also important from a biotechnological point of view, in lowering anthropic methane emissions from landfills, eutrophicated waters and also in decomposing some pollutants, such as chlorinated hydrocarbons [39, 40].

The issue of methanogenesis and methanotrophy also draws attention to the crucial ecological significance of *wetlands* and wetland soils. A wetland is basically any ecosystem characterized by three major features: *hydric soils* (meaning soils that are subjected to permanent or periodic water saturation, leading to accumulation of fine mineral fractions, such as silt and clays, and also of periodic organic matter accumulation, but also to a partial oxygen deficit, that influences microbiota and biochemical processes), *hydrophyte plants* (adapted to sometimes variable water levels and hypoxia) and a *hydroperiod* (a specific temporal pattern of water levels, due to precipitations, floods, tides, *etc.*) [46, 47].

Wetlands can be coastal or inland, freshwater or saltwater and they include marshes (nutrient-rich and periodically flooded), swamps (constantly saturated with water), bogs (with acidic water and usually dominated by peat-forming *Sphagnum* sp. moss), and fens (similar to bogs, but less acidic and having groundwater rather than precipitation as the main water source).

The importance of these ecosystems is crucial and multiple. First of all, due to their relatively hypoxic conditions, wetland soils tend to be less effective in decomposing organic matter into carbon dioxide. This way, carbon gets sequestered in soils (the most extreme version involving the formation of peat deposits in bogs and fens) over long periods, thus functioning as a sink for excess atmospheric carbon. Wetland soils and vegetation also tend to filtrate and store other types of compounds, including excess nitrates (up to 80%) and various pollutants (although microbial populations might complicate the issue: mercury, for instance, gets mostly sequestered by wetland soils; however, a large part of the amount that passes is converted from chemically-inert to more reactive forms such as methyl-mercury). The methanogenic-methanotrophic cycle also plays a role in climate regulation through the release or moderation of methane production.

Wetlands also host a huge biodiversity, including a variate vegetation, having carbon sink and pollutant removal functions by itself. Finally, they control coastal erosion, provide flood and storm protection, ensure water quality, and offer valuable natural products and recreation sites [46 - 48].

CONCLUSION

The main process linked to the carbon cycle that occurs in soils is decomposition. Bacteria and fungi are the main organisms that break complex and simple saccharides, lignin, proteins, lipids, and even hydrocarbons down to simpler compounds. The more stable and heavier to degrade fractions form humus, a key component of soil fertility.

Photosynthesis occurs in the upper layers of soil and is due to photosynthetic bacteria, algae, and lichens, while methanogenesis and its reverse, methanotrophy, are characteristic of hypoxic soils.

REFERENCES

[1]   Bot, A., Benites, J., The Importance of Soil Organic Matter. Key to Drought-Resistant Soil and Sustained Food Production. Food and Agriculture Organization of the United Nations, 2005. Available from: https://www.fao.org/3/a0100e/a0100e00.htm#Contents

[2]   The Carbon Cycle and the Nitrogen Cycle. Flexi 2.0, 2017. Available from: https://www.ck12.org/book/ck-12-earth-science-for-high-school/section/18.2

[3]   Crivoi, L., Sechestrarea carbonului în sol: fermierii pot obține certificate și le vinde implementând practici agricole durabile. Agrobiznes.ro, 2022. Available from: https://agrobiznes.ro/articole/sechestrarea-carbonului-in--ol-fermierii-pot-obtine-certificate-si-le-vinde-implementand-practici-agricole-durabile

[4]   Light & Plants. Let's Talk Science, 2022. Available from: https://letstalkscience.ca/educational-resources/backgrounders/light-plants

[5]   Nel, A.P., 2010. The influence of different winemaking techniques on the extraction of grape tannins. M.Sc. thesis, Stellenbosch University, 2010.

[6]   Bay SK, Waite DW, Dong X, *et al.* Chemosynthetic and photosynthetic bacteria contribute differentially to primary production across a steep desert aridity gradient. ISME J 2021; 15(11): 3339-56.
        [http://dx.doi.org/10.1038/s41396-021-01001-0] [PMID: 34035443]

[7]   Ray AE, Zhang E, Terauds A, Ji M, Kong W, Ferrari BC. Soil microbiomes with the genetic capacity for atmospheric chemosynthesis are widespread across the Poles and are associated with moisture, carbon, and nitrogen limitation. Front Microbiol 2020; 11: 1936.
        [http://dx.doi.org/10.3389/fmicb.2020.01936] [PMID: 32903524]

[8]   De Willigen P, Janssen BH, Heesmans HIM, Conijn JG, Velthof GJ, Chardon WJ. Decomposition and accumulation of organic matter in soil; comparison of some models. Wageningen: Alterra 2008.

[9]   McClaugherty C. Soils and decomposition În Encyclopedia of Life Sciences. Hoboken: John Wiley & Sons 2001.
        [http://dx.doi.org/10.1002/9780470015902.a0003187.pub2]

[10]   Wetterstedt, M., 2010. Decomposition of Soil Organic Matter. Experimental and Modelling Studies of the Importance of Temperature and Quality. Ph.D. thesis, Swedish University of Agricultural Sciences, Uppsala, 36.

[11]   Karyaningsih I. Types of organisms decomposers of soil pollutants. J For Environ 2018; 1: 16-21.
        [http://dx.doi.org/10.25134/jfe.v1i01.1044]

[12]   Condron LM, Stark C, O'Callaghan M, Clinton PW, Huang Z. The role of microbial communities in the formation and decomposition of soil organic matter. In: Dixon G, Tilston E, Eds. Soil

Microbiology and Sustainable Crop Production. Dordrecht: Springer 2010; pp. 81-118.
[http://dx.doi.org/10.1007/978-90-481-9479-7_4]

[13]   Singh S, Moholkar VS, Goyal A. Isolation, identification, and characterization of a cellulolytic *Bacillus amyloliquefaciens* strain SS35 from rhinoceros dung. ISRN Microbiol 2013; 2013(4): 1-7.
[http://dx.doi.org/10.1155/2013/728134] [PMID: 23762763]

[14]   Smith H, Ed. The Molecular Biology of Plant Cells. Berkeley: University of California Press 1977.

[15]   Kong L, Li G, Zhang B, He W, Wang H. Hydrogen production from biomass wastes by hydrothermal gasification. Energy Sources A Recovery Util Environ Effects 2008; 30(13): 1166-78.
[http://dx.doi.org/10.1080/15567030701258246]

[16]   Ghanbarzadeh B, Almasi H. Biodegradable polymers. In: Chamy R, Ed. Biodegradation - Life of Science. London: InTech Open 2013; pp. 141-85.
[http://dx.doi.org/10.5772/56230]

[17]   Cárdenas-Toro F, Alcázar-Alay SC, Forster-Carneiro T, Angela M, Meireles A. Obtaining oligo- and monosaccharides from agroindustrial and agricultural residues using hydrothermal treatments. Food Public Health 2014; 4(3): 123-39.
[http://dx.doi.org/10.5923/j.fph.20140403.08]

[18]   Leung, H., 2014. Long-term effects of timber harvesting on hemicellulolytic microbial communities in north American coniferous forest soils. M.Sc. Thesis, University of British Columbia, Vancouver, 2014, 89.

[19]   Thevenot M, Dignac MF, Rumpel C. Fate of lignins in soils: A review. Soil Biol Biochem 2010; 42(8): 1200-11.
[http://dx.doi.org/10.1016/j.soilbio.2010.03.017]

[20]   Datta R, Kelkar A, Baraniya D, *et al.* Enzymatic degradation of lignin in soil: A review. Sustainability (Basel) 2017; 9(7): 1163.
[http://dx.doi.org/10.3390/su9071163]

[21]   DeAngelis KM, Allgaier M, Chavarria Y, *et al.* Characterization of trapped lignin-degrading microbes in tropical forest soil. PLoS One 2011; 6(4): e19306.
[http://dx.doi.org/10.1371/journal.pone.0019306] [PMID: 21559391]

[22]   Bugg TDH, Ahmad M, Hardiman EM, Rahmanpour R. Pathways for degradation of lignin in bacteria and fungi. Nat Prod Rep 2011; 28(12): 1883-96.
[http://dx.doi.org/10.1039/c1np00042j] [PMID: 21918777]

[23]   Lincoln   University,   Aspergillus   soil   testing,   2020.   Available   from:
https://research.lincoln.ac.nz/testing-analytical-services/aspergillus-soil-testing

[24]   University of California, Phanerochaete chrysosporium RP-78. Mycocosm. The Fungal Genomics Resource, 2022. Available from: https://mycocosm.jgi.doe.gov/Phchr4_2/Phchr4_2.home. html

[25]   Schwarz, C., Observation 228256: Marasmius quercophilus Pouzar (Site ID) (Collybiopsis quercophila).   Mushroom   Observer,   2016.   Available   from:
https://mushroomobserver.org/observations/228256

[26]   Hayano K. Protease activity in a paddy field soil: Origin and some properties. Soil Sci Plant Nutr 1993; 39(3): 539-46.
[http://dx.doi.org/10.1080/00380768.1993.10419794]

[27]   Chakraborty A, Karmakar S. Isolation of protease producing bacteria from soil and characterization of the protease. Int J Curr Microbiol Appl Sci 2020; 9(3): 2974-83.
[http://dx.doi.org/10.20546/ijcmas.2020.903.341]

[28]   Suryawanshi HK, Pandya ND. Screening, identification of alkaline proteases producing fungi from soil of different habitats of Amalner Tahsil [Maharashtra] and their applications. Int J Appl Sci Biotechnol 2017; 5(3): 397-402.

[http://dx.doi.org/10.3126/ijasbt.v5i3.18304]

[29]   Ioan BG, Manea C, Hanganu B, Statescu L, Gheuca Solovastru L, Manoilescu I. The chemistry decomposition in human corpses. Revista de Chimie 2017; 68(6): 1352-6.
[http://dx.doi.org/10.37358/RC.17.6.5672]

[30]   Adamczyk B. Root-Derived Proteases as a Plant Tool to Access Soil Organic Nitrogen; Current Stage of Knowledge and Controversies. Plants 2021; 10(4): 731.
[http://dx.doi.org/10.3390/plants10040731] [PMID: 33918076]

[31]   Stevenson FJ. Lipids in soil. J Am Oil Chem Soc 1966; 43(4): 203-10.
[http://dx.doi.org/10.1007/BF02641088]

[32]   Mueller KE, Eissenstat DM, Müller CW, Oleksyn J, Reich PB, Freeman KH. What controls the concentration of various aliphatic lipids in soil? Soil Biol Biochem 2013; 63: 14-7.
[http://dx.doi.org/10.1016/j.soilbio.2013.03.021]

[33]   Warren CR. A liquid chromatography–mass spectrometry method for analysis of intact fatty-acid-based lipids extracted from soil. Eur J Soil Sci 2018; 69(5): 791-803.
[http://dx.doi.org/10.1111/ejss.12689]

[34]   Bridson JN. Lipid fraction in forest litter: Early stages of decomposition. Soil Biol Biochem 1985; 17(3): 285-90.
[http://dx.doi.org/10.1016/0038-0717(85)90062-8]

[35]   Silva, P. The chemical logic behind... fatty acid metabolism. Universidade Fernando Pessoa, Available from: http://homepage.ufp.pt/pedros/bq/fatty.htm

[36]   Atlas RM. Microbial degradation of petroleum hydrocarbons: an environmental perspective. Microbiol Rev 1981; 45(1): 180-209.
[http://dx.doi.org/10.1128/mr.45.1.180-209.1981] [PMID: 7012571]

[37]   Korda A, Santas P, Tenente A, Santas R. Petroleum hydrocarbon bioremediation: sampling and analytical techniques, in situ treatments and commercial microorganisms currently used. Appl Microbiol Biotechnol 1997; 48(6): 677-86.
[http://dx.doi.org/10.1007/s002530051115] [PMID: 9457796]

[38]   Ponge JF. Humus: Dark side of life or intractable "aether"? Pedosphere 2022; 32(4): 660-4.
[http://dx.doi.org/10.1016/S1002-0160(21)60013-9]

[39]   Topp E, Pattey E. Soils as sources and sinks for atmospheric methane. Can J Soil Sci 1997; 77(2): 167-77.
[http://dx.doi.org/10.4141/S96-107]

[40]   Serrano-Silva N, Sarria-Guzmán Y, Dendooven L, Luna-Guido M. Methanogenesis and methanotrophy in soil: A review. Pedosphere 2014; 24(3): 291-307.
[http://dx.doi.org/10.1016/S1002-0160(14)60016-3]

[41]   Angle JC, Morin TH, Solden LM, et al. Methanogenesis in oxygenated soils is a substantial fraction of wetland methane emissions. Nat Commun 2017; 8(1): 1567.
[http://dx.doi.org/10.1038/s41467-017-01753-4] [PMID: 29146959]

[42]   Yang J, Li G, Qian Y, Zhang F. Increased soil methane emissions and methanogenesis in oil contaminated areas. Land Degrad Dev 2018; 29(3): 563-71.
[http://dx.doi.org/10.1002/ldr.2886]

[43]   Galagan JE, Nusbaum C, Roy A, et al. The genome of *M. acetivorans* reveals extensive metabolic and physiological diversity. Genome Res 2002; 12(4): 532-42.
[http://dx.doi.org/10.1101/gr.223902] [PMID: 11932238]

[44]   Methanothrix thermoacetophila PT is an anaerobe, thermophilic archaeon that was isolated from sludge, thermophilic anaerobic digester. BacDive, Available from: https://bacdive.dsmz.de/strain/7050

[45]   Methanosarcina mazei S-6 is an anaerobe, mesophilic archaeon that was isolated from sewage sludge

plant. BacDrive, Available from: https://bacdive.dsmz.de/strain/7096

[46]   Badiou P. The importance of freshwater mineral soil wetlands in the global carbon cycle Ducks Unlimited Canada. Stonewall 2017.

[47]   Trettin CC, Kolka RK, Marsh AS, *et al.* Wetland and Hydric Soils. In: Pouyat RV, Page-Dumroese DS, Patel-Weynand T, Geiser LH, Eds. Forest and Rangeland Soils of the United States Under Changing Conditions A Comprehensive Science Synthesis. Cham: Springer 2020; pp. 99-126. [http://dx.doi.org/10.1007/978-3-030-45216-2_6]

[48]   Balwan WK, Kour S. Wetland- an ecological boon for the environment. East African Scholars J. Agri Life Sci 2021; 4(3): 38-48.

CHAPTER 5

Cycles of Matter in Soil, Nitrogen Cycle

Abstract: Nitrogen is another bioelement of crucial importance, being a part of amino acids, proteins, nucleic acids, and many other organic compounds. It is also an object to a complex natural cycle occurring, among others, at the soil level. Ammonification is one of the main components of this cycle, consisting of the decomposition of nitrogen-containing organic compounds and releasing ammonium ions, essential nutrients for plants and microorganisms. Another nitrogen input source in soils is the fixation of atmospheric dinitrogen by some bacteria, free-living or in symbiosis with certain plant species. Nitrification converts ammonium into nitrate, another valuable nutrient, soluble and easily disseminated in soil solution and hydrosphere. Microbial denitrification closes the cycle by transforming nitrate into nitrogen oxides and, then, dinitrogen that returns to the atmosphere.

Keywords: Ammonification, Denitrification, Fixation, Nitrification, Nitrogen.

INTRODUCTION

Nitrogen is one of the most important biogenic elements. It is part of some common organic and inorganic substances. First of all, as molecular nitrogen or dinitrogen (N_2), it forms 78% of the Earth's atmospheric mass. Nitrogen oxides (NO, NO_2, N_2O) are other components of our atmosphere, albeit minor ones, due to their instability.

In water and soils, various nitrogen salts are found, such as those featuring the nitrate (NO_3^-), nitrite (NO_2^-) and ammonium (NH_4^+) ions. Organic nitrogen compounds are much more variate, including amines, amides aromatic nitrogen compounds, enamines, nitramines, nitriles, imines, nitrosamines, organic nitrates, some vitamins and alkaloids, but most importantly, amino acids, peptides, proteins, nucleobases, nucleotides and their polymers, nucleic acids [2].

All these compounds undergo continuous syntheses and degradations, thus ensuring both the necessary nutrients to all lifeforms on Earth and maintaining the normal composition of the atmosphere. This is the biogeochemical cycle of nitrogen, whose four stages occur in diverse environments, including soil (Fig. (**1**).

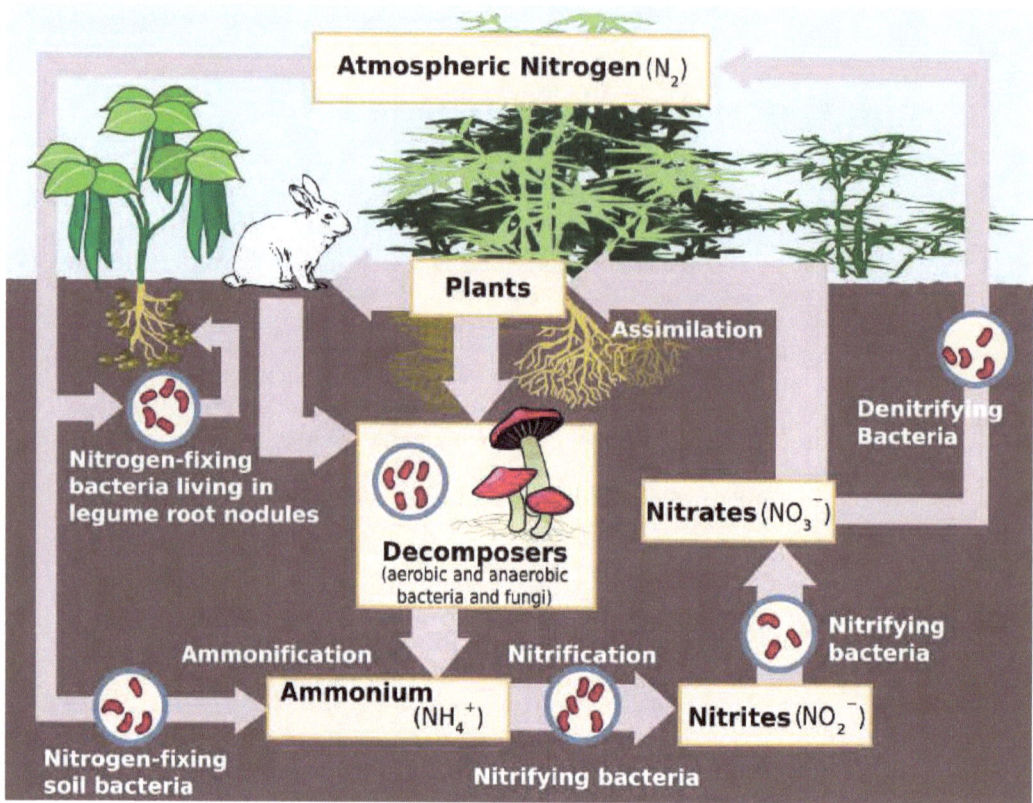

Fig. (1). Nitrogen cycle in soil [1].

Ammonification

Ammonification or nitrogen mineralization is a key process, leading to the release of nitrogen from various organic compounds and its conversion into ammonium ion (NH_4^+) salts; these salts are water-soluble and easily accessible to primary producers (especially to plants).

It is actually a form of decomposition of these substances (mostly byproducts of protein and nucleic acids breakdown). It is mostly due to bacteria. Among the main ammonifiers, we may find Gram-positive species (genera *Bacillus* and *Clostridium* and, most of all, actinomycetes), or Gram-negative ones (genera *Pseudomonas, Serratia, Vibrio, etc.*) [3].

There are also some fungi involved in this process, such as species of *Alternaria, Aspergillus* or *Mucor*. All these organisms can degrade proteins and their subdivisions, by secreting proteases (proteolytic enzymes, see previous chapter). Furthermore, the production of ribonucleases and deoxyribonucleases, allows the breaking down of nucleic acids.

However, these are not the only sources of organic nitrogen. Urea (a byproduct of decomposition, but also a commonly used fertilizer) is degraded by ureases, produced by certain species of *Bacillus*, *Micrococcus*, *Proteus,* or *Sarcina*. Amines are the target of aminooxidases produced by species of *Mycobacterium*, *Protoaminobacter,* and *Pseudomonas*. Amides are hydrolysed by amidases and, among the organisms responsible for this, we can mention the green alga *Chlorella* sp [4].

Populations of ammonifying microorganisms in the soil (mainly bacteria) commonly reach densities of $1\text{-}5\times10^6$ culturable organisms per gram of dry soil (real densities being, probably, much higher) [5]. The total amount of mineralized nitrogen is usually a few milligrams per kilogram of soil per day (between 0.3-9 mg/kg/day, for instance, in a study conducted on different types of soils in tropical and temperate regions of China) [6].

Among the factors that may determine the density and composition of ammonifying microbiota, as well as its efficiency, we should mention agricultural practices. Fertilization with urea, for instance, tends to enhance ammonification, while mineral amendments (calcium chloride, potassium sulfate) may have mixed effects. Likewise, mixed effects can be due to pesticides: some enhance the responsible microbiota (just up to a specific dose), while others inhibit it. Ecological crops seem to yield higher ammonification rates than conventional ones [7 - 9].

Nitrogen Fixation

One of the most interesting and important processes in the living world is the biological fixation of nitrogen (diazotrophs). Dinitrogen (N_2), a molecule rather chemically inert, makes up around 78% of our planet's atmosphere. However, in this state, it is not truly bioavailable. Its conversion to more accessible compounds is done electrically (by lightning) or by using nitrogenases, enzymes specific only to some groups of bacteria.

These complex enzymes, containing iron and, often, molybdenum or vanadium ions, can catalyze the reduction of nitrogen to ammonium, which, in turn, will be used in organic syntheses. Molecular oxygen, above a certain concentration, inhibits the enzymes so the microorganisms involved need to find various protection mechanisms: thick cell walls, abundant mucus, enzymes that immobilize oxygen, or symbioses with other lifeforms.

Diazotrophy is not really a common feature, but not even a very rare one. It is found in diverse groups of bacteria, some are aerobic, others are microaerophilic or anaerobic, with some photosynthesizing, and others being nonphotosynthesizing.

Among non-symbiotic bacteria able to fix nitrogen, we can mention members of the genera *Azotobacter, Azospirillum, Azoarcus, Campylobacter, Beggiatoa, Rhodobacter, Rhodospirillum, Clostridium, Herbaspirillum, Pantoea, Klebsiella* and also numerous cyanobacteria (*Anabaena, Nostoc, etc.*) Fig. (**2**). Among cyanobacteria we may find solitary (*Aphanothece, Gloeocapsa*) or colonial forms, without heterocysts (thick-walled cells, specialized in nitrogen fixation: *Cyanothece, Gloeothece, Lyngbia*) or with such modified cells (*Anabaena, Trichodesmium*) [2, 3, 10].

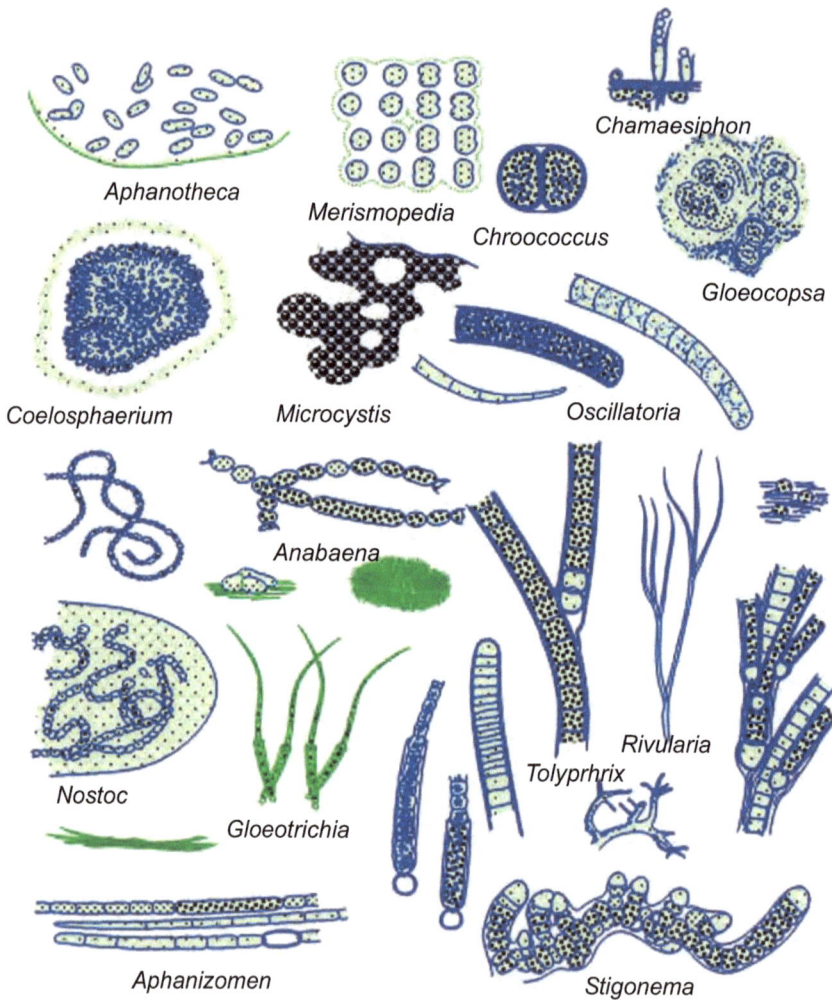

Fig. (2). A few genera of nitrogen-fixing cyanobacteria [10].

Of course, cyanobacteria, like all photoautotrophic organisms, only reside in the upper layers of soil. Yet, they are an important component of local microbiota. Inoculating agricultural fields with such microbes is becoming a more and more widely used technique to enrich, but also to stabilize soil, with significant effects on fertility [11].

Besides free microorganisms, this process also involves some associative or symbiotic forms (described in detail in the last chapter). Species of *Azospirillum* often form non-symbiotic associations with the roots of some plants (Poaceae, Brassicaceae, *etc.*, including plants of agro-horticultural interest). Diazotrophic cyanobacteria can be a part of some lichens (*Lobaria* sp., *Peltigera* sp.), but also endosymbionts of some bryophytes (*Blasia*) or upper plants (*Azolla, Cycas, Gunnera*, but in their case, the symbiosis occurs in aboveground organs) [2, 3, 10].

In addition, of course, there are extremely important symbioses between rhizobia (*Bradyrhizobium, Mesorhizobium, Rhizobium, Sinorhizobium,* and other related genera) and the roots of plants in the Fabaceae family, where they form nitrogen-fixing nodules, as well as those involving the actinobacteria *Frankia* sp. Also, at roots of some members of the Betulaceae, Casuarinaceae, Coriariaceae, Datiscaceae, Elaeagnaceae, Myricaceae, Rhamnaceae, and Rosaceae families, they form associations called actinorrhizae [2].

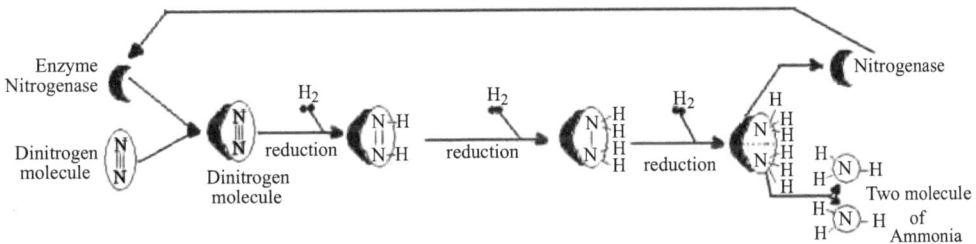

Fig. (3). General pathway of biological nitrogen fixation [12].

Globally, there are several pathways of fixation, one of the most important being due to anthropic activity. However, the main natural one is due to biological fixation (Fig. **3**), with an average of 61-88 Tg/year. Of this, just legume symbionts are responsible for 11-34 Tg/year. The ratio between free-living and plant-associated nitrogen fixers is highly variable. It tends to favor non-symbiotic fixation in cooler and moist climates. Boreal forests, wetlands, but also some steppes and prairies, and tropical forests are places where non-symbiotic fixation dominates, while the contrary is true for tundras, temperate forests, or savannahs [13 - 15].

Nitrification

The next stage of the cycle is the biological oxidation of ammonium ions or, shortly, nitrification. Nitrification is a process that, in turn, has two phases: ammonium (NH_4^+) oxidation to nitrite (NO_2^-) and, respectively, nitrite oxidation to nitrate (NO_3^-).

The two phases require two different sets of enzymes, thus two different groups of microorganisms – chemoautotrophic or sometimes heterotrophic (mainly bacteria but also some species of archaea and fungi). The process is usually aerobic.

During this process, the various biochemical transformations can involve both organic and inorganic nitrogen compounds (Fig. (**4**).

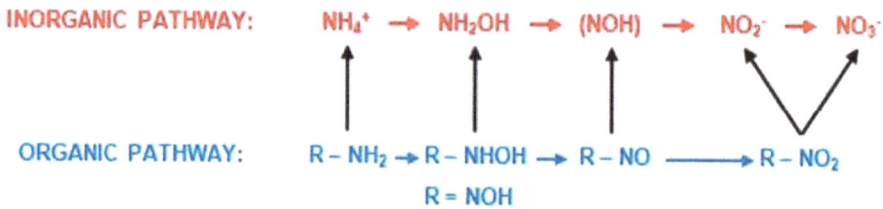

Fig. (4). Biochemical pathways of nitrification [2].

The first stage of this process is due to **ammonia-oxidizing bacteria** (AOB), also called **nitrite bacteria** or **nitrosobacteria**: genera *Nitrosomonas* (Fig. **5**), *Nitrosococcus*, *Nitrosospira*, *Nitrosovibrio*, and *Nitrosolobus*. There are also some **ammonia-oxidizing archaea** (AOA): *Nitrosoarchaeum*, *Nitrosopumilus*, and *Nitrososphaera*.

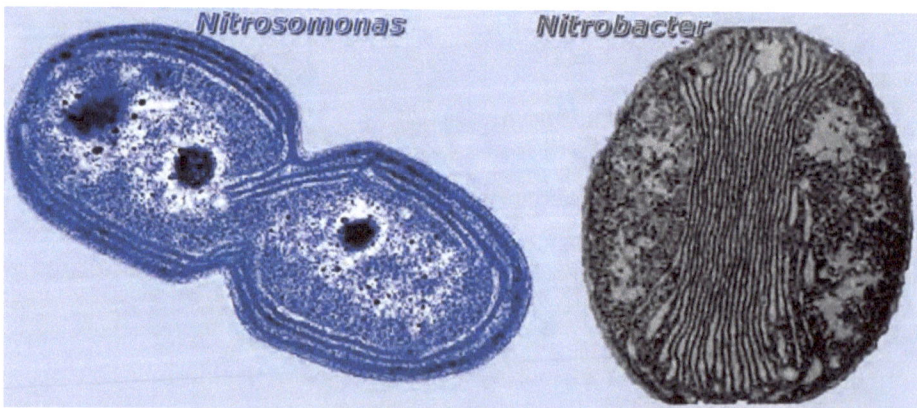

Fig. (5). *Nitrosomonas* sp. and *Nitrobacter* sp., are some of the most common ammonia-oxidizing bacteria, respectively nitrite-oxidizing bacteria [16].

The second stage involves mostly **nitrite-oxidizing bacteria** (NOB) or **nitrate bacteria**: *Nitrobacter* (Fig. **5**), *Nitrococcus*, *Nitrospina*, and *Nitrospira*. Some species of *Nitrospira*, as well as *Thiosphaera pantothropha*, are able to perform both transformations.

Heterotrophic oxidation of nitrogen compounds to nitrites or nitrates is another common process in soil, involving bacteria in the genera *Agrobacter*, *Alcaligenes*, *Arthrobacter*, *Nocardia,* and even fungi, such as *Aspergillus flavus* [2].

To make things even more complicated, there is another component of the nitrogen cycle, namely, the **anaerobic ammonia oxidation** (*anammox*), with a direct pathway to dinitrogen (N_2) and its release into the atmosphere. Although this process is more common in aquatic ecosystems, it also occurs in soils (wetland soils, but not only: in areas with natural vegetation or agroecosystems). It is due to some bacteria in the genera *Brocadia*, *Kuenenia*, *Anammoxoglobus,* and *Jettenia* (all belonging to phylum Planctomycetota) Their particular adaptations include a special enzymatic apparatus and a massive intracellular vesicle (anammoxosome), that stores both energy and toxic byproducts [17].

Among the factors influencing soil nitrification, we can mention soil microtopography and composition (certain soils, especially clayey ones, can immobilize nitrogen compounds by adsorbing them on mineral structures, thus inhibiting nitrifying microbiota), moisture (long-term drought is a strong inhibitor), temperature, oxygen, pH and eventual fertilizers. Some agrochemicals like urease inhibitors (hydroquinone, for instance) or nitrification inhibitors (dicyandiamide) that either limit ammonium bioavailability or directly act on nitrifying microbiota, have been applied for a while by farmers, in order to enhance nitrogen fertilization efficiency [18 - 20].

Nitrification is extremely important for the soil. Ammonium compounds, although easily bioavailable, are less water-soluble. Nitrates, on the other hand, can be easily absorbed by plants and microbes (albeit at a lower rate) and are extremely soluble, being easily disseminated within soil solution. Under this form, nitrogen bioavailability in the entire ecosystem is greatly enhanced.

Furthermore, nitrification plays a complex role in nitrogen sink in soils. Ammonium compounds are more prone to being decomposed to gaseous ammonia, which is lost to the atmosphere, while nitrification limits this loss. Yet, nitrate is the basis of the next stage of the nitrogen cycle, namely microbial denitrification, a process that also leads to dinitrogen formation and its loss to the atmosphere (this is the main reason some farmers use the abovementioned chemical inhibitors). Finally, the anammox pathway leads directly to dinitrogen formation [2, 17, 18, 20].

Denitrification

Of course, the nitrogen cycle needs to be closed by returning this element to the atmosphere. Total denitrification is the conversion of nitrate ions to nitrogen oxides (mostly N_2O) and N_2 (nitrogen oxides are instable in Earth's atmospheric conditions). There is also a so-called partial (dissimilatory) denitrification, which is basically the reverse of nitrification and ammonification: nitrate conversion to nitrite or even directly to ammonium.

Total denitrification (the dominant form) is a reductive process, practically a version of anaerobic respiration, where the position of oxygen as the final electron acceptor is taken by nitrates (Fig. **6**). Microorganisms involved can be aerobic, as well as anaerobic, and are always bacteria (the most common in soil being species of *Pseudomonas*, followed by *Achromobacter*, *Bacillus,* and *Micrococcus*; other important genera are *Aeromonas*, *Agrobacterium*, *Alcaligenes*, *Chromobacterium*, *Flavobacterium*, *Hyphomicrobium*, and *Streptomyces*; some species of *Alcaligenes* can also perform partial denitrification to ammonium) [2, 21].

There are various factors influencing the rate of this process (usually, the upper values are somewhere around 1 mg N/kg/h, while the lower limit can be around 0.25 mg/kg/h). It seems that the determinant factor is the pH of soil solution (optimum between 6-8; acidic conditions are usually inhibitory). But it is not the only one: moisture, organic matter content, and, obviously, the amount of nitrates available (higher when fertilizers are applied) are positively correlated with the denitrification rate. Oxygen (in turn influenced by water imbibition) is an inhibitor. Vegetation type is also relevant: grassland soils have higher denitrification than those in forests [22 - 25].

The role of denitrification in nature is multiple and complex. First of all, it continuously regenerates the amount of atmospheric dinitrogen, essential as buffer gas in breathing.

Yet, for a long time, denitrification was regarded as a negative phenomenon, due to its reduced efficiency of fertilizer treatment . In the last decades, however, it is the excess of nitrate treatments to cause trouble. Reckless use of fertilizers tends to pollute both soils and groundwater. In this context, denitrifying microbiota proves to be a useful ally, just as in the case of wastewater treatment. Finally, these bacteria are also able to degrade various organic pollutants produced by the petrochemical industry: toluene, resorcinol, and other aromatic compounds [2, 20, 23, 24].

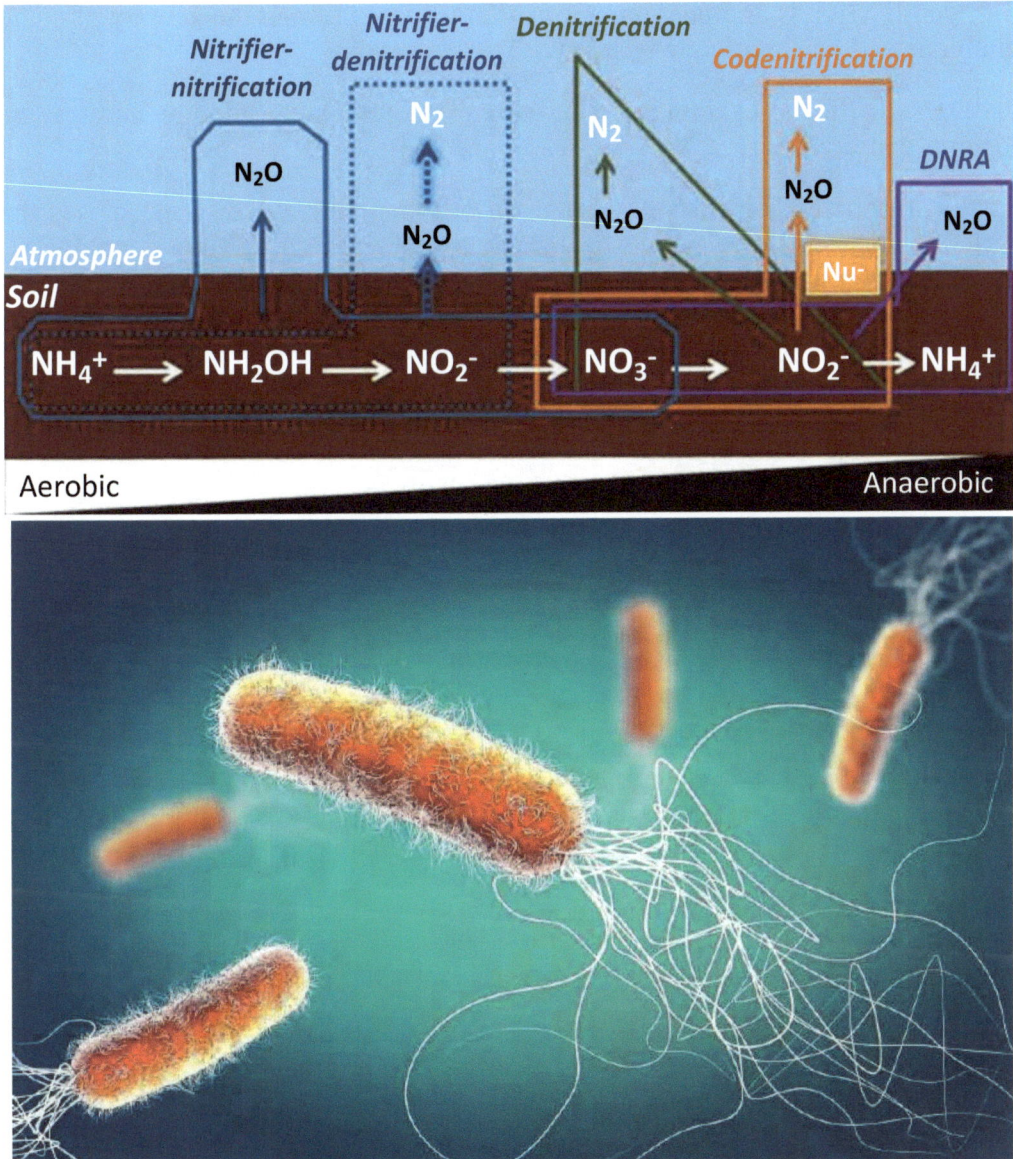

Fig. (6). Pathways of denitrification [26] and *Pseudomonas aeruginosa*, one of the most common denitrifying species in soils [27].

CONCLUSION

Ammonification is one of the main stages of nitrogen cycling that occurs in soil. It consists of decomposing organic nitrogen to ammonium ions and involves heterotrophic bacteria, fungi, and even some microalgae.

Nitrogen fixation is another source of soil nitrogen, through the activity of some symbiotic and non-symbiotic bacteria.

Through nitrification, ammonium is converted into more mobile nitrates, by bacteria and archaea.

Finally, denitrification provides the main nitrogen sink in soils and closes the cycle, returning this element to the atmosphere. Denitrifying bacteria are responsible for this process.

REFERENCES

[1]   Chaffey, N., 2014. Spotlight on macronutrients (Part 2): Nitrogen, in a bit of a fix... Botany One, 2014, Avialable from: https://botany.one/2014/05/spotlight-macronutrients-part-2-nitrogen-bit-fix/

[2]   Paśmionka IB, Bulski K, Boligłowa E. The participation of microbiota in the transformation of nitrogen compounds in the soil — A review. Agronomy (Basel) 2021; 11(5): 977.
[http://dx.doi.org/10.3390/agronomy11050977]

[3]   Herbert RA. Nitrogen cycling in coastal marine ecosystems. FEMS Microbiol Rev 1999; 23(5): 563-90.
[http://dx.doi.org/10.1111/j.1574-6976.1999.tb00414.x] [PMID: 10525167]

[4]   Meenakshi,   R.T.,   Nitrogen   cycle.   Slideshare,   2016.   Avialable   from: https://www.slideshare.net/ThulasiMeenakshi/nitrogen-cycle-67284749

[5]   Semenov AM, Khvatov IL, Olenin AV. Determination of the number of ammonification bacteria and activity of the ammonification process in soils and their relevance for the development of the of soil health parameter. Curr Investig Agric Curr Res 2019; 6(2): 779-86.
[http://dx.doi.org/10.32474/CIACR.2019.06.000231]

[6]   Wang C, Wang N, Zhu J, *et al.* Soil gross N ammonification and nitrification from tropical to temperate forests in eastern China. Funct Ecol 2018; 32(1): 83-94.
[http://dx.doi.org/10.1111/1365-2435.13024]

[7]   Rangaswamy V, Venkateswarlu K. Ammonification and nitrification in soils, and nitrogen fixation by *Azospirillum* sp. as influenced by cypermethrin and fenvalerate. Agric Ecosyst Environ 1993; 45(3-4): 311-7.
[http://dx.doi.org/10.1016/0167-8809(93)90079-5]

[8]   Omar SA, Ismail MA. Microbial populations, ammonification and nitrification in soil treated with urea and inorganic salts. Folia Microbiol (Praha) 1999; 44(2): 205-12.
[http://dx.doi.org/10.1007/BF02816244] [PMID: 10588055]

[9]   Burger M, Jackson LE. Microbial immobilization of ammonium and nitrate in relation to ammonification and nitrification rates in organic and conventional cropping systems. Soil Biol Biochem 2003; 35(1): 29-36.
[http://dx.doi.org/10.1016/S0038-0717(02)00233-X]

[10]   Issa AA, Abd-Alla MH, Ohyama T. Nitrogen fixing cyanobacteria: Future prospect. In: Ohyama T, Ed. Advances in Biology and Ecology of Nitrogen Fixation InTechOpen. Londra 2014; pp. 23-48.

[11]   Chamizo S, Mugnai G, Rossi F, Certini G, De Philippis R. Cyanobacteria inoculation improves soil stability and fertility on different textured soils: Gaining insights for applicability in soil restoration. Front Environ Sci 2018; 6: 49.
[http://dx.doi.org/10.3389/fenvs.2018.00049]

[12]   Kumar, P. Introduction to Botany. Chapter 10: Nitrogen fixation and nitrogen metabolism, Avialable from: https://www.peoi.org/Courses/Coursesen/bot/bot10.html

[13] Cleveland CC, Townsend AR, Schimel DS, *et al.* Global patterns of terrestrial biological nitrogen (N$_2$) fixation in natural ecosystems. Global Biogeochem Cycles 1999; 13(2): 623-45.
[http://dx.doi.org/10.1029/1999GB900014]

[14] Davies-Barnard T, Friedlingstein P. The global distribution of biological nitrogen fixation in terrestrial natural ecosystems. Global Biogeochem Cycles 2020; 34(3): e2019GB006387.
[http://dx.doi.org/10.1029/2019GB006387]

[15] Yu T, Zhuang Q. Modeling biological nitrogen fixation in global natural terrestrial ecosystems. Biogeosciences 2020; 17(13): 3643-57.
[http://dx.doi.org/10.5194/bg-17-3643-2020]

[16] AquaPortail, Nitrosomonas: définition, explications. AquaPortail.com, 2018. Avialable from: https://www.aquaportail.com/definition-12688-nitrosomonas.html

[17] Nie S, Zhu GB, Singh B, Zhu YG. Anaerobic ammonium oxidation in agricultural soils-synthesis and prospective. Environ Pollut 2019; 244: 127-34.
[http://dx.doi.org/10.1016/j.envpol.2018.10.050] [PMID: 30321707]

[18] Sahrawat KL. Factors affecting nitrification in soils. Commun Soil Sci Plant Anal 2008; 39(9-10): 1436-46.
[http://dx.doi.org/10.1080/00103620802004235]

[19] Zaman T, Qazi W, Asad SA, *et al.* Nitrification resilience and response of ammonia-oxidizing bacteria upon heat-drought extremes across three soil ecosystems in lower Himalaya. Int J Agric Biol 2020; 24: 1107-14.
[http://dx.doi.org/10.17957/IJAB/15.1538]

[20] Cui X, Wang J, Wang J, *et al.* Soil available nitrogen and yield effect under different combinations of urease/nitrate inhibitor in wheat/maize rotation system. Agronomy (Basel) 2022; 12(8): 1888.
[http://dx.doi.org/10.3390/agronomy12081888]

[21] Alexander M. Denitrifying bacteria. In: Norman AG, Ed. Methods of Soil Analysis: Part 2 Chemical and Microbiological Properties, 92. Madison: American Society of Agronomy 1965; pp. 1484-6.

[22] Sun P, Zhuge Y, Zhang J, Cai Z. Soil pH was the main controlling factor of the denitrification rates and N$_2$/N$_2$O emission ratios in forest and grassland soils along the Northeast China Transect (NECT). Soil Sci Plant Nutr 2012; 58(4): 517-25.
[http://dx.doi.org/10.1080/00380768.2012.703609]

[23] Denitrification Fact Sheet Northern Region Reducing Potential N Losses GRDC. Barton 2014.

[24] International Plant Nutrition Institute, Nitrogen Notes: Denitrification. IPNI, 2016. Available from: http://www.ipni.net/publication/nitrogen-en.nsf/0/668099AE825517CB85257DD600054B8C/$FILE/NitrogenNotes-EN-5.pdf

[25] Rohe L, Apelt B, Vogel HJ, Well R, Wu GM, Schlüter S. Denitrification in soil as a function of oxygen availability at the microscale. Biogeosciences 2021; 18(3): 1185-201.
[http://dx.doi.org/10.5194/bg-18-1185-2021]

[26] Sánchez-García M, Roig A, Sánchez-Monedero MA, Cayuela ML. Biochar increases N$_2$O emissions produced by nitrification-mediated pathways. Front Environ Sci 2014; 2: 2.
[http://dx.doi.org/10.3389/fenvs.2014.00025]

[27] Dr. Max, 2022. Infecția cu Pseudomonas aeruginosa: cauze, manifestări și opțiuni de tratament. Dr. Max, 2022, Avialable from: https://www.drmax.ro/articole/infectia-cu-pseudomonas-aerugin-sa-cauze-manifestari-tratament

CHAPTER 6

Cycles of Matter in Soil: Phosphorus, Sulfur, Metals

Abstract: Phosphorus and sulfur, together with alkaline, alkaline earth and transitional metals are important nutrients and constituents of living matter. The sulfur cycle involves an atmospheric phase, but its main stages are due to terrestrial biota, through processes like sulfate reduction, sulfide oxidation, anoxygenic photosynthesis, *etc.* The cycles of phosphorus and metals lack significant atmospheric stages. The main biogeochemical processes involving soil microorganisms are those of solubilization and precipitation, that determine their general bioavailability.

Keywords: Potassium, Phosphorus, Calcium, Sulfur, Sodium, Transitional metals.

INTRODUCTION

While carbon and nitrogen (together with oxygen and hydrogen, of course) are the main bioelements, found in all organic compounds, they are not alone.

The "recipe" of life also includes other key ingredients like phosphorus or sulfur, but also oligo- and microelements, including a wide variety of metals: sodium, potassium, calcium, iron, manganese, copper, *etc.*

All these bioelements are subjected to continuous recycling in soil. Furthermore, oxidoreductive processes involving some of them (like transitional metals) provide a source of energy for various microorganisms.

Phosphorus Cycle

Phosphorus is one of the key ingredients of living matter. Phospholipids that make up cell membranes, adenosine triphosphate/diphosphate that is used by all organisms to store their energy, as well as DNA, and RNA, essential to storing and transmitting genetic information, are just a few examples.

Besides these, phosphorus is a quite common constituent of minerals in the Earth's crust, especially apatites ($Ca_5(PO_4)_3X$; hydroxy-/chloro-/fluoroapatites), strengite, and variscite. A certain amount of such minerals is also found in soils.

Yet, the most common form of inorganic phosphorus compound in soil is that of orthophosphates (PO_4^{3-}). Part of these salts is found adsorbed on clay particles and iron, calcium, and aluminium ions. They can be slowly released into the soil solution, thus becoming bioavailable to plants and microorganisms. Finally, there are some soluble phosphates in the soil solution (albeit not in high concentrations), which are easily bioavailable [1 - 3].

It is easy to notice that this cycle lacks an atmospheric component. Actually, there is a gaseous compound, phosphine (PH_3), produced by some microorganisms, as well as industry, but in very low amounts.

The main phosphorus source in the soil is the decomposition of dead organic matter (see previous chapters), a process due to a wide array of bacteria, fungi, *etc.* Also, in agroecosystems, some important sources are chemical or biological (especially poultry manure) fertilizers.

Besides decomposition, microorganisms are involved in other two important phases: phosphorus precipitation in insoluble forms, and its mobilization (solubilization; Fig. **1**) [1 - 6].

Phosphorus Solubilization

Insoluble forms of phosphorus are hardly available to living organisms. This can be remediated by secreting organic acids, phosphatases, or hormones, that can mobilize phosphorus (as phosphate ions) in chemical forms that are more soluble and easier to transport by soil solution.

Part of this process is due to plants, through their own radicular secretions. Another part involves microorganisms, especially **phosphate-solubilizing bacteria** (PSB). Finally, a substantial part is due to the interspecific collaboration between plant root systems and microbial associations within the immediately neighbouring soil region, an environment called the rhizosphere (see the next chapter). Plant secretions favor solubilizing microbiota, which, in turn, mobilizes phosphates in soil.

The process is of extreme importance to plant growth (thus, also to agricultural productivity), since phosphorus is an essential nutrient, absorbed in large amounts and with a tendency to be depleted fast around roots, at least in its easily accessible forms [2, 5, 6].

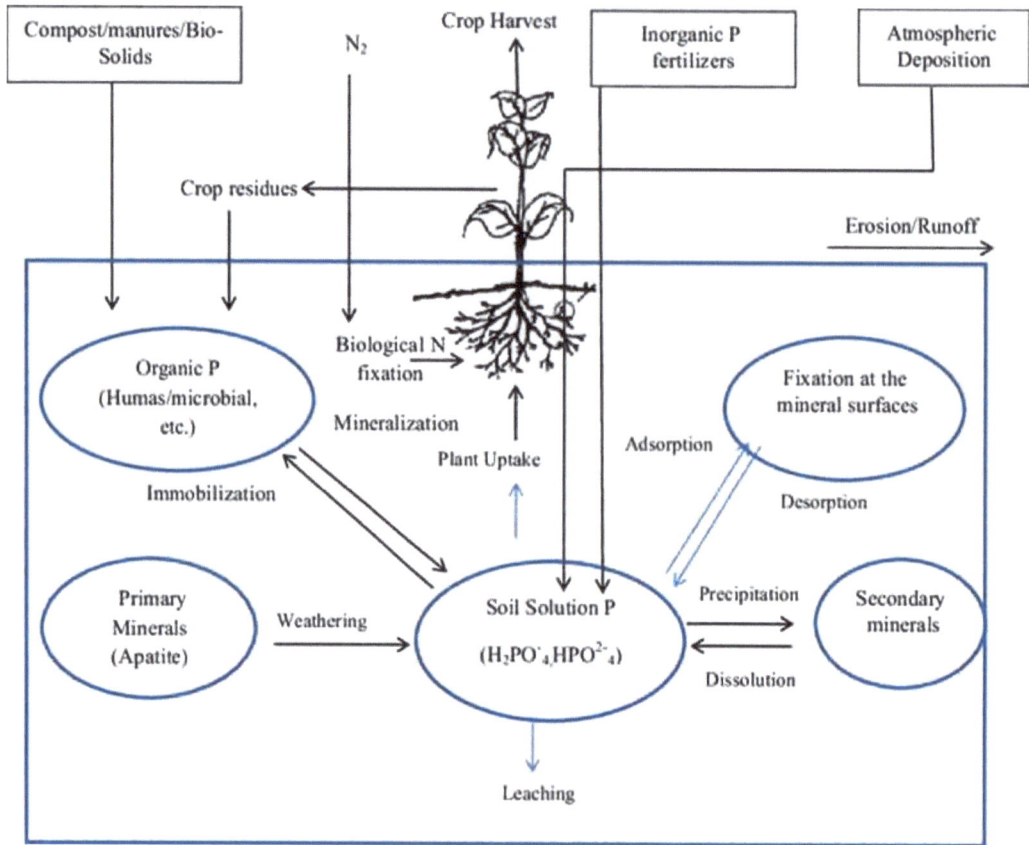

Fig. (1). Phosphorus cycle in soil [7].

Among the bacteria involved are members of the genera *Azotobacter*, *Bacillus*, *Beijerinckia*, *Burkholderia*, *Enterobacter*, *Erwinia*, *Flavobacterium*, *Microbacterium*, *Pseudomonas*, *Rhizobium* and its relatives or *Serratia*. Among fungi, we can mention *Aspergillus* sp. and *Penicillium* sp. Their main way of action is by secreting acids (rich in carboxyl and hydroxyl groups), that chelate metals associated with phosphate, thus releasing the latter into the soil solution. Other mechanisms involve direct oxidations, acidification of soil solution, the use of enzymes to release phosphate from organic structures, *etc.* (Fig. **2**).

As mentioned above, the process is extremely important and knowledge of these microorganisms is of great value for agriculture: inoculation with PSB may significantly enhance crop output in soils with low phosphorus levels (for instance, in calcareous soils, where it tends to precipitate easily). Thus, those microorganisms can be used as biofertilizers [6, 9].

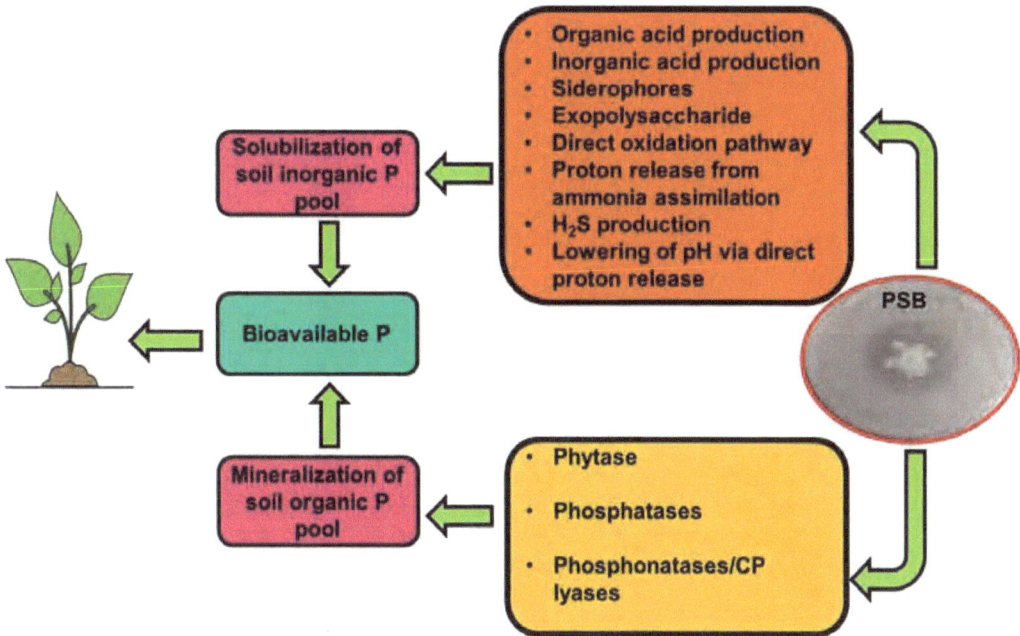

Fig. (2). Ways of action of phosphate solubilizing bacteria [8].

Phosphorus Precipitation

The opposite process of mobilization is also often mediated by microorganisms. Some of them (such as the archaea *Halobacterium distributum* and *H. salinarum*) act by alkalinizing their environment, which favors extracellular precipitation as magnesium phosphate. Bacteria in the genus *Brevibacterium* can accumulate ammonium and magnesium phosphate (struvite) inside their cell. *Kuraishia capsulata* is a yeast capable of accumulating phosphomanan (an extracellular phospho saccharide complex).

However, most of the species involved accumulate polyphosphate granules (polymers with hundreds of phosphate groups) as a relatively stable nutritive reserve (Fig. **3**). These granules can be released when the bacterium dies. Among the organisms involved are some bacteria (genera *Accumulibacter*, *Acinetobacter*, *Dechloromonas*, *Friedmaniella*, *Gemmatimonas*, *Microlunatus*, *Microthrix* and some other actinobacteria, *Nocardia*, *Rhodococcus*, *Rhodocyclus*, *Tessaracoccus*, *Tetrasphaeraetc.*). We can add some fungal species (*Mucor circinelloides*), green algae (*Chlorella*, *Coelastrella*), and diatoms [10 - 12].

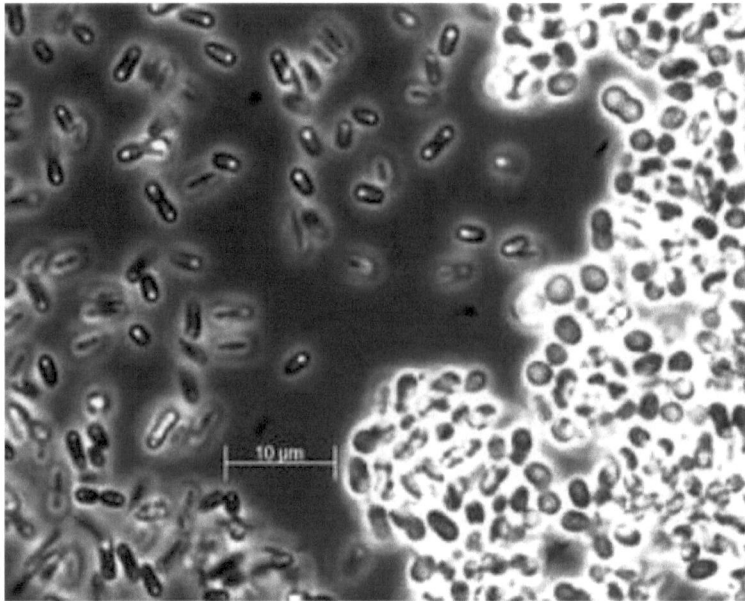

Fig. (3). Population of *Accumulibacter* sp. (left) and *Competibacter* sp. (right), polyphosphate-accumulating bacteria, with polyphosphate granules visible inside their cells [13].

This process is also of great importance since excess phosphorus can lead to explosive growth of microbes. If not in that specific area, through infiltration in soil solution, groundwater, and surface water, it reaches larger water bodies, causing eutrophication. This is a growing problem, due to the massive usage of chemical and biological fertilizers.

Some of these polyphosphate-accumulating organisms, such as members of the genera *Accumulibacter* and *Tetrasphaera*, are of biotechnological interest, in wastewater treatment. Other functions that some PAO may perform at the same time are denitrification or precipitation of excess calcium and heavy metals [10 - 12].

Sulfur Cycle

The sulfur cycle is a rather complex one, having additional gaseous, atmospheric phases. On a global scale, it involves processes like volcanic eruptions, pollution caused by burning fossil fuels (with SO_2 emissions), acid rain (with sulfuric acid), and dry deposition on soil surface and in water [15].

Among these stages, some also occur in soil, with the active participation of local microbiota (Fig. **4**).

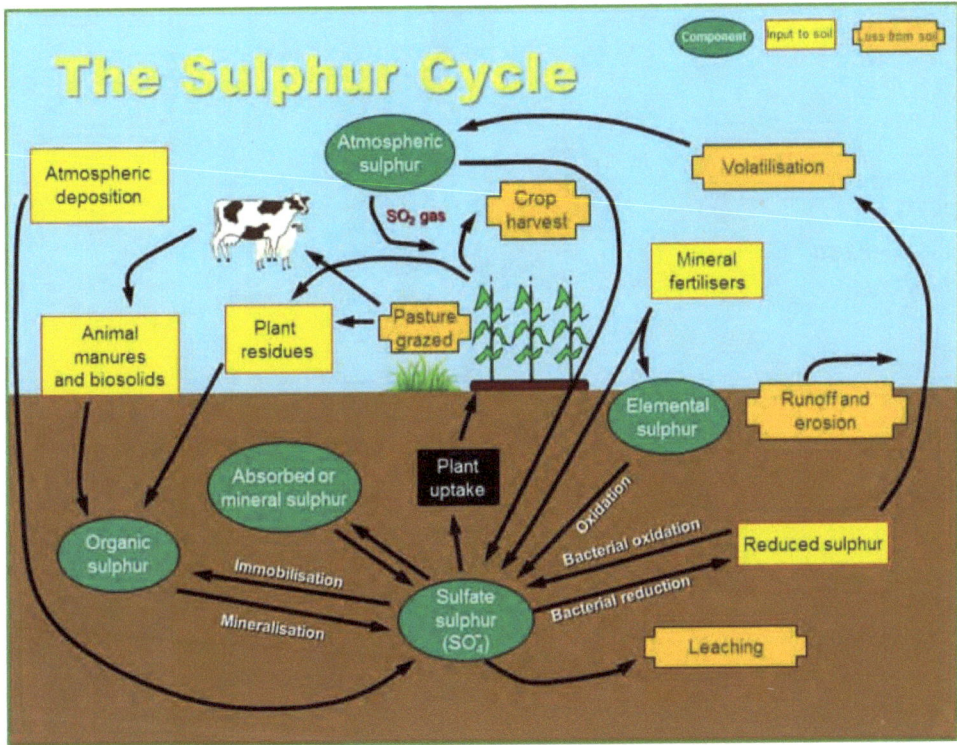

Fig. (4). Sulfur cycle in soil [14].

Organic Sulfur Mobilization

Total 95% of sulfur in soil is found in organic compounds like sulfate esters and sulfonates. The mobilization or mineralization process consists of the decomposition of the respective substances to simple monomers and, then, releasing sulfur, especially as sulfate ions (SO_4^{2-}).

There are numerous bacterial species (from genera *Acidovorax, Burkholderia, Comamonas, Cupriavidus, Enterobacter, Hydrogenophaga, Klebsiella, Polaromonas, Pseudomonas, Rhodococcus, Salmonella, Serratia, Variovorax* and some actinobacteria), which are often associated with plant root systems, as well as some symbiotic fungi (in mycorrhizae).

The process (Fig. **5**) is of major importance, allowing the presence of sulfur, in a soluble and easily accessible form, in soil solution. It is an extremely important nutrient to plants and many other organisms [16].

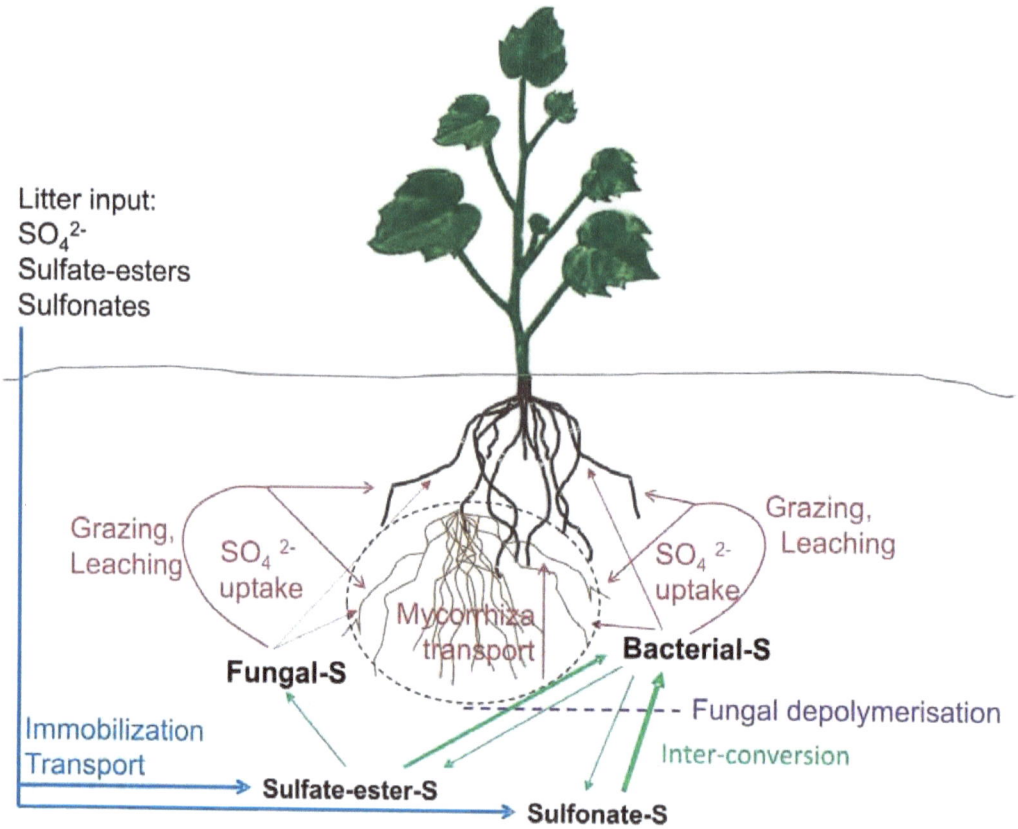

Fig. (5). Sulfur mineralization in soil [16].

Sulfate Reduction

Sulftes (but also other compounds, such as sulfites, thiosulfates, thionates polysulfides), of biogenic or abiogenic origin, are present, in various concentrations, in soil solution. Even elemental sulfur (S) can be found in volcanic soils.

Under specific conditions, these compounds can undergo a reduction process, up to sulfide ions (S^{2-}). These, as hydrogen sulfide (H_2S) is released in the environment, quickly reacting with cations and forming sulfides (while a small part reaches the atmosphere).

The process is made possible by the action of **sulfate-reducing bacteria** (SRB). Sulfate reduction is a mechanism of anaerobic respiration, in which the sulfate ion (or thiosulfate, sulfite, *etc.*) takes the place of oxygen and which requires particular metabolic pathways. Of these bacteria, in soils, the genus *Desulfovibrio* is clearly dominant, but we may also find species of *Desulfobacterium*,

Desulfobulbus,   Desulfococcus,   Desulfonema,   Desulfosporosinus,
Desulfotomaculum,etc., often forming interspecific consortia together with
various heterotrophic microorganisms [17 - 19].

Due to the necessary environmental conditions (anoxia, substantial reserves of
sulfur compounds), bacterial sulfur reduction mainly takes place in certain types
of soil, that are moist and rich in decomposing organic matter such as, swamps,
peatlands, and rice fields. Such areas can be spotted by the dark color of the soil
(given by sulfides) and the rotten egg smell (due to the release of hydrogen
sulfide). Nevertheless, small populations of such bacteria are distributed in almost
all types of soil, thriving in locally available anoxic microniches. Pollution is also
among the favorable factors [17 - 20].

Sulfate reduction has great practical importance. Hydrogen sulfide reacts with a
wide variety of metals, causing them to precipitate as relatively stable sulfides.
This way, the ambient toxicity in soils chronically polluted with heavy metals
(mining or industrial areas), including radionuclides, is reduced; this can be used
in bioremediation (see next chapter). The process also limits excess sulfates in
places where this is an issue, such as in gypsum-rich soils or areas affected by
acid rain, industrial spills, *etc.* Finally, sulfate reduction raises the soil's pH,
helping to improve acidic soils [17, 19, 21, 22].

Anoxygenic Photosynthesis

A marginal process in soils, but still part of the sulfur cycle, is this particular form
of photoautotrophy, in which the place of water as the electron donor is taken by
hydrogen sulfide (H_2S), elemental sulfur (S), or sulfates (SO_4^{2-}).

It should be noted that not all anoxygenic photosynthetic processes (Fig. **6**)
involve sulfur compounds and not all require anaerobiosis. The most often
involved are bacteria belonging to the order Chromatiales (γ-Proteobacteria). The
process is not a very common one, but still present, especially in moist soils,
where significant sulfur sources are found (swamps, *etc.*), obviously in the upper
layers, exposed to sunlight. In other regions, anoxygenic phototrophic bacteria
may take part in biocrust formation (see Chapters 2 and 3) [24, 25].

Sulfide Oxidation

Hydrogen sulfide is a gas that is released, as seen above, from those types of soil
hosting hypoxic niches, and rich in organic matter undergoing decomposition.
This way, a significant amount of sulfur would be lost to the atmosphere. Also,
soil can naturally contain a certain amount of metal sulfides (in minerals such as
greigite, and Fe_3S_4). Elemental sulfur (S) can be added as a fertilizer or sometimes

can be present in volcanic areas. Finally, all these types of compounds can derive from industrial pollution (for example, sulfur from the rubber industry).

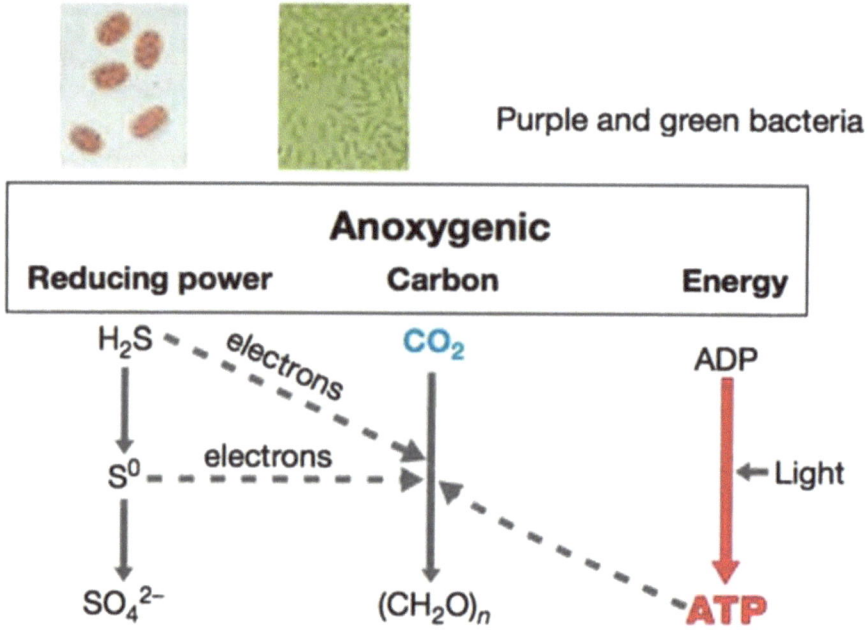

Fig. (6). Anoxygenic photosynthesis: general scheme [23].

The reinsertion of this element in its natural cycle is done through oxidation to sulfates, soluble compounds that are accessible to plants and other organisms. This process has an abiotic side (through exposure to atmospheric oxygen) and a biotic one. **S**ulfur-oxidizing **bacteria** (SOB), such as some species of *Pseudomonas, Burkholderia, Klebsiella, Thiobacillus* or *Acidithiobacillus* (in acidic soil, mine drainage areas *etc.*) are mainly responsible for the latter. Some archaea (*Sulfolobus* sp., only in hot, volcanic soils) and fungi (species of *Aspergillus, Mucor, Trichoderma, Monilia, Amanita, etc.*) are included [26 - 30].

Sodium, Potassium, Calcium and Magnesium Cycles

Alkaline and alkaline earth metals are key ingredients of all living matter. Especially potassium is an essential nutrient to plant growth, thus present in most commercial fertilizers. Calcium is another vital nutrient, but is also present in mineral form (calcium carbonate) in soils and rocks. Some soils, namely calcareous ones, even have calcium in excess, with a major impact on the local biota. Sodium is another important nutrient, but also present as sodium chloride, in saline soils.

All these elements are continuously recycled, passing from solid and adsorbed forms to soluble ones, as well as being transferred along trophic chains (Figs. **7** and **8**). Plants, microorganisms, animals, and humans are all involved in these circuits. Soil microbiota plays a key role in precipitation and solubilization processes, while plant root exudates stimulate microbial activity [32, 33].

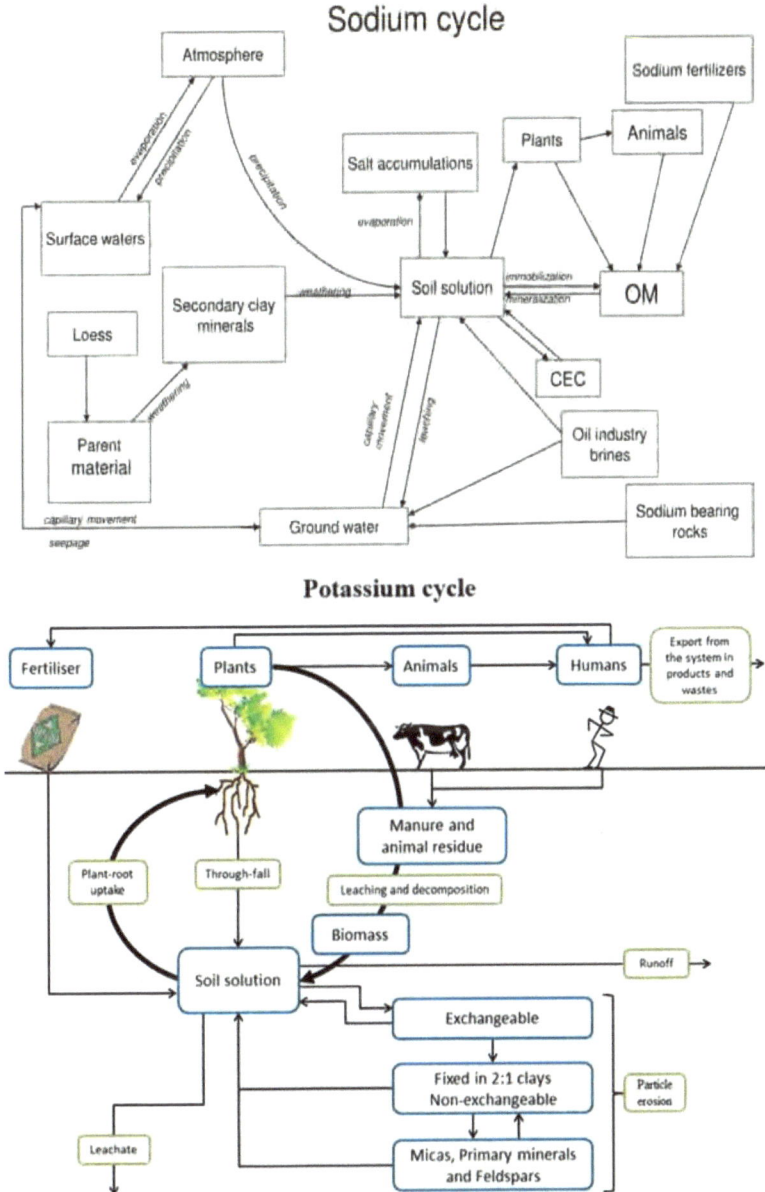

Fig. (7). Sodium [31] and potassium [32] cycles.

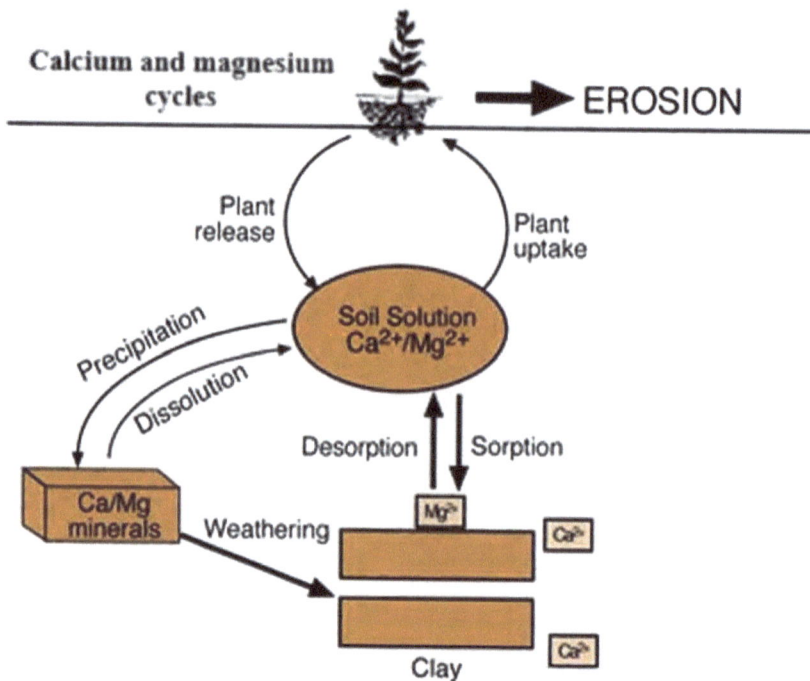

Fig. (8). Calcium and magnesium cycles [33].

Transitional Metals

Iron, manganese, copper, aluminium and many other transitional metals are present in different forms in soil. They are also oligo- or micronutrients for living organisms and are found in the composition of certain organic compounds.

Characteristic of these elements is the formation of different cations, with different valences (ferrous/ferric, manganous/manganic, cuprous/cupric ions, *etc.*). These are found in different minerals, have different solubilities and their concentration in soil solution is highly dependent on pH.

Oxidation and reduction reactions involving cations are a source of energy for some groups of microorganisms. We are especially talking about iron and, in the second place, manganese (Fig. **9**). Oxidation of ferrous ions (Fe^{2+}) is specific to some chemoautotrophic, mostly acidophilic bacteria and archaea (*Gallionella* sp., *Thiobacillus ferooxidans*, *Ferroplasma* sp. *etc.*). Reduction of ferric ions (Fe^{3+}), on the other hand, is important to the mobilization of this highly valuable nutrient in bioavailable forms. Responsible for this are bacterial species belonging to the genera such as *Shewanella*, *Geothrix*, *Geobacter*, and *Anaeromyxobacter*, but the process also takes place, to a certain degree, in the cells of plant roots [34].

The Iron Cycle

Fe^{+2}   **Fe^{+3}**

Common ferrous minerals
Magnetite Fe$_3$O$_4$
Pyrite   FeS$_2$
Hydrolysis products
FeOH$^+$. Fe(OH)$_2^0$

Common ferric minerals
Iron hydroxide Fe(OH)$_3$
Goethite FeOOH
Hematite Fe$_2$O$_3$
Jarosite KFe$_3$(SO$_4$)$_2$(OH)$_6$

Weathering   Precipitation   Precipitation   Weathering

Thiobacillus ferrooxidans
(strict acidophile)
Gallionella ferroginea
Leptrothrix ochracea

Fe^{+2} in Solution
pH 5 10^{-14} m/l
pH 7 10^{-18} m/l

Oxidation   Reduction

Shewenella putrefaciens

Fe^{+3} in Solution
pH 5 10^{-12} m/l
pH 7 10^{-18} m/l

Exists in solution as
Fe^{+2} pH<6.75
FeOH$^+$ pH>6.75
Fe^{+2} chelates

Exists in solution as
Fe^{+3}
Fe(OH)$_2^+$(predominant)
Fe^{+3} chelates

Soil Solution

Plant exudates
Plant residue

Plant uptake
as Fe^{+2} form

Plants

Iron exists in plants as components of
proteins
enzymes
cells

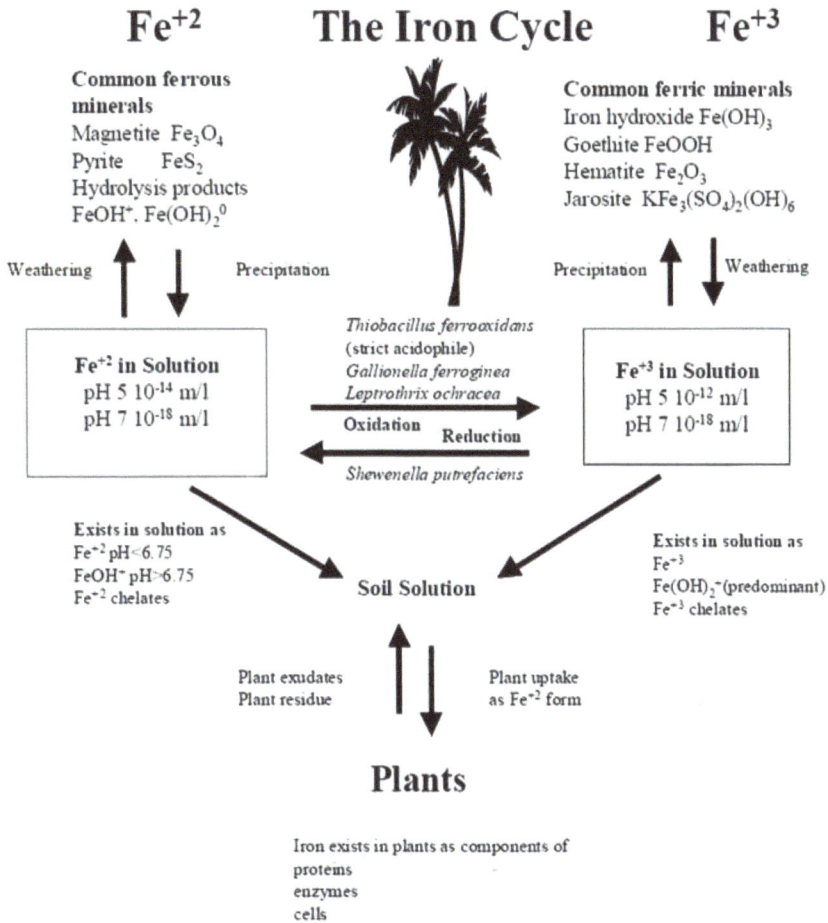

Metals Cycling

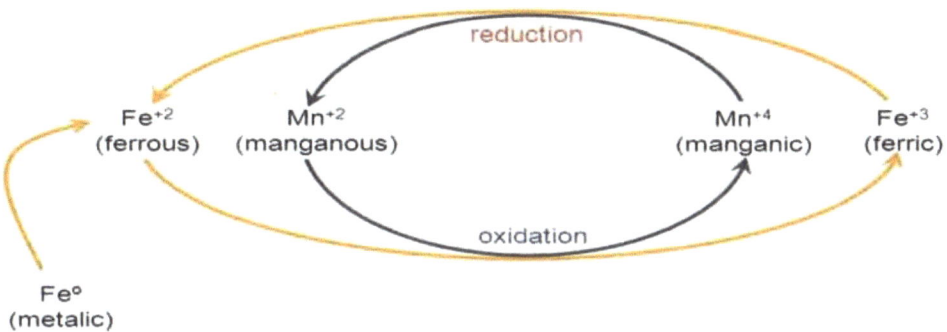

reduction

Fe^{+2} Mn^{+2} Mn^{+4} Fe^{+3}
(ferrous)   (manganous)   (manganic)   (ferric)

oxidation

Fe^o
(metalic)

Fig. (9). Iron and manganese cycles [34, 35].

CONCLUSION

Phosphorus in soil is subject to decomposition processes, from organic to inorganic forms, precipitation to insoluble forms, and its opposite, mobilization. Through these processes, soil microbiota, including phosphate-solubilizing bacteria and polyphosphate-accumulating organisms regulate the levels of this crucial element available to plants.

Sulfur in soil is mostly found in organic compounds, from where it is mineralized by a wide array of bacteria and fungi. Sulfur reduction and its reverse, sulfur oxidation, are rather important processes in hypoxic soils .

Alkaline and alkaline earth metals are key life ingredients, subject to recirculation in organic forms, but also solubilization and precipitation processes are important. In addition to these, transitional metals such as iron and manganese can undergo reduction and oxidation cycles in different soil layers, serving as energetic substrates to various bacteria. Such processes are also connected to the availability of these nutrients to plants.

REFERENCES

[1] Espinoza L, Norman R, Staton N, Daniels M. The Nitrogen and Phosphorous Cycle in Soils. Little Rock: University of Arkansas Cooperative Extension Service 2005.

[2] Du Pont Pioneer Agronomy Sciences, Phosphorus Behavior in Soil. Intel Seed, 2017. Available from: https://intelseed.ca/uploads/Phosphorus_Behavior_in_Soil-2017.pdf

[3] Prasad, R., Chakraborty, D., Phosphorus Basics: Understanding Phosphorus Forms and Their Cycling in the Soil. Alabama Cooperative Extension System, 2019. Available from: https://www.aces.edu/wp-content/uploads/2019/04/ANR-2535-Phosphorus-Basics_041719L.pdf

[4] Mullins, G., Phosphorus, Agriculture & the Environment. Virginia Cooperative Extension, 2009. Available from: https://efotg.sc.egov.usda.gov/references/public/va/PhosphorousAgEnv.pdf

[5] Tembhurne SS, Paradhi AA. Phosphorus transformation in soil and plants. Krishi Science 2021; 2(4): 11-4.

[6] Ibrahim M, Iqbal M, Tang YT, Khan S, Guan DX, Li G. Phosphorus mobilization in plant–soil environments and inspired strategies for managing phosphorus: A review. Agronomy (Basel) 2022; 12(10): 2539.
[http://dx.doi.org/10.3390/agronomy12102539]

[7] Mitran T, Meena RS, Lal R, Layek J, Kumar S, Datta R. Role of soil phosphorus on legume production. In: Meena R, Das A, Yadav G, Lal R, Eds. Legumes for Soil Health and Sustainable Management. Singapore: Springer 2018; pp. 487-510.
[http://dx.doi.org/10.1007/978-981-13-0253-4_15]

[8] Rawat P, Das S, Shankhdhar D, Shankhdhar SC. Phosphate-solubilizing microorganisms: Mechanism and their role in phosphate solubilization and uptake. J Soil Sci Plant Nutr 2021; 21(1): 49-68.
[http://dx.doi.org/10.1007/s42729-020-00342-7]

[9] Namlı A, Mahmood A, Sevilir B, Özkır E. Effect of phosphorus solubilizing bacteria on some soil properties, wheat yield and nutrient contents. Eurasian J Soil Sci 2017; 6(3): 249-58.
[http://dx.doi.org/10.18393/ejss.293157]

[10]   Tarayre C, Nguyen HT, Brognaux A, *et al.* Characterisation of phosphate accumulating organisms and techniques for polyphosphate detection: A review. Sensors (Basel) 2016; 16(6): 797.
[http://dx.doi.org/10.3390/s16060797] [PMID: 27258275]

[11]   Akbari A, Wang Z, He P, *et al.* Unrevealed roles of polyphosphate-accumulating microorganisms. Microb Biotechnol 2021; 14(1): 82-7.
[http://dx.doi.org/10.1111/1751-7915.13730] [PMID: 33404187]

[12]   Vučić V, Müller S. New developments in biological phosphorus accessibility and recovery approaches from soil and waste streams. Eng Life Sci 2021; 21(3-4): 77-86.
[http://dx.doi.org/10.1002/elsc.202000076] [PMID: 33716607]

[13]   Welles L, Lopez-Vazquez CM, Hooijmans CM, van Loosdrecht MCM, Brdjanovic D. Prevalence of 'Candidatus *Accumulibacter phosphatis*' type II under phosphate limiting conditions. AMB Express 2016; 6(1): 44.
[http://dx.doi.org/10.1186/s13568-016-0214-z] [PMID: 27376945]

[14]   Crop Management Network Inc., 2023. Gypsum as a sulfur source is smart for your soil. Crop Management Network, 2023. Available from: https://www.cropmanagement.com/gypsum

[15]   Sulfur cycle. Encyclopaaedia Britannica, Available from: https://www.britannica.com/science/sulfur-cycle

[16]   Gahan J, Schmalenberger A. The role of bacteria and mycorrhiza in plant sulfur supply. Front Plant Sci 2014; 5: 723.
[http://dx.doi.org/10.3389/fpls.2014.00723] [PMID: 25566295]

[17]   Ilori MO, Okonkwo AM, Bamidele M. Factors affecting growth of sulfate-reducing bacteria isolated from tropical soil. Z Naturforsch C J Biosci 1999; 54(7-8): 613-6.
[http://dx.doi.org/10.1515/znc-1999-7-826]

[18]   Hausmann B, Knorr KH, Schreck K, *et al.* Consortia of low-abundance bacteria drive sulfate reduction-dependent degradation of fermentation products in peat soil microcosms. ISME J 2016; 10(10): 2365-75.
[http://dx.doi.org/10.1038/ismej.2016.42] [PMID: 27015005]

[19]   Kusumawati E, Sudrajat S, Purnamasari I, Panggabean BC, Apriyanti M. Short Communication: The potential of Sulfate Reducing Bacteria of ex-coal mine sediment pond as sulfate reducing agents of acid land in Samarinda, Indonesia. Bonorowo Wetlands 2017; 7(2): 79-82.
[http://dx.doi.org/10.13057/bonorowo/w070204]

[20]   Wind T, Conrad R. Localization of sulfate reduction in planted and unplanted rice field soil. Biogeochemistry 1997; 37(3): 253-78.
[http://dx.doi.org/10.1023/A:1005760506957]

[21]   Kijjanapanich, P., Sulfate reduction for remediation of gypsiferous soils and solid wastes. Ph.D. thesis, Université Paris-Est, 2013, 170.

[22]   Mazlina M, Hanafiah AS, Rauf A, Sutarta ES. Potential of reducing sulphate bacteria on increasing soil ph and decreasing sulphate levels on acid sulphate soil. Int J Sci Technol Res 2020; 9(2): 4423-6.

[23]   MICRO 303 Exam 2 Chapters 3, 4, 13, 14, 19, 20, 22, Quizlet.com, Available from: https://quizlet.com/162341957/micro-303-exam-2-chapters-3-4-13-14-19-20-22-flash-cards

[24]   Csotonyi JT, Swiderski J, Stackebrandt E, Yurkov V. A new environment for aerobic anoxygenic phototrophic bacteria: biological soil crusts. Environ Microbiol Rep 2010; 2(5): 651-6.
[http://dx.doi.org/10.1111/j.1758-2229.2010.00151.x] [PMID: 23766251]

[25]   Hanada S. Anoxygenic photosynthesis —A photochemical reaction that does not contribute to oxygen reproduction. Microbes Environ 2016; 31(1): 1-3.
[http://dx.doi.org/10.1264/jsme2.ME3101rh] [PMID: 27021204]

[26]   Ward NJ, Sullivan LA, Fyfe DM, Bush RT, Ferguson AJP. The process of sulfide oxidation in some

acid sulfate soil materials. Soil Res 2004; 42(4): 449-58.
[http://dx.doi.org/10.1071/SR03135]

[27] Chaudhary S, nvi T, Dhanker R, Goyal S. Different applications of sulphur oxidizing bacteria: A review. Int J Curr Microbiol Appl Sci 2019; 8(11): 770-8.
[http://dx.doi.org/10.20546/ijcmas.2019.811.091]

[28] Suparjo. Isolation and characterization of sulfur-oxidizing bacteria (SOB) from waste of rubber factory and paper in Jambi. Int J Ecophysiol 2019; 1(2): 131-9.
[http://dx.doi.org/10.32734/ijoep.v1i2.1276]

[29] Juwanda M, Sakhidin , Saparso , Kharisun . Soil properties and sulfur-oxidizing bacterial diversity in response to different planting patterns of shallot (Allium ascalonicum). Biodiversitas (Surak) 2020; 21(6): 2832-9.
[http://dx.doi.org/10.13057/biodiv/d210661]

[30] Fertiliser Technology Research Centre. Technical bulletin: Oxidation of elemental sulfur in soils. Fertiliser Technology Research Centre, University of Adelaide, Available from: https://set.adelaide.edu.au/fertiliser/ua/media/74/factsheet-oxidation-of-elemental-sulfur-in-soils.pdf

[31] Tasha T., Sodium cycle. SlideServe, 2013. Available from: https://www.slideserve.com/tanith/sodium-cycle

[32] Schofield H.K., A biogeochemical study of nutrient dynamics in artificial soil. Ph.D. thesis, University of Plymouth, 2015, 285.

[33] Korb N, Jones C, Jacobsen J. Secondary macronutrients: Cycling, testing and fertilizer recommendations Nutrient Management Module No 6. Bozeman: Montana State University Extension Service 2002.

[34] Raun WR, Johnson GV, Mullen RV, Freeman KW, Westerman RL. Soil-plant nutrient cycling and environmental quality. Stillwater: Oklahoma State University 2002.

[35] Iron and Manganese Cycles – Steps, Importance. Microbiology Note, 2002. Available from: https://microbiologynote.com/iron-and-manganese-cycles

Ecological Relationships Between Soil Organisms, Symbioses, Applications of Soil Ecology

Abstract: Between soil organisms, various interspecific relationships are formed, some of which are positive, and others are negative for at least one of the parts involved. A mutually positive relationship is symbiosis. Endo- and ectosymbioses between nitrogen-fixing bacteria and plant roots, actinorrhizae, and, most of all, mycorrhizae play extremely important roles in plant productivity and maintaining soil quality. Relationships between plants and various groups of microorganisms at the rhizosphere level also ensure a matter and energy flow from one plant to another, leading to a true „mycorrhizal Internet". Knowledge and control over these complex relationships also have practical applications, in producing biofertilizers, biopesticides, and in bioremediation, *etc.*

Keywords: Interspecific relationships, Mycorrhizae, Rhizosphere, Symbiosis.

INTRODUCTION

Just like in any other environment, organisms that inhabit soil do not live isolated. They depend on each other, through a wide array of interspecific interactions.

Some of these relationships are negative for at least one of the partners. The most obvious that come to our minds are predation or parasitism.

Yet, many other such interactions are positive, or even essential to both sides involved and, first of all is symbiosis.

Types of Interspecific Ecological Relationships

The various organisms that inhabit any particular environment, including soil, can establish a wide variety of relationships.

Among the **positive**, or **associative** ones (beneficial for both parties involved) we can mention metabiosis, symbiosis, and commensalism.

Metabiosis is an indirect positive relationship: an organism alters the surrounding environment, through its metabolism, thus creating favorable conditions for another one (Fig. **1**). For instance, plants bring organic matter into the soil, thus contributing to pedogenesis and feeding a wide array of microorganisms. Earthworms aerate soils, favoring aerobic microbiota there. Some bacteria and plants help clean up pollutants from the soil, making it accessible again to the more sensitive species.

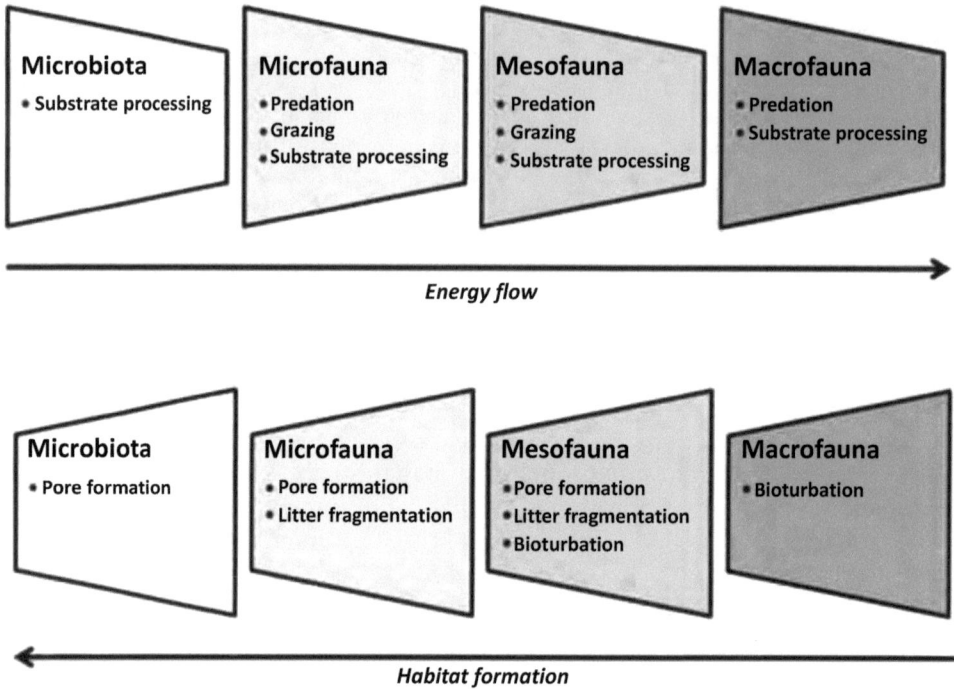

Fig. (**1**). Participation of soil biota in habitat alteration and energy flows [4].

In a wider sense, **symbiosis (mutualism)** is a relationship strictly necessary for at least one of the parts to thrive. In a stricter sense, we are talking about a relationship that is both compulsory and beneficial to both sides involved. Lichens, legume nodules (hosting nitrogen-fixing bacteria), actinorrhizae, and mycorrhizae are good examples of fruitful symbioses developed over millions of years of evolution (see subchapter 7.2).

Commensalism briefly means "to eat at someone else's table"; a coexistence profitable for one of the partners and indifferent to the other. For example, dead plant organs and root exudates provide food for the heterotrophic microbiota.

Among the **negative** relationships, we can mention amensalism, antibiosis, and predatorism.

Amensalism is neutral to one of the partners but harmful to the other. Many species can alter their environment (without any notable benefit for themselves), inhibiting the growth of other organisms. Acidification of soil solution by some acidophilic bacteria (*Thiobacillus* sp.) reduces the microbial populations that are less tolerant to low pH values [1 - 3].

Antibiosis is an active form of amensalism. An organism intentionally secretes toxins or inhibitors in order to wipe out any competition. The phenomenon is widespread among bacteria, fungi (*Penicillium* sp. being the best example) and even plants.

Competition occurs when more organisms compete for the same resources – especially trophic resources – and is stronger when the the amount of those resources is limited. For instance, a nitrogen deficit will cause a ruthless race between plants and microorganisms for that limited amount.

Finally, **predatorism** is mainly specific to protozoa and animals. An organism eats another and the same phenomenon occurs at successive, overlaying levels, leading to the formation of trophic chains (Fig. **2**). Such chains usually include primary producers, consumers of various levels, and decomposers.

A specific form of predatorism is **parasitism**, meaning that an organism can only thrive on behalf of another (its host) [1 - 3].

Symbioses

Nitrogen-fixing nodules

One of the main examples of symbiotic relationships present at the soil level is between legumes and nitrogen-fixing bacteria generally known as "**rhizobia**".

The plants involved are all part of the family Fabaceae (and the vast majority of the species in this family are involved). Rhizobia, on the other hand, is actually a very diverse group of bacterial taxa. Most are α-proteobacteria, belonging to several closely related genera, such as *Bradyrhizobium, Mesorhizobium, Rhizobium, Agrobacterium*, and *Sinorhizobium*. In some tropical legumes, such as those in the genus *Mimosa*, some of the endosymbionts may belong to β-proteobacteria: *Burkholderia, Cupriavidus*, and *Paraburkholderia*.

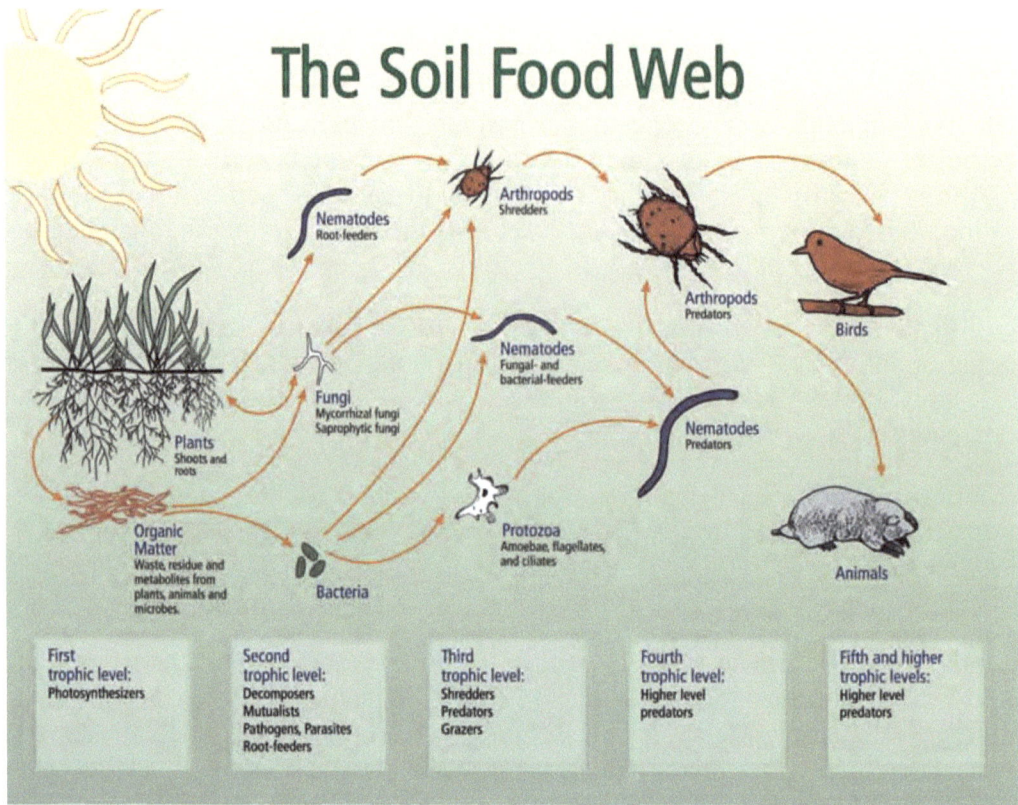

Fig. (2). Trophic chains in soil [5].

Many of the respective bacterial species or varieties (biovars) are strictly specialized on a small number of hosts. For example, *Rhizobium leguminosarum* bv. *trifolii* is a symbiont of clover species, while *R. leguminosarum* bv. *viciae* can be found in broad beans or lentils (*Vicia* sp.). *Mesorhizobium ciceri* is specific to chickpeas, *Bradyrhizobium japonicum* is specific to soybeans, and *B. Arachidis* is specific to peanuts. In other cases, the specificity of the relationship is lower, with the same plant species being able to host different bacterial endosymbionts, while the same bacteria can "infect" several different hosts [6, 7].

Among non-legumes, only *Parasponia* sp. (family Ulmaceae) can host rhizobia, yet researchers try (for the moment with moderate success) to induce artificial root nodulation in some crop plants, such as rice [8].

The abovementioned microorganisms are also able to live in free populations within soils, being also able to fix nitrogen, albeit at a lower rate (in fact, those bacteria genera are known to contain non-symbiotic and even non-diazotrophic varieties). Yet, symbiosis gives the process a significantly greater efficiency, with benefits for both partners.

The first phase of the symbiosis consists of attracting bacteria towards roots. The nodulation ability is genetically determined and is manifested by secreting, at the root hair level, nodulation factors (mostly flavonoids) that stimulate the proliferation of rhizobia around the root and their migration towards root hairs. At the same time, the reverse communication, from rhizobia to roots, is ensured by secreting some lipo chitinous polysaccharides.

Nodulation starts by infecting some of the root hairs (up to 25% of these) or, rarely, other rhizodermic cells. Bacteria proliferate, forming an infection thread, a branched tube actually representing an invagination of the plant cell membrane, "coated" with some compounds secreted by bacteria. The tube grows until it reaches cortical cells (Fig. **3**). Infected hairs curl, getting a specific shape.

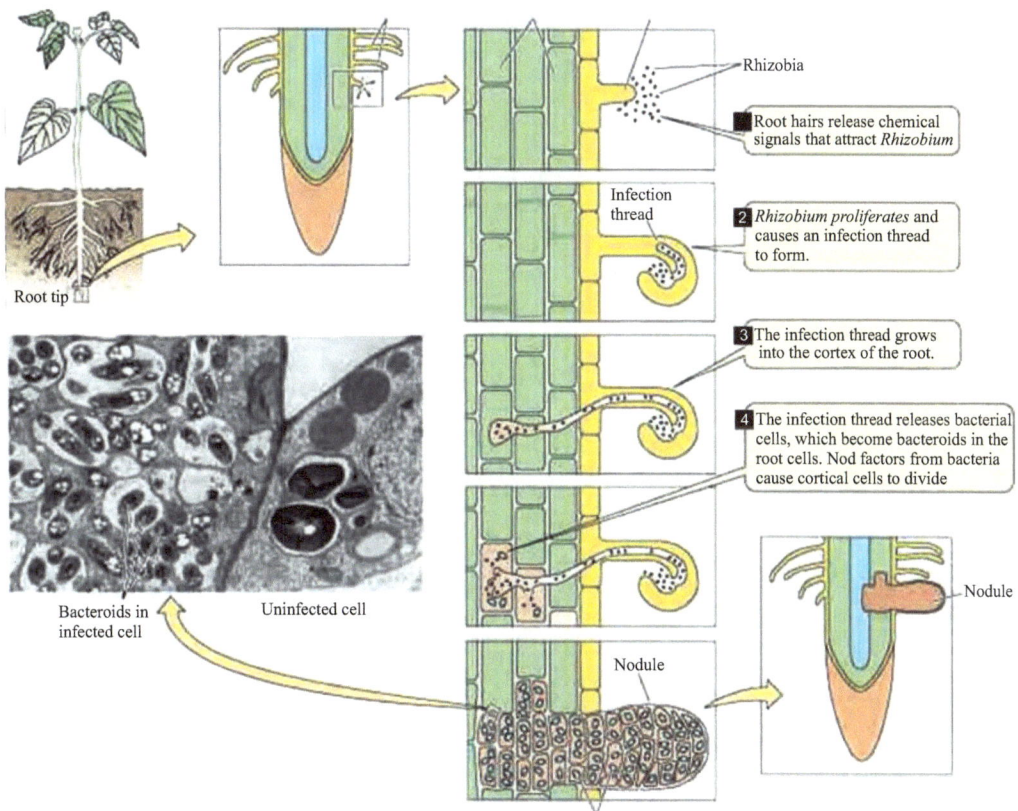

Fig. (3). Root nodulation process in Fabaceae [11].

The bacteria then determine a breach through cortical cell walls, through enzymatic lysis, thus forming the so-called **symbiosomes** – massive vacuoles filling most of the cell volume. Infected cells undergo major alterations: they rapidly divide, causing that particular root area to swell, hence the visible nodule, they also increase their respiratory rate and secrete large amounts of leghemoglobin, which lowers oxygen levels inside symbiosomes.

In turn, bacteria also undergo transformations: after an initial phase of fast divisions, the newly-formed cells become **bacteroids**, immobile bacteria, incapable of division and hosting an intense nitrogen fixation process [9, 10].

This symbiosis brings major benefits to both sides involved (Fig. **4**). Rhizobia provides the host with the excess fixed nitrogen, in the form of glutamine and ureides, as precursors to amino acids, or even whole amino acids and peptides. The hosts nourish their endosymbionts with saccharides and other compounds produced through photosynthesis.

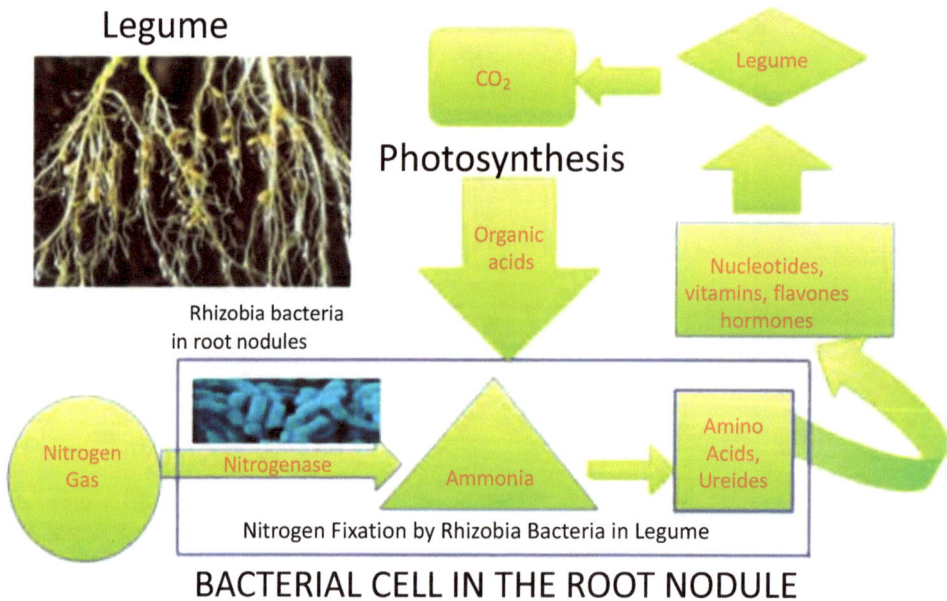

Fig. (4). Biochemical exchanges between rhizobia and host plants [13].

However, this is not the only role that nodules play. Researchers found that they also enhance phosphate and iron mobilization from the soil. They also improve plant resistance to various stress factors, such as salinity, heavy metals, *etc.* [12].

For soil biota as a whole and agricultural productivity, it is important that these symbioses replenish the available nitrogen stock. This is the main reason behind crop rotation, which always has at least one stage of legume cultivation.

Actinorrhizae

Other forms of radicular symbiosis are actinorrhizae. Considering their genesis and role, they are not essentially different from nodules (Fig. **5**).

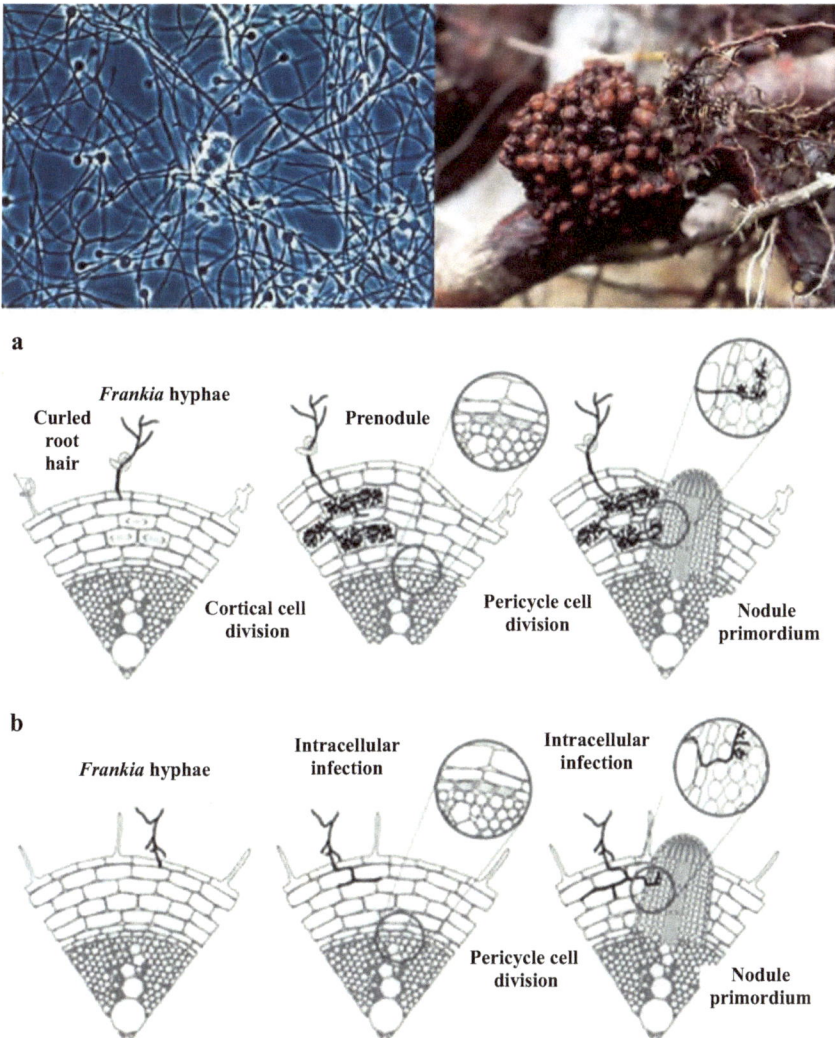

Fig. (5). *Frankia* sp., [16], actinorrhizal nodules in alder tree [17], and the two possible ways actinorrhizae can form [18].

The microbial partners, in this case, are represented by various species and varieties of the actinobacteria *Frankia* sp. Unlike rhizobia, this bacteria has a filamentous and extremely branched cell, similar to fungal mycelia. It is this network of hyphae that penetrates through intercellular spaces and then forms invaginations and intracellular vacuoles inside the root cortex of the host.

The vegetal partner may belong to some species of the orders Rosales (like silverberry – *Elaeagnus* sp., sea buckthorn – *Hippophae* sp., avens – *Dryas* sp. *etc.*), Fagales (in temperate areas mainly alders – *Alnus* sp., but also genera *Casuarina, Myrica etc.*) and, more rarely, Cucurbitales (*Coriaria* sp., *Datisca* sp.) [14, 15].

Nitrogen-fixing Ectosymbioses

Extremely important in both natural environments and agricultural production, is the symbiosis with species of *Azospirillum*. This is a genus of Gram-negative, nitrogen-fixing, aerobic or microaerophilic, mobile, rod-shaped bacteria belonging to the family Rhodospirillaceae (α-Proteobacteria). They are widespread in water and soils.

Some species (mainly *A. brasilense, A. amazonense, A. lipoferum, etc.*) can form symbiotic associations with the roots of certain plants (the existence of such relationships was proven for at least 110 species, belonging to 35 families). Unlike other bacteria mentioned above, *Azospirillum* does not colonize root tissues, but just forms dense populations outside the rhizodermis, only occasionally penetrating the interior. Due to their mobility, these bacteria can easily pass from one root to another, thus associating themselves with entire plant communities [19, 20].

Among the plants involved, we can mention wheat, maize, rice, sugarcane, sorghum, various wild Poaceae, spinach, cucumber, species of *Brassica, etc.* In some legumes (such as soybean), the ectosymbiosis with *Azospirillum* works along the endosymbiosis with rhizobia, greatly increasing the amount of nitrogen fixed [21, 22].

While for bacteria, benefits are obvious – feeding on root exudates and lowering oxygen concentration in the rhizosphere – for plants these are extremely numerous and variate. First of all, the nitrogen compounds in excess are transferred to the plant, leading to a major increase in the assimilation of this element (up to 30% in maize) [23].

Furthermore, bacteria secrete hormones like auxins, gibberellins or cytokines, stimulating plant growth. This way, individuals bearing such endosymbionts will get a larger size, higher biomass, a more developed root system, more root hairs and more leaves with a larger total area. Thus, the efficiency of water uptake from soil increases (meaning an enhanced drought resistance), likewise mineral nutrient uptake and photosynthetic rate. *Azospirillum* is considered to be one of the most important so-called **plant growth-promoting microbes** (PGPM; Fig. **6**) [21, 22, 24, 25].

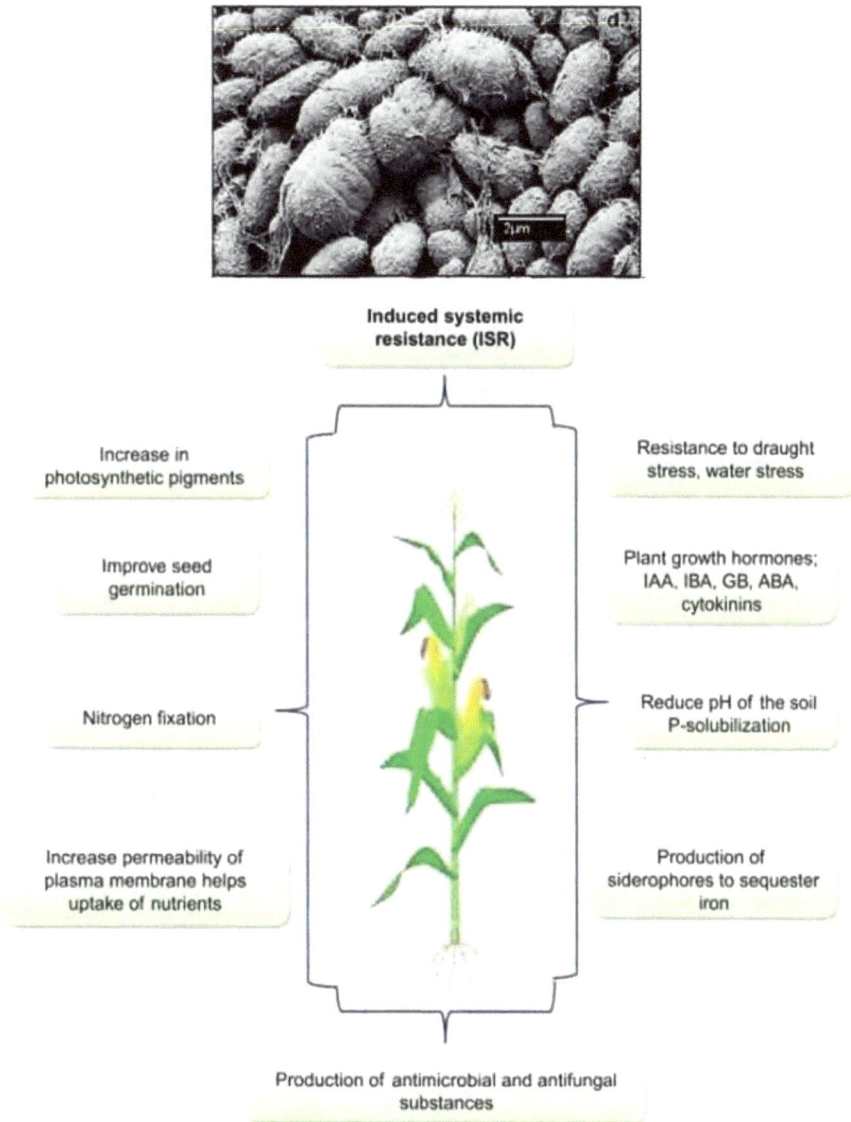

Fig. (6). *Azospirillum* sp. colony on plant rhizodermis seen in electron microscopy [26] and its role in plant life [27].

Mycorrhizae

Mycorrhizae are one of the most widespread and important types of symbiosis on Earth. Briefly, it is a relationship between filamentous fungi and the root system of a plant (although in some ferns, it rather involves rhizomes or other parts of the stem).

These relatipnships have evolved ever since the first stages of land colonization by plants and hugely diversified along tens of millions of years [28, 29].

The fungal partners (with a total of around 6,000 species) usually belong to ascomycetes and basidiomycetes, although there are some known cases of mycorrhizal zygomycetes. They include microscopic species, as well as some macroscopic ones, including edible mushrooms (*Amanita*, *Boletus*, *Cantharellus*, *Tuber*).

As for the plants involved, they belong to extremely variate groups and are believed to represent somewhere around 80 and 95% (or even more!) of the vegetal species known to humankind (these estimates are difficult to make, since the exact number of plant species is disputed, while the mycorrhizal or non-mycorrhizal status has only been proven for a tiny fraction).

Participation or non-participation in mycorrhizae is genetically determined. There are plants obligately involved (they cannot survive without the fungi), while for others, mycorrhizae are facultative. The same is true for fungi (true morel, *Morchella* sp. is often in symbiosis with plants, but can also survive on its own).

Its specificity also varies. Some fungi are strictly specialized on a particular host, others can form relationships with several different partners, sometimes even at the same time. The same goes for plants.

There are non-mycorrhizal plants. This feature is especially common among Brassicaceae (cabbage, cauliflower, kohlrabi, mustard, *etc.*). A relatively large number of non-mycorrhizal species is also found among Amaranthaceae (beet, spinach), Caryophylaceae (carnations), and Ericaceae (blueberry, lingonberry, azalea, rhododendron, *etc.*) [29, 30].

Just like in other symbioses, mycorrhizae start with an interspecific signalling stage, due to root and fungal secretions that facilitate spore germination in the proximity of roots and the growth of hyphae towards the latter. Considering the structure and anatomical changes induced, there are six main types of mycorrhizae (Fig. **7**).

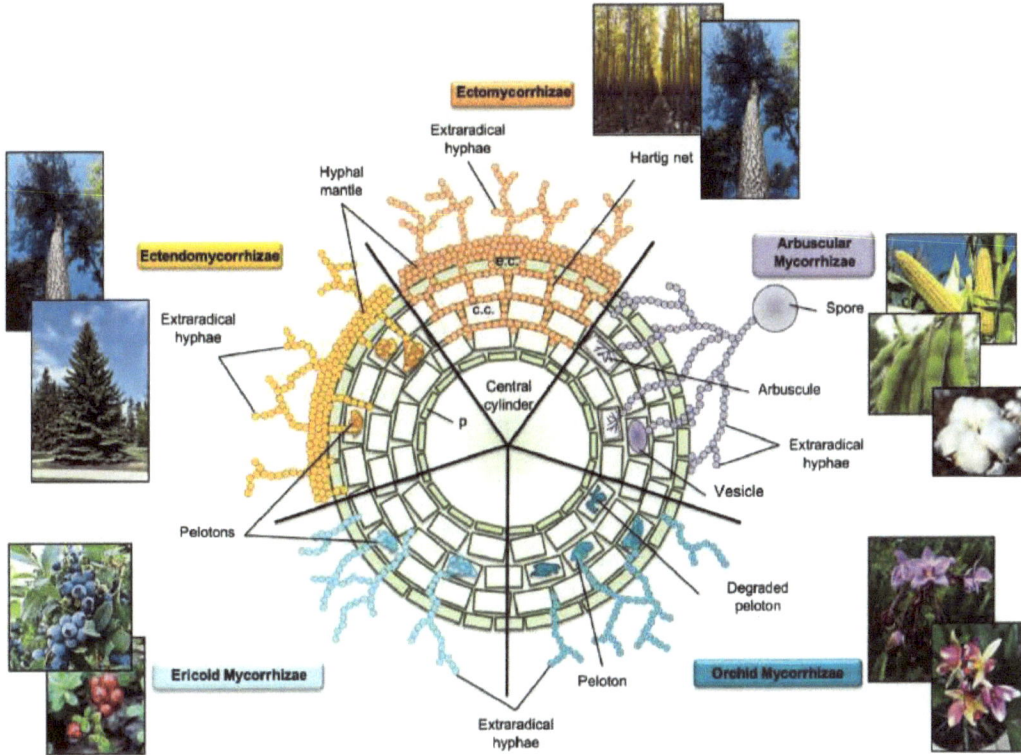

Fig. (7). Types of mycorrhizae [32].

Ectomycorrhizae involve anywhere between 2 and 10% of plant species (and mainly basidiomycetes). We are especially talking about woody species: pine, spruce, larch, thuja, beech, birch, hazel, chestnut, oak, linden, pecan, poplar, eucalypt, *etc*. In this case, fungal hyphae penetrate through the rhizodermis and grow between cortical cells, forming a dense, extremely branched network, with an extended contact area, called a **Hartig net**. Hyphae stay, in this case, within the intercellular spaces of the cortex, without passing through cell walls.

Ectendomycorrhizae or **arbutoid mycorrhizae** are characteristic of some Ericaceae. Basidiomycetes involved in this relationship form a Hartig net, as shown above, but some of their hyphae pierce through the cell walls of some cortical cells, forming coiled loops around the protoplast.

Arbuscular endomycorrhizae are, by far, the most common fungi (present in 80% of known plants). They belong to the class Glomeromycota. Their hyphae penetrate the cell walls of cortical parenchyma, causing the cell membrane to invaginate. In these invaginations, branched mycelial terminations (**arbuscules**) are formed, often ending with or being associated with vesicles. This abundant branching provides an enormous total contact area, while matter transfer occurs directly to and from each individual cell. The vesicles serve as storage organelles.

Ericoid endo mycorrhizae are found in Ericaceae and a few related families (the main particularity of Ericaceae is the environment they live in usually acidic soil). Ascomycetes in the genus *Pezoloma* (or related genera) pierce through cortical cell walls without causing invaginations and arbuscules. Instead, they form dense spiral nets in the space between the cell wall and the cell membrane.

Orchid mycorrhizae occur between orchids and basidiomycetes such as *Peloctonia* sp. or related genera. Cortical cell membrane invaginations host some dense coiled hyphal nets, ball-shaped, called **pelotons**. Their development leads to a major alteration of the host cortical cells (nuclei are hypertrophied, starch granules).

Monotropoid endomycorrhizae are rare, only present in some Ericaceae species with a heterotrophic way of life (lacking chlorophyll) or a mixotrophic one. In this case, the relationship is rather unilateral. Basically, the plant parasitizes the fungus.

Besides the massive intraarticular branching, hyphae are also found in dense groupings outside the rhizodermis, forming an external sheath (mantle). The "infected" roots are often easy to distinguish due to their larger diameter (due to cortex swelling) and different colors [29, 31]

The functioning of mycorrhizae involves complex processes of interspecific signaling. Root exudates consisting of some flavonoids, diterpenes, cytokines, *etc.* stimulate fungal spore germination; strigolactones direct hyphal growth towards and through the epidermis; simple saccharides secreted by the plant feed the fungi; hormones and other compounds secreted by the fungi stimulate plant growth (especially the root system).

The importance of mycorrhizae to the host plants is a multiple one. Due to the large outer surface and certain physiological features, fungi are very effective in absorbing some bioelements, such as potassium, phosphorus, and nitrogen, of which part will be directed to the host, thus supporting the plant's mineral nutrition. In the same way, mycorrhizae enhance water absorption.

Fungal hormones stimulate plant growth and development. Mycelia also works as an intermediary in relation to certain compounds in soil solution. This way, the host's tolerance to drought, salinity, pollutants, *etc.* is significantly increased. Furthermore, the plant-fungi complex can be extremely efficient in improving soil quality and bioremediating some toxic compounds (through biodegrading organic toxins, sequestering or translocating heavy metals, *etc.*)

By employing diverse mechanisms, mycorrhizae can help fight pathogens. These mechanisms can be direct (antibiosis, secretion of compounds that inhibit pathogenic microorganism growth, trophic competition or creating a mechanical barrier between soil and root) or indirect (stimulating the thickening of root cell walls or the secretion of antibiotic compounds by the plant) [31 - 35].

Thus, we can conclude that mycorrhizae are a key factor in sustaining vegetal productivity.

Rhizosphere

The concept of **rhizosphere** was first coined and defined in 1904, by Lorenz Hiltner. According to his definition, the rhizosphere would be that particular soil region enclosing plant roots, inhabited by specific communities of microorganisms that are influenced by the substances secreted by roots.

Practically, we are talking about a true microecosystem, comprising various species of micro- and macroorganisms, including the plant itself, mycorrhizal fungi, the endosymbionts in nodules and actinorrhizae, ectosymbionts, as well as a wide range of non-symbiotic organisms (phytopathogens included). This micro ecosystem is the frame where different types of interspecific relationships take place, such as mutualism/symbiosis, amensalism/antibiosis, parasitism, competition, and even predatorism.

Rhizosphere extends on just a few millimeters of soil around the root epidermis, but its total spatial expansion can be extremely variable, depending on the length and branching of the root system (see subchapter 3.3 and Fig. **9**) [36, 37].

The rhizosphere has three spatial components (Fig. **8**).

The endorhizosphere comprises the rhizodermis and parts of the root cortex. This is where the exchange of mineral and organic exchange between root and soil occurs and this is also the place where various microbial symbionts and pathogens dwell. All these interactions take place in the space between cells (apoplastic), and between cell walls and membranes, respectively in invaginations of cell membranes, as shown in the previous subchapter.

Rhizoplane is the actual interface between a plant and soil: the outer surface is the rhizodermis, which secretes the mucilages, some adhering soil grains or mineral depositions and hosting populations of microorganisms, which sometimes form compact sheaths (such as mycorrhizal ones).

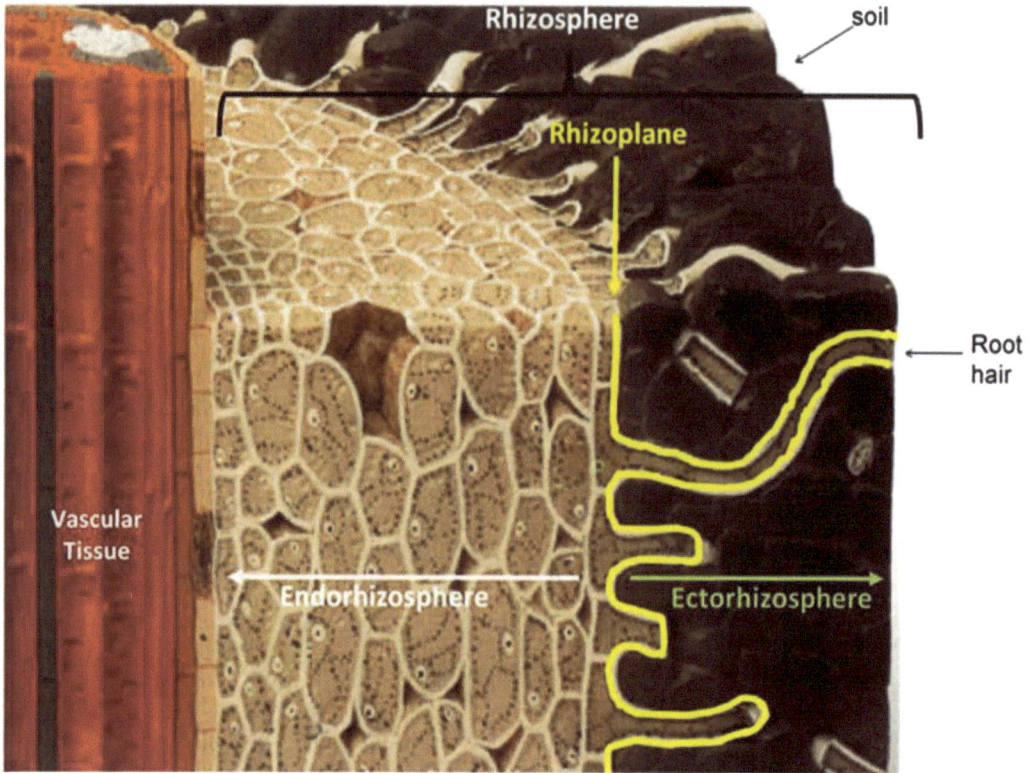

Fig. (8). The three zones of rhizosphere [36].

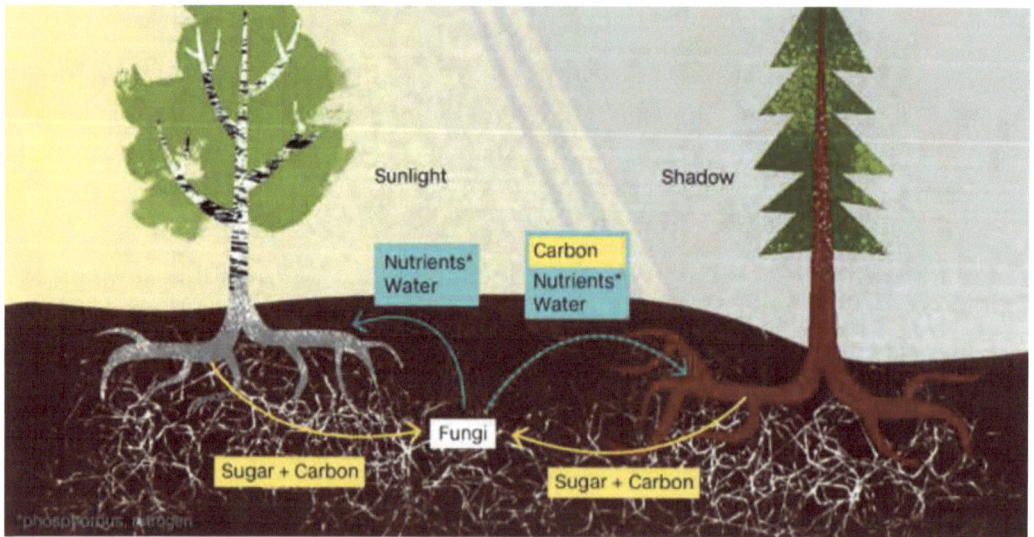

Fig. (9). Functioning of the "mycorrhizal Internet" [43].

The ectorhizosphere (exorhizosphere) is the adjacent soil region, significantly influenced by root exudates and mycorrhizal hyphal branching and also hosting a diverse microbiome. On the outside, it has non-rhizospheric soil around it, without a clearly defined limit between them [36].

While the roles of different symbiotic associations in the life of host plants were presented in the previous chapter, another important aspect to consider is the long-range intra- and interspecific communications, mediated by rhizospheric microorganisms (especially by mycorrhizal fungi).

Each plant can establish symbiotic relationships with one or more species of fungi. Each fungus can associate itself with one or more plants or can have relationships with other mycorrhizal fungi from neighboring plants. These mycelial networks tend to disseminate available nutrients so that they can be indirectly transferred from one plant to another. This is how a tree growing in a shaded place can benefit from organic chemicals synthesized by its neighbors living in more sunny areas. The same mechanism allows mature trees to "feed" their offspring, providing them with part of the necessary nutrients.

However, these interactions are not only trophic in nature. Through mycorrhizal networks, chemical signalling compounds can be transmitted. Experiments on tomato plants, of which some were infected with the pathogen *Alternaria solani*, have shown that uninfected plants "hear" soon enough of the presence of this threat and develop preemptive protection measures (secretion of inhibiting compounds, *etc.*). With the aboveground organs tightly sealed, the only logical explanation was interradicular communication. The same communication means were found in fava beans (and then in other species) regarding another type of threat: aphids and other damaging insects.

The interactions mediated by rhizospheric networks are not always positive. Some plants – saprophytic or parasitic, lacking chlorophyll, such as the orchid *Cephalanthera austiniae*, but also some invasive autotrophic species, like *Centaurea stoebe* or *Festuca idahoensis* – use mycorrhizal symbioses to drain resources from neighboring plants. Other plants use the same networks to spread toxins over large areas, thus inhibiting the growth of competing plants (such as the juglone secreted by walnut roots) or that of their symbionts (the case of garlic mustard, *Alliaria petiolata*).

Due to all these possibilities of long-range communications, researchers often talk of a true "**mycorrhizal Internet**", or use the even more catchy name given by Peter Wohlleben, that of "**Wood Wide Web**" [38 - 41].

Research in this field has only started during the last few decades, so there are still many unknown details, regarding both the biochemical aspects of such transfers and their evolutionary significance. Are these networks "capitalist" (a way to ensure their own position of each composing individual or community within the intra- and interspecific competition), "socialist" (implying a rather homogenous distribution of available resources over large areas), or even do they behave as "superorganisms"? [41]

This latter interpretation paves the way for a new manner of understanding life on Earth. When looking from this point of view, each individual lifeform plays the role of a component of a superior "organism" (fungi, for instance, working as the equivalent of a "nervous system"). Considering that such associations of plants, fungi, and various microorganisms cover most land areas on Earth, it would not be difficult to imagine some sort of a global "superorganism" that is able to maintain the equilibrium of the various environmental parameters around the planet, such as that put forward by James Lovelock in his "Gaia Hypothesis" [41, 42].

Applications

Knowledge of the complex ecological interactions in soil has extremely important practical applications, in agriculture.

Microbial Fertilizers

In the previous chapters and subchapters, some of the **plant growth-promoting microorganisms** (PGPM) were mentioned. These are organisms (bacteria, fungi, *etc.*) that are normally found in plant rhizosphere biota, and some are symbiotic.

The isolation, controlled multiplication in bioreactors, conditioning for commercialization and transport and their dispersal on agricultural fields (Fig. **10**) of such lifeforms represents a growing industry: these microorganisms can work as **biofertilizers**, thus reducing the need for chemical fertilizers. Compared to the latter, which have high costs of production and are dangerous pollutants when in excess, biofertilizers have the advantages of being 100% natural and self-reproducing through regular cell division.

Among the most often used are nitrogen-fixing bacteria: being symbiotic like rhizobia (for legume crops), or non-symbiotic, like *Azospirillum* sp. (useful for a wide range of crops, especially maize) or even cyanobacteria (for rice fields).

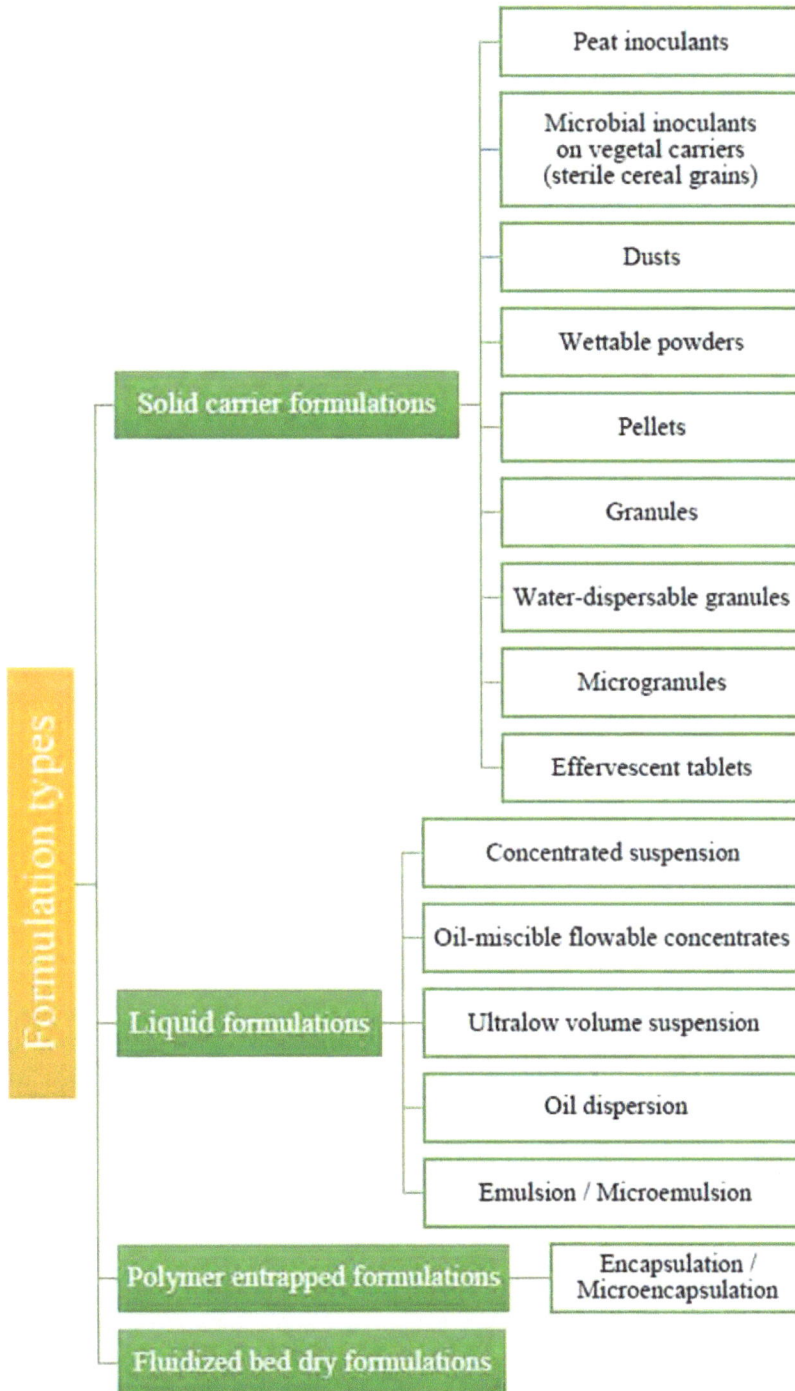

Fig. (10). Formulation types of microbial fertilizers [46].

Another important category is that of phosphate-solubilizing bacteria (PSB), mainly species of *Bacillus* and *Pseudomonas*, that increase the bioavailability of this key nutrient. Other species also help mobilize some micronutrients, such as silica or zinc (*Bacillus* sp.)

Mycorrhizal fungi may also constitute a valuable inoculum, enhancing symbiotic relationships with plant roots, helping to mobilize phosphate and other nutrients, increasing tolerance to adverse environmental conditions, and overall productivity.

Last but not least, many microorganisms, including bacteria (*Azotobacter*, *Serratia*, *Cellulomonas*), fungi – mycorrhizal (*Beauveria*, *Trichoderma*), and also several microalgae (*Chlorella*, *Dunaliella, etc.*) have the ability to secrete plant hormones or analogues, stimulating the growth of plant organs and increasing tolerance to hydric and oxidative stress, pathogens, *etc.* [44 - 46].

Biological Pathogen Control

Another biotechnological application gaining more and more popularity currently is the production of biopesticides. The procedure is basically similar to the isolation of some microorganisms of interest, cultivation and inoculation, using means such as those shown in Fig. (**10**).

However, in this case, the selected microorganisms help control various pests affecting crops.

Not all **biopesticides** act at the soil level (the classic case of *Bacillus thuringiensis*-based insecticides, applied on leaves), but some do. Most often, their action is due to competition and/or antibiosis processes. Some species (*Penicillium* sp.) secrete natural antibiotics, thus limiting the growth of other microbes, including pathogenic ones.

Others, such as some species of *Bacillus* and *Pseudomonas*, also produce siderophores, compounds that efficiently chelate iron, limiting the access of competitors to this important nutrient.

There are also organisms (*Penicillum* sp.) that easily colonize lesions occurring in outer root tissues. By doing this, they prevent the access of opportunistic parasites.

Finally, there are biopesticides with a more direct approach, through hyperparasitism (some species of *Clonostachys* and *Trichoderma* parasitize other, phytopathogenic fungi) or even predatorism (such as the bacteriovores of bacterium *Bdelovibrio*).

According to the target of such biopesticides, we can distinguish bactericides (such as some strains of *Bacillus subtilis*), fungicides (species of *Bacillus, Pseudomonas, Trichoderma, etc.*), insecticides, and acaricides (*Bacillus thuringiensis, Beauveria bassiana*, the protozoan *Nosema* or even parasitic nematodes belonging to families Heterorhabditidae and Steinernematidae), *etc.* [47 - 49].

One of the most successful examples of biological control is that of crown gall disease. The pathogen responsible is *Rhizobium radiobacter* var. *tumefaciens* (formerly known as *Agrobacterium radiobacter* or *A. tumefaciens*), which is a Gram-negative bacterium in the family Rhizobiaceae.

Unlike its symbiotic relatives, this is an opportunistic parasite, attracted by glucidic and phenolic root exudates of plants. Once the root is reached, some bacterial strains (those possessing plasmid Ti) enter through rhizodermal microlesions, spreading through the plant and causing inflammations or tumors at various root or stem levels (Fig. **11**). Among the species commonly affected are fruit trees (stone fruit trees, walnuts), roses, raspberry, grapevine, beet, horseradish, rhubarb, *etc.*

Fig. (11). Crown gall in peach tree and the pathogen responsible: *Rhizobium radiobacter* var. *tumefaciens* [51].

The bacterium is easily transmittable from one vegetation cycle to another and from one region to another through sap droplets, dead plant organs, and cuttings. The disease has a serious impact on plant viability and productivity.

The solution to this problem came from other strains of the same species, *Rhizobium radiobacter*, strains that are saprophytic and directly compete with the pathogens for trophic resources. They inhibit their competitors by secreting bacteriocins – bacterial antibiotics – thus preventing root infection. The best-known and most effective is strain K84. These bacteria are grown in bioreactors and applied in suspension on cuttings prior to plantation, significantly lowering the occurrence of crown gall [50, 51].

A very similar disease is found in grapevine (grapevine crown gall), caused by *Allorhizobium Vitis* (formerly *Rhizobium vitis*) that can be successfully battled the same way, using non-pathogenic, bacteriocin-producing strains such as ARK-1, ARK-2, ARK-3 and VAR03-1 [52].

Biological Herbicides

Besides pathogens, another major problem for agriculture is that of weeds. Also, in many regions of the world, the proliferation of certain invasive plant species threatens local ecosystems.

Just as any other chemical pesticides, chemical herbicides cause serious environmental issues, due to both toxicity (especially when used in excess) and the resource and energy demand of the synthesis process.

This is why bioherbicides appear as a preferable alternative. We are talking about pathogenic microorganisms (viruses, bacteria, fungi) that selectively infect target weeds, without causing any damage to crops.

The first such herbicide was produced in 1994 after Jack Johnson discovered the effect that a specific strain of *Xanthomonas campestris* has on annual meadow grass (*Poa annua*), a common invasive grass [53].

Since then, the bioherbicide industry has greatly advanced and today there are many available solutions for controlling a wide variety of weeds.

For instance, the parasite ascomycete fungus *Ascochyta caulina* helps fight wild spinach or white goosefoot (*Chenopodium album*), species of *Fusarium* (*F. oxysporum, F. orthoceras, etc.*) keep under control broomrape (*Orobanche* sp., a noxious parasitic), species of *Xanthomonas* or fungi in the genera *Alternaria*, *Stagonospora*, *Phyllosticta*, *Phoma*, *Sclerotinia* eliminate creeping thistle (*Cirsium arvense*), etc.

Aquatic invasive plants can also require biological control; this is the case with the common water hyacinth (*Pontederia crassipes*), targeted by the phytopathogens *Alternaria eichorniae* and *Cercospora piaropi*.

Last but not least, this method can be used to limit the proliferation of some woody plants on agricultural fields.

The parasitic basidiomycete fungus *Chondrostereum purpureum* is successfully used against alder trees (*Alnus* sp.), black cherry (*Prunus serotina*), and many other trees and shrubs, while in tropical regions *Cylindrobasidium leave* is used to keep acacias under control [54, 55].

Biological Frost Control

Frost is one of the most damaging environmental factors to agriculture, horticulture, pomiculture, and viticulture. Although somewhat counter-intuitive, it is not the actual cold that causes damage, but the formation of small ice crystals outside plant organs or even in intercellular lacunae. They can inflict direct lesions on those tissues or cause cell dehydration.

The respective lesions often become gateways for various pathogens. Roots, stems and buds are among the most affected organs.

The formation of ice crystals is favored by the presence of certain nucleation particles and among those are some proteins of bacterial origin (INP: *Ice Nucleation Proteins*). It is now acknowledged that there are some bacteria commonly found in epiphytic microbiota, such as species of *Pseudomonas* (especially *P. syringae*), *Xanthomonas,* or *Erwinia* that secrete such proteins, enhancing the destructive effects of frost on host plants.

The solution is quite simple: inoculation with bacteria that either secrete antifreeze compounds or remove, through competition, the noxious strains. The most common are some species of *Pseudomonas* and *Erwinia* (mainly *E. herbicola*) [56 - 58].

Bioremediation

Soils worldwide are currently subjected to strong pressure due to anthropic activities. We are talking about the countless sources of pollution. Spills of noxious chemicals or solid wastes that are difficult to biodegrade affect soil micro and macrobiota, its fertility, and, finally, agriculture, livestock (when animals graze on contaminated soil), and human health.

Traditional remediation methods include excavating chronically polluted soil, treatments with various chemical compounds, *etc.* All these methods are energy-consuming, need technology and workforce, and can be rather destructive themselves.

The alternative is **bioremediation**: using micro- and/or macroorganisms to remove the contaminants, thus restoring that ecosystem to its initial state as soon as possible.

The targets of bioremediation can be quite diverse classes of chemicals: heavy metals, hydrocarbons and derivatives, pesticides, plastic material, *etc.* The mechanisms of this process can also be extremely variate, and so are the lifeforms involved [59].

One of the main strategies currently used is microbial bioremediation, which consists of using microorganisms (indigenous or introduced) to clean up the pollutants. This process is based on their ability to biodegrade the troublesome compounds (but also their eventual toxic byproducts) up to benign substances, easy to metabolize by local microbiota. This requires microbes (usually bacteria or fungi) to have the appropriate enzymatic apparatus.

A typical case is the biodegradation of crude oil and derivatives, that reach soils due to accidental spills from tanks, pipelines, *etc.*, or by low-intensity but constant spills (refineries, auto workshops, *etc.*). As mentioned before (subchapter 4.3), there are strains of microorganisms that have the required enzyme set (usually this is an adaptation of metabolic pathways involved in oxidizing fatty acids) to break down a wider or narrower array of hydrocarbons.

We can also add the need to decontaminate soils chronically polluted with hydroxylated or halogenated derivatives or hydrocarbons and various other synthetic compounds used as pesticides or being part of plastic materials. The biofuel industry can also be a source of pollution, this time involving lipid oils, whose cleanup requires an effective usage of lipolytic microbiota. Finally, a new frontier in bioremediation research is finding efficient organisms (microbes, fungi, insect larvae, *etc.*) that consume plastic waste.

The actual bioremediation strategies greatly vary from one case to another. Microorganisms of interest can be selectively grown and then inoculated in the polluted environment (a process called **bioaugmentation**). In theory, we can also design and use multivalent microorganisms through genetic engineering (such as bacterial strains that decompose a very wide range of hydrocarbons), however, current legislations tend to limit the release of such microbes in the environment. Also, the activity of indigenous (or introduced) degradative microbiota can be supported by adding some key nutrients, in a process called **biostimulation**. We are talking about nitrates, but most of all oxygen, is essential to biodegradation processes, mainly aerobic (Fig. **12**). Usually, oxygen is brought in by pumping hydrogen peroxide [59 - 62].

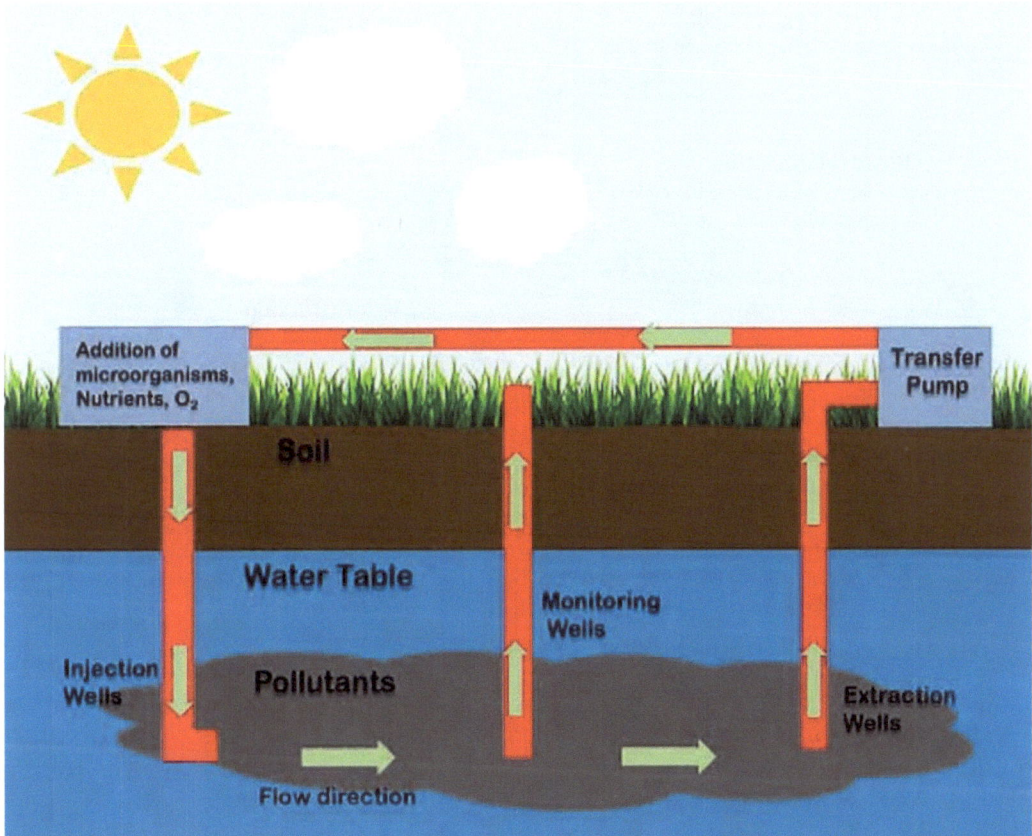

Fig. (12). The general design of an *in-situ* microbial bioremediation process, through bioaugmentation, and biostimulation [63].

There is also another option: using native or introduced vegetation (or, very often, the associations between plants and mycorrhizal fungi) to decontaminate soil, a process called **phytoremediation**.

Many plants are rather sensitive to soil pollutants or toxins. Yet, there are also many resistant ones, and some of them can contribute to the biodegradation of these pollutants, through several mechanisms (Fig. **13**).

Phytoremediation

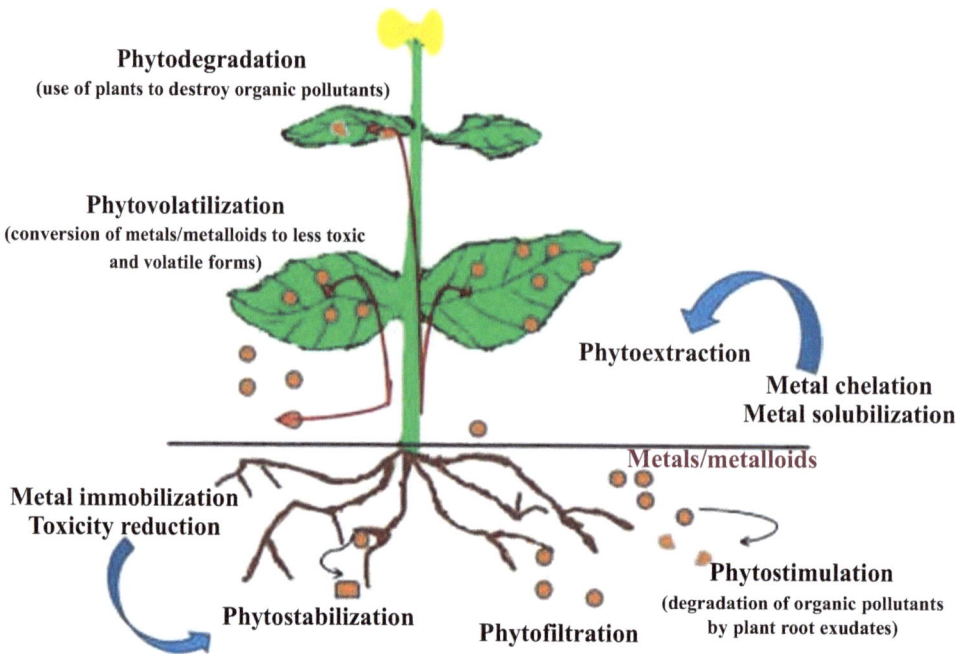

Fig. (13). Mechanisms of phytoremediation [67].

Phytostimulation is most often involved, especially when dealing with organic pollutants. It is an indirect process, by which the plant enhances the microbial degradative activity in the soil, by providing nutritive root exudates or by oxygen "injection". This is the case of some plant species whose tissue is permeable enough to oxygen and allows its diffusion towards deeper layers of the rhizosphere. This may prove extremely useful, for example, in remediating hydrocarbon pollution.

Phytodegradation involves the direct use, by the plant, of its enzymatic apparatus in order to break down the pollutant. The phenomena can occur at the root level or after the compound is absorbed into the plant.

Phytofiltration means filtering the pollutant out of the soil solution, usually at the root level (**rhizofiltration**), through adsorption or absorption.

Phytostabilization involves the uptake and accumulation of the pollutant at the root level. This way, its concentration in soil solution may significantly decrease.

This is extremely useful when dealing with heavy metals, for instance, although metals or any other type of stable pollutants can return to the environment after plants die and decompose.

Phytoextraction is the active or passive (with soil water flow) uptake of the pollutant and its translocation to aboveground organs. It can be followed by phytodegradation in case of organic compounds. For heavy metals, the main way to remove them from the environment is by harvesting the plants (see the discussion on bioaccumulation below).

Phytovolatilization is mostly used for certain organic compounds. Once absorbed into the plant and transported through xylem vessels, they (or their decomposition byproducts) are released into the atmosphere under a gaseous state, through the transpiration process [64 - 66].

Bioaccumulation

Bioaccumulation means the accumulation of a certain chemical element or compound in the cells or tissues of an organism, in a higher concentration than that in the surrounding environment.

Basically, it may involve a wide range of chemicals but is most important in case of heavy metals, elements that can be highly toxic and, obviously, cannot undergo any sort of biodegradation.

Metals such as iron, aluminium, copper, zinc, chromium, lead, but also cadmium, rare metals (gold, platinum), radionuclides (uranium, thorium), or semimetals (selenium, arsenic, thallium) are found in any type of soil, in variable amounts. However, local mineralogical conditions or, more often, chronic pollution due to metal and paint industries, fossil fuel burning, waste storage, nuclear industry, *etc.* may lead to much higher concentrations than normal. In such amounts, some metals become toxic to living beings.

It is now known that there are some tolerant species that can help us in many ways. We are mostly talking about plants, and in this case, the key process is **phytoaccumulation**. While most plant species tend to forcefully exclude or to simply limit the uptake of such elements in excess, there are others that preferentially absorb them, translocate them to various organs, and store them there, under non-toxic forms (and preferably, as far away as possible from the photosynthetic apparatus, the most sensitive to heavy metal toxicity; Fig. (**14**).

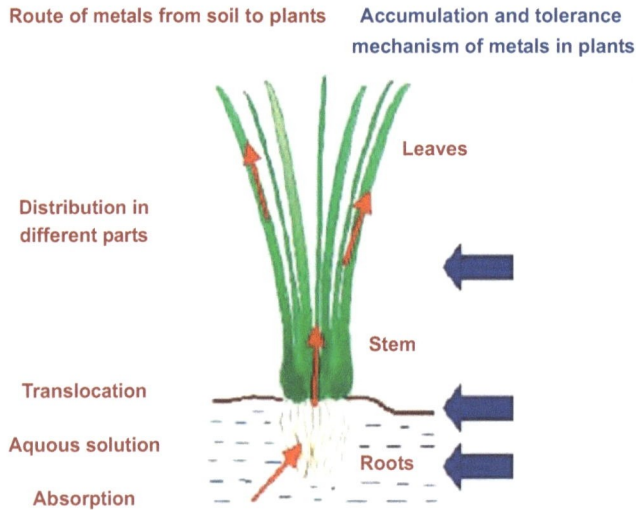

Fig. (14). General mechanism of metals and semimetal phytoaccumulation [75].

These are **bioaccumulating** plants. And if the tissular concentration of metallic ions surpasses by ten, hundred or even a thousand times that in regular vegetation, such plants are called **hyperaccumulators**. Hyperaccumulation is a trait most often found in plants growing on saline or ultramafic soils (also known as serpentine soils; they form through the breakdown of ultramafic rocks, rich in nickel, chromium, cobalt and other metals, while relatively poor in essential nutrients), but there are some species that can simply become hyperaccumulating under proper environmental conditions.

The minimal thresholds of hyperaccumulation may vary from one metal to another: from 10,000 (according to some researchers, 3,000) mg/kg for Fe, Mn, Zn, to 1,000 (alternatively, 300) mg/kg for As, Co, Cr, Cu, Ni, Pb, Sb, Se, Tl, or just 100 (or 30 mg/kg) for Cd, and even lower, for rare elements [68 - 70].

There are many possible applications of this process, this is why surveying global flora for potentially hyperaccumulating species is a promising research direction in botany. Among the first to be discovered were nickel-accumulating species, such as *Alyssum bertolonii* and *Thalaspi caerulescens*, followed by many other plants, mostly living in tropical regions rich in nickel (New Caledonia) or cobalt (Congo), or even poly accumulating species like *Brassica juncea* (Indian mustard, capable of accumulating As, Cu, Zn, *etc*; this trait is most often found among Brassicaceae, probably due to their non-mycorrhizal roots) [68 - 70]. But plants with a certain bioaccumulating potential can be also found within the common temperate flora [71].

Phytoremediation of soils polluted with heavy metals is, of course, one of the main applications for these plants. It works by using species capable of phytoextraction (see above; it can be entirely natural or artificially stimulated by dispersing some chelating chemicals in the soil), followed by metal storage in aboveground organs. Their harvesting means the removal of the pollutant from the environment.

Phytostabilization occurs in plants that do not translocate metal ions to aerial organs, but store them inside the root. In this case, harvesting is more difficult, but the metal is at least sequestered for a long period of time in forms that are less accessible to soil biota and thus, non-toxic [68 - 70].

Phytoprospection works by detecting abnormally high metal amounts in local vegetation. This might be a clue to the presence of metal deposits worth exploring in that area.

Phytomining is a field of research still in its beginnings. It paves new ways in the exploitation of subeconomic metalliferous ore deposits. In this case, plants, through phytoextraction, translocation, and bioconcentration, make the metal easily available to humans. All that we need to do is to grow suitable plants on that terrain, harvest them, and process their tissues in order to get the desired metal. And, yes, there are plants and fungi are able to accumulate gold [72 - 74].

CONCLUSION

Ecological interactions occurring in soil are multiple and complex. Among the most important are those involving underground plant organs, *i.e.* those occurring at the rhizosphere level.

These include root nodulation with rhizobia, actinorrhizae, mycorrhizae, and root-*A zospirillum* symbioses. They have a profound impact on plant productivity, including crops. They also allow long-distance matter and information exchanges, allowing plant associations to work as communities.

Knowledge of these aspects is essential to the modern human economy, allowing for the production and application of biofertilizers and biopesticides, biological frost control, bioremediation, and bioaccumulation, with its numerous potential uses.

REFERENCES

[1]   Ryczkowski A. Five types of ecological relationships. Sciencing, 2018. Available from: https://sciencing.com/five-types-ecological-relationships-7786.html

[2]   Zabrodskii PF. The main directions and tasks of ecological microbiology. Acta Sci Microbiol 2019; 2(6): 30-3.

[3]   Brown R. Ecological relationships definition. Jotscroll, 2023. Available from: https://www.jotscroll.com/ecological-relationships-definition

[4]   Briones MJI. Soil fauna and soil functions: a jigsaw puzzle. Front Environ Sci 2014; 2. [http://dx.doi.org/10.3389/fenvs.2014.00007]

[5]   Why Living Roots Matter Year-Round. Farmers, Center for Regenerative Agriculture. University of Missouri, Available from: https://cra.missouri.edu/farmers/why-living-roots-matter-year-round

[6]   Willems A. The taxonomy of rhizobia: an overview. Plant Soil 2006; 287(1-2): 3-14. [http://dx.doi.org/10.1007/s11104-006-9058-7]

[7]   Grains Research and Development Corporation, 2016. Rhizobial Inoculants Fact Sheet. Northern, Southern and Western Regions. Harvesting the Benefit of Inoculating Legumes. GRDC, Barton, 4.

[8]   Al-Mallah MK, Davey MR, Cocking EC. Formation of Nodular Structures on Rice Seedlings by Rhizobia. J Exp Bot 1989; 40(4): 473-8. [http://dx.doi.org/10.1093/jxb/40.4.473]

[9]   Nap JP, Bisseling T. Developmental biology of a plant-prokaryote symbiosis: the legume root nodule. Science 1990; 250(4983): 948-54. [http://dx.doi.org/10.1126/science.250.4983.948] [PMID: 17746918]

[10] Jiao YS, Liu YH, Yan H, *et al.* Rhizobial diversity and nodulation characteristics of the extremely promiscuous legume *Sophora flavescens*. Mol Plant Microbe Interact 2015; 28(12): 1338-52. [http://dx.doi.org/10.1094/MPMI-06-15-0141-R] [PMID: 26389798]

[11] Domergue, O., Diversité fonctionnelle de rhizobia associés à la féverole, en agro-écosystème Sud de France. Ph.D. thesis, Université Paris Sciences et Lettres, Paris, 2017, 232.

[12] Wekesa C, Asudi GO, Okoth P, *et al.* Rhizobia contribute to salinity tolerance in common beans (*Phaseolus vulgaris* L.). Cells 2022; 11(22): 3628. [http://dx.doi.org/10.3390/cells11223628] [PMID: 36429056]

[13] Symbiotic Nitrogen Fixation. Pediaa, Available from: https://pediaa.com/tag/symbiotic-nitroge--fixation

[14] Diaga D, Tahir AD, Ibrahima N. Actinorhizal, mycorhizal and rhizobial symbioses: how much do we know? Afr J Biotechnol 2003; 2(1): 1-7. [http://dx.doi.org/10.5897/AJB2003.000-1001]

[15] Russo RO. Nitrogen-Fixing Trees with Actinorhiza in Forestry and Agroforestry. In: Werner D, Newton WE, Eds. Nitrogen Fixation in Agriculture, Forestry, Ecology, and the Environment Nitrogen Fixation: Origins, Applications, and Research Progress. Dordrecht: Springer 2005; 4: pp. 143-71. [http://dx.doi.org/10.1007/1-4020-3544-6_8]

[16] Jaiswal, S., Frankia. Alchetron, 2022. Available from: https://alchetron.com/Frankia

[17] Frankia alni. Plant Parasites of Europe. Leafminers, Galls and Fungi, 2023. Available from: https://bladmineerders.nl/parasites/bacteria/actinobacteria/actinomycetales/frankia/frankia-alni

[18] Perrine-Walker F, Doumas P, Lucas M, *et al.* Auxin carriers localization drives auxin accumulation in plant cells infected by *Frankia* in *Casuarina glauca* actinorhizal nodules. Curr Protein Pept Sci 2011; 12(2): 156-64. [http://dx.doi.org/10.2174/138920311795684896] [PMID: 21348842]

[19] Okon Y, Kapulnik Y. Development and function ofAzospirillum-inoculated roots. Plant Soil 1986; 90(1-3): 3-16. [http://dx.doi.org/10.1007/BF02277383]

[20] Bashan Y, Holguin G. Inter-root movement of *Azospirillum brasilense* and subsequent root colonization of crop and weed seedlings growing in soil. Microb Ecol 1995; 29(3): 269-81. [http://dx.doi.org/10.1007/BF00164890] [PMID: 24185346]

[21]   Gamo T. *Azospirillum* spp. from crop roots: a promoter of plant growth. Jpn Agric Res Q 1991; 24(4): 253-9.

[22]   Gamo T, Ahn SB. Growth-promoting *azospirillum* spp. isolated from the roots of several non-gramineous crops in Japan. Soil Sci Plant Nutr 1991; 37(3): 455-61.
[http://dx.doi.org/10.1080/00380768.1991.10415058]

[23]   Baldani VLD, Baldani JI, Döbereiner J. Effects of *Azospirillum* inoculation on root infection and nitrogen incorporation in wheat. Can J Microbiol 1983; 29(8): 924-9.
[http://dx.doi.org/10.1139/m83-148]

[24]   Mehdipour Moghaddam MJ, Emtiazi G, Salehi Z. Enhanced auxin production by *Azospirillum* pure cultures from plant root exudates. J Agric Sci Technol 2012; 14: 985-94.

[25]   Marques DM, Magalhães PC, Marriel IE, Gomes Júnior CC, Silva AB, Souza TC. Gas exchange, root morphology and nutrients in maize plants inoculated with *Azospirillum brasilense* cultivated under two water conditions. Braz Arch Biol Technol 2021; 64: e21190580.
[http://dx.doi.org/10.1590/1678-4324-2021190580]

[26]   Guerrero-Molina MF, Winik BC, Pedraza RO. More than rhizosphere colonization of strawberry plants by *Azospirillum brasilense*. Appl Soil Ecol 2012; 61: 205-12.
[http://dx.doi.org/10.1016/j.apsoil.2011.10.011]

[27]   Raffi MM, Charyulu PBBN. *Azospirillum*-biofertilizer for sustainable cereal crop production: Current status. In: Viswanath B, Ed. Recent Developments in Applied Microbiology and Biochemistry. Cambridge: Academic Press 2021; pp. 193-209.
[http://dx.doi.org/10.1016/B978-0-12-821406-0.00018-7]

[28]   Bonfante P, Genre A. Plants and arbuscular mycorrhizal fungi: an evolutionary-developmental perspective. Trends Plant Sci 2008; 13(9): 492-8.
[http://dx.doi.org/10.1016/j.tplants.2008.07.001] [PMID: 18701339]

[29]   Albornoz FE, Dixon KW, Lambers H. Revisiting mycorrhizal dogmas: Are mycorrhizas really functioning as they are widely believed to do? Soil Ecol Lett 2021; 3(1): 73-82.
[http://dx.doi.org/10.1007/s42832-020-0070-2]

[30]   Mycorrhizal Applications, Types of mycorrhizal plants. Mycorrhizal Applications, 2017. Available from: https://mycorrhizae.com/wp-content/uploads/2017/04/Types-of-Mycorrhizal-Plants-v2.1.pdf

[31]   Habte M. Mycorrhizal fungi and plant nutrition. In: Silva JA, Uchida R, Eds. Plant Nutrient Management in Hawaii's Soils, Approaches for Tropical and Subtropical Agriculture. Manoa: University of Hawaii 2000; pp. 127-31.

[32]   Howard, J., Fungi fertilize the future. Crop and Soil Sciences News, 2020. Available from: https://cals.ncsu.edu/crop-and-soil-sciences/news/fungi-fertilize-the-future

[33]   Bücking, H., Liepold, E., Ambliwade, P., Nutrient uptake of plants and the regulatory mechanisms underlying these transport processes. In Dhal, N.K., Sahu, S.C. (eds.), Plant Science, InTechOpen, Londra, 2012. pp. 107-138.

[34]   Begum N, Qin C, Ahanger MA, *et al*. Role of arbuscular mycorrhizal fungi in plant growth regulation: implications in abiotic stress tolerance. Front Plant Sci 2019; 10: 1068.
[http://dx.doi.org/10.3389/fpls.2019.01068] [PMID: 31608075]

[35]   Khrieba MI. Mycorrhizae's role in plant nutrition and protection from pathogens. Curr Investig Agric Curr Res 2019; 8(1): 1037-45.
[http://dx.doi.org/10.32474/CIACR.2019.08.000277]

[36]   McNear, D.H., The rhizosphere - Roots, soil and everything in between. Nat. Educ. Knowl. 2013; 4(3), Available from: https://www.nature.com/scitable/knowledge/library/the-rhizosphere-roots-s-il-and-67500617

[37]   Adedeji AA, Babalola OO. Rhizosphere: A complex determinant of soil microbial community. Ann.

Univ. Oradea. Fasc Biol 2020; 27(1): 71-81.

[38]   Groasis. Plants communicate using an internet of fungus. Groasis, Available from: https://www.groasis.com/en/technology/plants-communicate-using-an-internet-of-fungus

[39]   Groasis. Plants communicate using an internet of fungus. Groasis, Available from: https://www.nationalforests.org/blog/underground-mycorrhizal-network

[40]   Yih D. Food, poison, and espionage: Mycorrhizal networks in action. Arnoldia, 2017; 75(2), Available from: https://arboretum.harvard.edu/stories/food-poison-and-espionage-mycorrhizal-netwo-ks-in-action

[41]   Figueiredo AF, Boy J, Guggenberger G. Common mycorrhizae network: A review of the theories and mechanisms behind underground interactions. Frontiers in Fungal Biology 2021; 2: 735299. [http://dx.doi.org/10.3389/ffunb.2021.735299] [PMID: 37744156]

[42]   Doolittle, W.F., Is the Earth an organism? Aeon, 2020. Available from: https://aeon.co/essays/the-gaia-hypothesis-reimagined-by-one-of-its-key-sceptics

[43]   Chen A. The Wood Wide Web: Underground fungi-plant communication network. The Aggie Transcript,   2020,   Available   from: https://aggietranscript.ucdavis.edu/the-wood-wide--eb-underground-fungi-plant-communication-network

[44]   Rai MK, Ed. Handbook of Microbial Fertilizers. Binghamton: Food Products Press 2006. [http://dx.doi.org/10.1201/9781482277760]

[45]   Stamenković S, Beškoski V, Karabegović I, Lazić M, Nikolić N. Microbial fertilizers: A comprehensive review of current findings and future perspectives. Span J Agric Res 2018; 16(1): e09R01.
[http://dx.doi.org/10.5424/sjar/2018161-12117]

[46]   Barbu LDN, Boiu-Sicuia OA. Plant-beneficial microbial inoculants and their formulation – A review. Rom J Plant Prot 2021; 14: 32-43.
[http://dx.doi.org/10.54574/RJPP.14.05]

[47]   Karnwal A, Kapoor D. Soil microbes as biopesticides: agricultural applications and future prospects. In: Yadav AN, Singh J, Singh C, Yadav N, Eds. Current Trends in Microbial Biotechnology for Sustainable Agriculture. Singapore: Springer 2020; pp. 499-524.

[48]   Kumar J, Ramlal A, Mallick D, Mishra V. An overview of some biopesticides and their importance in plant protection for commercial acceptance. Plants 2021; 10(6): 1185.
[http://dx.doi.org/10.3390/plants10061185] [PMID: 34200860]

[49]   Ayilara MS, Adeleke BS, Akinola SA, *et al.* Biopesticides as a promising alternative to synthetic pesticides: A case for microbial pesticides, phytopesticides, and nanobiopesticides. Front Microbiol 2023; 14: 1040901.
[http://dx.doi.org/10.3389/fmicb.2023.1040901] [PMID: 36876068]

[50]   Kerr A. Biological control of Crown Gall through production of Agrocin 84. Plant Dis 1980; 64(1): 25-30.

[51]   Kerr A. Biological control of Crown Gall. Australas Plant Pathol 2016; 45(1): 15-8.
[http://dx.doi.org/10.1007/s13313-015-0389-9]

[52]   Kawaguchi A, Kirino N, Inoue K. Biological control for grapevine crown gall evaluated by a network meta-analysis. Plants 2023; 12(3): 572.
[http://dx.doi.org/10.3390/plants12030572] [PMID: 36771655]

[53]   Li Y, Sun Z, Zhuang X, Xu L, Chen S, Li M. Research progress on microbial herbicides. Crop Prot 2003; 22(2): 247-52.
[http://dx.doi.org/10.1016/S0261-2194(02)00189-8]

[54]   Chutia M, Mahanta JJ, Bhattacharyya N, Bhuyan M, Boruah P, Sarma TC. Microbial Herbicides for Weed Management: Prospects, Progress and Constraints. Plant Pathol J 2007; 6: 210-8.

[http://dx.doi.org/10.3923/ppj.2007.210.218]

[55]   Stubbs TL, Kennedy AC. Micorbial weed control and microbial herbicides. In: Alvarez-Fernandez R, Ed. Herbicides InTech Open. Londra 2012; pp. 135-66.

[56]   Zonouri SS, Fatehinia M, Nuritabar S, Manuchehri S. Characterization of ice nucleation bacteria and their applications. Cumhur Sci J 2015; 36(3): 1726-32.

[57]   Eskandari A, Leow TC, Rahman MBA, Oslan SN. Antifreeze proteins and their practical utilization in industry, medicine, and agriculture. Biomolecules 2020; 10(12): 1649.
[http://dx.doi.org/10.3390/biom10121649] [PMID: 33317024]

[58]   Lukas M, Schwidetzky R, Eufemio RJ, Bonn M, Meister K. Toward bacterial ice nucleation understanding. J Phys Chem B 2022; 126: 1861-7.
[http://dx.doi.org/10.1021/acs.jpcb.1c09342] [PMID: 35084861]

[59]   Doboş L, Puia C. Rolul microorganismelor în procesul de remediere a solurilor poluate cu hidrocarburi. Pro Environ 2010; 3: 185-8.

[60]   Atlas RM. Microbial degradation of petroleum hydrocarbons: an environmental perspective. Microbiol Rev 1981; 45(1): 180-209.
[http://dx.doi.org/10.1128/mr.45.1.180-209.1981] [PMID: 7012571]

[61]   Korda A, Santas P, Tenente A, Santas R. Petroleum hydrocarbon bioremediation: sampling and analytical techniques, in situ treatments and commercial microorganisms currently used. Appl Microbiol Biotechnol 1997; 48(6): 677-86.
[http://dx.doi.org/10.1007/s002530051115] [PMID: 9457796]

[62]   Aluyor EO, Obahiagbon KO, Ori-Jesu M. Biodegradation of vegetable oils: A review. Sci Res Essays 2009; 4: 543-8.

[63]   Amruta, P., In-situ bioremediation techniques – Environment notes. Prepp, 2023. Available from: https://prepp.in/news/e-492-in-situ-bioremediation-techniques-environment-notes

[64]   La Banca, S., 2020. In phytoremediation, plants extract toxins from soils. JSTOR Daily, 2020, Available from: https://daily.jstor.org/in-phytoremediation-plants-extract-toxins-from-soils

[65]   Yan A, Wang Y, Tan SN, Mohd Yusof ML, Ghosh S, Chen Z. Phytoremediation: A promising approach for revegetation of heavy metal-polluted land. Front Plant Sci 2020; 11: 359.
[http://dx.doi.org/10.3389/fpls.2020.00359] [PMID: 32425957]

[66]   Sharma JK, Kumar N, Singh NP, Santal AR. Phytoremediation technologies and their mechanism for removal of heavy metal from contaminated soil: An approach for a sustainable environment. Front Plant Sci 2023; 14: 1076876.
[http://dx.doi.org/10.3389/fpls.2023.1076876] [PMID: 36778693]

[67]   Karki, G., Phytoremediation: classification, mechanisms, applications and limitations. Online Biology Notes, 2020, Available from: https://www.onlinebiologynotes.com/phytoremediation-classificatio--mechanisms-applications-and-limitations

[68]   Rascio N, Navari-Izzo F. Heavy metal hyperaccumulating plants: How and why do they do it? And what makes them so interesting? Plant Sci 2011; 180(2): 169-81.
[http://dx.doi.org/10.1016/j.plantsci.2010.08.016] [PMID: 21421358]

[69]   Tang YT, Deng THB, Wu QH, *et al.* Designing cropping systems for metal-contaminated sites: a review. Pedosphere 2012; 22(4): 470-88.
[http://dx.doi.org/10.1016/S1002-0160(12)60032-0]

[70]   van der Ent A, Baker AJM, Reeves RD, Pollard AJ, Schat H. Hyperaccumulators of metal and metalloid trace elements: Facts and fiction. Plant Soil 2013; 362(1-2): 319-34.
[http://dx.doi.org/10.1007/s11104-012-1287-3]

[71]   Popoviciu DR, Negreanu-Pîrjol B-Ş, Făgăraş M, Düzgüneş E, Negreanu-Pîrjol T. Bioaccumulation of copper, zinc and manganese in some common herbaceous species from marine coastal area. J Environ

Prot Ecol 2017; 18(1): 22-9.

[72] Carobene, A., Piante e funghi in cerca dell'oro. Il Sole 24 Ore, 2010, Available from: https://st.ilsole24ore.com/art/editrice/2010-07-01/piante-funghi-cerca-081949.shtml?uuid= AY0HHs3B

[73] Choi, C.Q., 2013. There's gold in them thar trees. Live Science, 2013, Available from: https://www.livescience.com/40603-gold-found-in-eucalyptus-trees.html

[74] Van der Ent A. Heavy metal farming. Australas. Sci., 2015: 26-27.

[75] Kumar V, Chopra AK. Toxicity of chromium in agricultural crops with respect to its chemical speciation - A review. World Appl Sci J 2015; 33(6): 944-69.
[http://dx.doi.org/10.5829/idosi.wasj.2015.33.06.9533]

SUBJECT INDEX

A

Abiotic factors 3
Absorbing water 43
Accumulation, periodic organic matter 72
Acids 19, 23, 40, 55, 63, 64, 67, 68, 69, 70, 77, 78, 89, 92, 124
  alkanoic 67
  fatty 67, 68, 124
  formic 70
  Fulvic 69
  galacturonic 63
  humic 69
  hydroxy 67
  nucleic 23, 55, 77, 78
  organic 40, 89
  phenolic 64
  sulfuric 92
Adhesion forces 6
Agro-horticultural interest 81
Algae 23, 24, 25, 26, 27, 42, 57, 73, 91
  green 24, 25, 91
  yellow-green 25, 26, 27, 42
Allorhizobium vitis 122
Amino acid-peptidases 66
Aminooxidases 79
Ammonia-oxidizing bacteria (AOB) 82
Anaerobiosis 95
Anoxygenic 18, 57
  photoautotrophic species 18
Anthropic activities 24, 81, 123
Antibiosis 15, 105, 115
Antibiotics 9, 120, 122
  bacterial 122
  natural 120
Ascomycetes 37, 38, 39, 112, 114
Atmospheric 18, 96
  nitrogen 18
  oxygen 96
Autotrophic 57, 59
  feeding process 57
  nutrition 59

B

Bacillus thuringiensis 121
Bacteria 18, 46, 85, 103, 105, 118
  green non-sulfur 18
  heterotrophic 85
  nitrogen-fixing 103, 105, 118
  protein-rich 46
Bacterial adhesion 14
Bacteriophages 21
Biochemical pathways 71, 82
  of methanogenesis 71
  of nitrification 82
Biodegradation 67, 68
  of hydrocarbons 67
  pathways 68
Biofertilizers 90, 103, 118, 129
  producing 103
Biogenic chemical elements 55
Biological herbicides 122
Bioremediation, microbial 124
Biospheric processes 4
Bioturbation effect 48

C

Carbon 14, 15, 21, 46, 47, 55, 56, 59, 65, 67, 72
  atmospheric 72
  dioxide, atmospheric 14
Cell 21, 22, 123
  dehydration 123
  destruction 21, 22
Cellulomonas 61, 120
Cellulose fibers 63
Chemoautotrophs 12, 14
Chemoautotrophy 55
Chemosynthesis 55, 56, 59
Chymotrypsin 66
Concentration, fulvic acids 69
Crop(s) 15, 46, 79, 109, 118, 120, 122, 129
  agricultural 46

www.ingramcontent.com/pod-product-compliance
Lightning Source LLC
Chambersburg PA
CBHW041420290326
41932CB00042B/34